W9-BXY-813

Bloom's Modern Critical Interpretations

The Adventures of
  Huckleberry Finn
The Age of Innocence
All Quiet on the
  Western Front
Animal Farm
As You Like It
The Ballad of the
  Sad Café
Beloved
Beowulf
Billy Budd, Benito
  Cereno, Bartleby the
  Scrivener, and Other
  Tales
The Bluest Eye
Brave New World
Cat on a Hot Tin
  Roof
The Catcher in the
  Rye
Catch-22
Cat's Cradle
The Color Purple
Crime and
  Punishment
The Crucible
Daisy Miller, The
  Turn of the Screw,
  and Other Tales
Darkness at Noon
David Copperfield
Death of a Salesman
The Divine Comedy
Don Quixote
Dracula
Dubliners
Emma
Fahrenheit 451
A Farewell to Arms
Frankenstein
The General Prologue
  to the Canterbury
  Tales

The Glass Menagerie
The Grapes of Wrath
Great Expectations
The Great Gatsby
Gulliver's Travels
Hamlet
The Handmaid's Tale
Heart of Darkness
I Know Why the
  Caged Bird Sings
The Iliad
The Interpretation of
  Dreams
Invisible Man
Jane Eyre
The Joy Luck Club
Julius Caesar
The Jungle
King Lear
Long Day's Journey
  Into Night
Lord of the Flies
The Lord of the Rings
Love in the Time
  of Cholera
Macbeth
The Man Without
  Qualities
The Merchant of
  Venice
The Metamorphosis
A Midsummer Night's
  Dream
Miss Lonelyhearts
Moby-Dick
My Ántonia
Native Son
Night
1984
The Odyssey
Oedipus Rex
The Old Man and the
  Sea
On the Road

One Flew Over the
  Cuckoo's Nest
One Hundred Years of
  Solitude
Othello
Paradise Lost
The Pardoner's Tale
A Passage to India
Persuasion
Portnoy's Complaint
A Portrait of the Artist
  as a Young Man
Pride and Prejudice
Ragtime
The Red Badge of
  Courage
The Rime of the
  Ancient Mariner
Romeo & Juliet
The Rubáiyát of Omar
  Khayyám
The Scarlet Letter
A Scholarly Look at
  The Diary of Anne
  Frank
A Separate Peace
Silas Marner
Slaughterhouse-Five
Song of Myself
Song of Solomon
The Sonnets of
  William Shakespeare
Sophie's Choice
The Sound and the
  Fury
The Stranger
A Streetcar Named
  Desire
Sula
The Sun Also Rises
A Tale of Two Cities
The Tale of Genji
The Tales of Poe
The Tempest

Bloom's Modern Critical Interpretations

Tess of the
    D'Urbervilles
Their Eyes Were
    Watching God
Things Fall Apart

To Kill a Mockingbird
Ulysses
Waiting for Godot
Walden
The Waste Land

White Noise
Wuthering Heights
Young Goodman
    Brown

Bloom's Modern Critical Interpretations

Edith Wharton's
THE AGE OF INNOCENCE

Edited and with an introduction by
Harold Bloom
Sterling Professor of the Humanities
Yale University

CHELSEA HOUSE
PUBLISHERS
A Haights Cross Communications Company
Philadelphia

Printed and bound in the United States of America

10 9 8 7 6 5 4 3 2 1

Library of Congress Cataloging-in-Publication Data

The Age of Innocence / Harold Bloom, ed.
    p. cm. — (Modern critical interpretations)
  Includes bibliographical references and index.
  ISBN 0-7910-8126-5 (alk. paper)
  1. Wharton, Edith, 1862-1937. Age of innocence. I. Bloom, Harold. II. Series.
  PS3545.H16A73 2004
  813'.52—dc22

                                    2004012649

Contributing editor: Pamela Loos

Cover design by Keith Trego

Cover: Courtesy Library of Congress

Layout by EJB Publishing Services

All links and web addresses were checked and verified to be correct at the time of
publication. Because of the dynamic nature of the web, some addresses and links may
have changed since publication and may no longer be valid.

Every effort has been made to trace the owners of copyrighted material and secure
copyright permission. Articles appearing in this volume generally appear much as they did
in their original publication with little to no editorial changes. Those interested in
locating the original source will find bibliographic information in the bibliography and
acknowledgments sections of this volume.

Contents

Editor's Note   vii

Introduction   1
    Harold Bloom

Complementary Portraits:
James's Lady and Wharton's Age   3
    Cushing Strout

The Age of Innocence   13
    David Holbrook

Ironic Structure and
Untold Stories in *The Age of Innocence*   33
    Kathy Miller Hadley

Filters, Portraits, and History's Mixed Bag:
A Lost Lady and *The Age of Innocence*   45
    John J. Murphy

Silencing Women in
Edith Wharton's *The Age of Innocence*   55
    Clare Virginia Eby

"Edith Agonistes"   71
    Dale M. Bauer

Forms of Disembodiment:
The Social Subject in *The Age of Innocence*   83
    Pamela Knights

Studies of Salamanders:
The Fiction, 1912–1920   109
    Cynthia Griffin Wolff

Archer's Way   133
    John Updike

The Age of Innocence:
Branching Thematic Allusions   141
    Helen Killoran

The Price of a Conscious Self
in Edith Wharton's *The Age of Innocence*   155
    Jill M. Kress

Chronology   187

Contributors   191

Bibliography   193

Acknowledgments   197

Index   199

Editor's Note

My Introduction emphasizes Edith Wharton's intense nostalgia for the Old New York of her childhood, with its tribal expulsion of Ellen Olenska.

Cushing Strout deftly compares the Isabel Archer of Henry James's *The Portrait of a Lady* to Newland Archer in Wharton's *The Age of Innocence*.

Newland Archer's self-defeat is ably chronicled by David Holbrook, while Wharton's skill at irony is studied by Kathy Miller Hadley.

John J. Murphy juxtaposes Willa Cather's beautiful *A Lost Lady* to Wharton's novel, seeing in each complex visions of the social contextualizatism of eros.

Wharton speaks out against the social *silence* of Old New York, according to Clare Virginia Eby, after which Dale M. Bauer discerns a Whartonian recognition of scientific developments in the story of Ellen and Newland.

Pamela Knights defines social "innocence" in the book, while Cynthia Griffin Wolff praises Wharton's sure control of "tradition."

The celebrated popular novelist, John Updike, admires the "classic lines" of Wharton's narrative, after which Helen Killoran considers the Whartonian art of allusion.

In this volume's final essay, Jill M. Kress meditates upon the cost of acute consciousness in Newland's divided self.

HAROLD BLOOM

Introduction

A profound study of Edith Wharton's own nostalgias, *The Age of Innocence* (1920) achieved a large discerning audience immediately and has retained it since. For Wharton herself, the novel was a prelude to her autobiography, *A Backward Glance*, published 14 years later and three years before her death. Wharton, who was 57 in 1919 when *The Age of Innocence* was in most part composed, associated herself with both her protagonists, Newland Archer and Ellen Olenska. *The Age of Innocence* is a historical novel set in socially prominent Old New York of the early 1870s, a vanished world indeed when seen from a post–World War I perspective. Wrongly regarded by many critics as a novel derived from Henry James, *The Age of Innocence* is rather a deliberate complement to *The Portrait of a Lady*, seeking and finding a perspective that James was conscious of having excluded from his masterpiece. Wharton might well have called her novel *The Portrait of a Gentleman*, since Newland Archer's very name is an allusion to Isabel Archer, a far more attractive and fascinating character than Wharton's unheroic gentleman of Old New York.

Not that Newland is anything but a very decent and good man who will become a useful philanthropist and civic figure. Unfortunately, however, he has no insight whatsoever as to the differences between men and women, and his passion is of poor quality compared to Ellen's. R.W.B. Lewis, Wharton's

1

biographer, regards *The Age of Innocence* as a minor masterpiece. Time so far has confirmed Lewis's judgment, but we now suffer through an age of ideology, and I am uncertain as to whether *The Age of Innocence* will be strong enough to endure. I have no doubts about Wharton's *The House of Mirth* and *The Custom of the Country*, but I wonder whether Newland Archer may yet sink his own book. The best historical novel of Old New York, *The Age of Innocence* retains great interest both as social history and as social anthropology. One is always startled by the farewell dinner of Ellen Olenska, where Newland realizes that he is attending "the tribal rally around a kinswoman about to be eliminated from the tribe." Wharton's own judgment, as narrator, sums up this tribal expulsion.

> It was the Old New York way of taking life "without effusion of blood": the way of people who dreaded scandal more than disease, who placed decency above courage, and who considered that nothing was more ill-bred than "scenes," except the behavior of those who gave rise to them.

That seems a condemnation of Old New York, and yet it is not. Throughout the novel, Wharton acknowledges that Newland's world centers upon an idea of order, a convention that stifles passion and yet liberates from chaos. The old order at least was an order; Wharton was horrified at the post–World War I United States. Newland Archer is flawed in perception: of his world, of his wife, most of all of Ellen. And yet Wharton subtly makes it clear that even a more courageous and perceptive Newland would not have made a successful match with Ellen. Their relationship in time must have dissolved, with Newland returning to the only tribe that could sustain him. Henry James's Isabel Archer, returning to her dreadful husband Osmond, also accepts an idea of order, but one in which her renunciation has a transcendental element. Wharton, shrewder if less sublime than her Friend James, gives us a more realistic yet a less consequential Archer.

CUSHING STROUT

Complementary Portraits:
James's Lady and Wharton's Age

In his *Portrait of Edith Wharton* (1947) Percy Lubbock suggested that Henry James first saw her as a novel of his own, "no doubt in his earlier manner." For Lubbock he was the "master of her art" and the "master of her ceremonies" as well, whenever she visited him for one of their exhilarating tours in her car. We are led to see her as a "dazzling intruder" on the great man's solitary dedication to his art. Lubbock's memoir, almost parodically Jamesian in style and temper, ends with a vision of Wharton and James talking together as they disappear over the hill. This biographer's accolade is to say that the development of Wharton's serious literary talent has made her even more Jamesian, as if she were now a "creation of his latest manner." Wharton is engulfed in the legend of the master.

No wonder more recent admirers of Wharton have had to disassociate her from James, as she did herself from his later novels, which she found lacking in "thick nourishing human air." Irving Howe inaugurated this modern trend by arguing that since the observation of manners was only an aspect of her work, subordinated (as it was with James) to "the strength of her personal vision and the incisiveness of her mind," then it was at most only "the lesser James that influenced the lesser Mrs. Wharton." In her most important novels Howe found it hard to detect "any *specific* Jamesian influence." Cynthia Wolff in 1977 completed this process of severance with

From *The Hudson Review 35*, no. 3 (Autumn 1982): 405–415. © 1982 by The Hudson Review, Inc.

the purpose of establishing Wharton as a major writer in her own terms. Resonating with the women's movement's interest in reclaiming female writers, *A Feast of Words: The Triumph of Edith Wharton* decisively repudiated the patronizing older tradition of seeing her as merely a clever disciple of James.

There is an odd assumption, however, in these admirable attempts to do justice to Edith Wharton, an unintended premise that Jamesian comparisons are bound to be invidious. Moreover, the fear of linking her to James reduces the idea of influence to discipleship. I find it indicative of these tendencies that Cynthia Wolff draws back from exploring the striking relationship between James's *The Portrait of a Lady* and Wharton's *The Age of Innocence*, their two most widely read and admired works. She recognizes what she calls an "antiphonal" connection between these novels and points out that Wharton's hero (Newland Archer) and James's heroine (Isabel Archer) are further linked when a character in *The Age of Innocence* remarks that Wharton's protagonist looks like a painting, "The Portrait of a Gentleman." Moreover, Wolff knows that both novels involve issues of individual freedom and the sanctity of the marriage bond. But, in the end, the New World setting of Wharton's story, contrasted with the Old World setting of James's, and the mood of "equilibrium and acceptance" in one, contrasted with the tragic hue of the other, lead Wolf to drop the comparison as a misleading one.

The strong case for considering the two novels together goes beyond Wharton's allusions. It notices what James felt he left out of *The Portrait of a Lady*. He tells us that he pressed "least hard" on rendering the male satellites of his heroine, while focusing his attention on Isabel Archer in a way that was vulnerable to the charges of being "too exclusively psychological" and of failing to see the heroine "to the end of her situation." James felt that his book did have the unity of what "groups together," but he added that "the rest may be taken up or not, later." Because Wharton and James were close and mutually admiring friends, it is reasonable to believe that she took seriously these remarks about a work which she considered to be the perfection of his art. His observations gave her an opening for her own talent to take up "the rest" by putting the psychological in a social context, telling the male side of the story more fully, and seeing the heroine and the hero through to the end of their situation. These are the virtues, in fact, of *The Age of Innocence*, which, in this sense, complements *The Portrait of a Lady*.

To understand how it does may leave us with a clearer sense not only of their different ways of telling a story, but also of their joint interest in a moral theme. Irving Howe emphasizes their different milieux: James's ties through his theological father to New England philosophical idealism and

Wharton's ties through parents and husband to "the provincial ruling class of 'old New York.'" But what justifies her reference to their common origins in "old America," whose "last traces" could be found in Europe, is, I suggest, their mutual capacity for appreciating renunciation as both a moral decision and a culturally formed trait or disposition.

Wharton's novel begins with the return to America of Ellen Olenska, who is thinking of divorcing a corrupt Count. It is as if her creator had asked herself what might have happened to James's heroine after she returned to her hateful husband in Rome. The irony of James's story hinged on Isabel Archer's thinking herself unconventional and generous in making a marriage which actually caused her to be "ground in the very mill of the conventional" by a Europeanized dilettante with fraudulent pretensions to unworldliness. (His former mistress, Madame Merle, had also plotted to bring about his marriage with an eye on Isabel's inheritance.) *The Age of Innocence* mirrors this irony in reverse by dramatizing a conventional but decent marriage and making Ellen Olenska conspire to strengthen it for the most moral of reasons. In this story the protagonist, Newland Archer, is the dilettante, who is fascinated with Ellen for her flavor of Europeanized sophistication.

There is a matching central irony here also. When Archer, in his capacity as a lawyer, reluctantly gives Ellen conventional, second-hand advice not to make a family fuss by divorcing her husband, she surprises him by taking this advice seriously in genuinely moral terms as a respect for his own social code and the stability of its life, including the happiness of May Welland, who wants to marry him. He is finally thwarted in his pursuit of Ellen by her own vote for decency, rather than for the courage she might have urged him to have on their own behalf. May has not scrupled after her marriage to put an end to her husband's intrigue with Ellen by confronting her with the premature claim of being pregnant. Ellen returns to Europe, leaving Archer to the muted sorrows and pleasures of living with his conventional wife.

Isabel's deluded generosity is counterpointed by Ellen's clear-sighted recognition of what an affair would mean and by her generous respect for the stability of May's life. Wharton's heroine acts as if she were an older Isabel, sobered by sorrow, but still unimpaired in her generosity of spirit. When Newland Archer naively tells Ellen that he wants to get away from categories like "mistress" and "wife" in order to be "simply two human beings who love each other," she reminds him that she's known many who have tried to find that country and "believe me, they all got out by mistake at wayside stations: at places like Boulogne, or Pisa, or Monte Carlo—and it wasn't at all different from the old world they'd left, but only rather smaller and dingier and more promiscuous." If she has had to look at the Gorgon, as she puts it, because of her mistaken marriage, it has not only dried her tears, but grimly fastened her eyes open "so that they're never again in the blessed darkness."

Mary McCarthy has observed regretfully in her *Ideas and the Novel* that James's characters rarely have opinions on politics, religion, or art. They discuss only other people. Wharton is more interested in opinions because, as its title announces, *The Age of Innocence* focuses on a milieu, rather than on an individual's state of mind. We may speculate, of course, that Isabel Archer's innocence is also representative, a legacy of a transcendentalist enthusiasm for the possibilities of "free expansion," but James provides her with a minimum of specific social circumstances: dead parents, two nearly invisible married sisters, and pleasant memories of her grandmother's house in Albany and three brief trips across the Atlantic. Isabel's wish is "to leave the past behind her and, as she said to herself, to begin afresh." The impulse is typically American, but it is not peculiar to the personal circumstances of her life. She is comparable to Huck Finn in this respect even though she has been brought up on the music of Gounod, the poetry of Browning, and the prose of George Eliot, as James tells us in an unusually concrete reference.

Newland Archer's marriage, on the other hand, is a tribal rite, as Wharton presents it. It is part of a social pattern that allows a man a foolish fling with a married woman before his marriage, abhors the scandal of divorce, keeps a gentleman out of politics (given over to immigrants and their bosses), deprecates intellectual interests, and socially ostracizes those whose business failures can be traced to unethical practices. It is the New York social world of the 1870s, the same decade at the end of which James had conceived the idea for his story about Isabel Archer. She is surrounded not by a society, however; but by displaced persons. (Mrs. Touchett, her aunt, is virtually separated from her husband, who himself lives in England, as an American, with his son, Ralph; Isabel's successful suitor, Gilbert Osmond, is an American expatriate in Rome; his former lover, Madame Merle, is also an expatriated and Europeanized American.) Isabel is vulnerable to serious misinterpretations of her new circumstances because of her romantic imagination and a lack of social cues or clues in a world of displaced persons.

Newland Archer, by contrast, is aware that "in reality they all lived in a kind of hieroglyphic world, where the real thing was never said or done or even thought, but only represented by a set of arbitrary signs," a system of shared assumptions. In this society May's frankness and innocence, he reflects, "were only an artificial product ... a creation of factitious purity, so cunningly manufactured by a conspiracy of mothers and aunts and grandmothers and long-dead ancestresses, because it was supposed to be what he wanted, what he had a right to, in order that he might exercise his lordly pleasure in smashing it like an image made of snow." If Isabel's reputation as an intellectual young lady hangs about her "like the cloudy envelope of a goddess in an epic," May's status is that of a familiar product of social codes.

When Ellen Olenska comes home to America, she trails some of the same clouds of glory for Newland Archer's eyes that had earlier enveloped James's heroine, and she is now also marked by the scars of a bad marriage to a corrupt man. The two female principals are alike also in making renunciation the crucial action of their lives. Just as Isabel Archer gives up the social and erotic possibilities offered to her, respectively, by Lord Warburton and Caspar Goodwood, so does Ellen carry on this rite of sacrifice by respecting Newland Archer's marriage, rather than the personal claims of her own emotional interest in him. In the end, he also earns the right to the name he shares with Isabel by making his own milder act of renunciation. After the death of his wife, he returns at the age of fifty-seven to Ellen's Parisian apartment, where she has lived her life, separated from her husband, who has now died. "There is nothing now to keep them apart," Wharton tells us. But only his son, a child of a freer time, actually visits Madame Olenska. Her former lover concludes that she is more real as a memory than she would be as a living person, and he returns alone to his hotel. Wharton has shown us to the end of their situation, as James deliberately did not do with Isabel and Caspar Goodwood.

These melodious chimings of antiphony also include the novelists' presentation of an inner consistency in the protagonists' characters. Both pay a heavy price in their marriages, both resign themselves to the payment, and both miss a chance for a more sexually fulfilling relationship, because there are other values to consider and because their temperaments tend to incline them as well in directions that are congruent with fidelity to their marriage vows. Newland Archer honors his own past as he looks back on it, yet he also knows that his wife had been "so lacking in imagination, so incapable of growth, that the world of her youth had fallen into pieces and rebuilt itself without her ever being conscious of the change." He may have been a good citizen, responsive enough to Theodore Roosevelt's appeal for active service in politics to work for a year in the State Assembly and to chair civic committees for philanthropy, but "something he knew he had missed: the flower of life." It is incarnated for him in Ellen Olenska as an "imaginary beloved in a book or a picture," the "composite vision of all that he had missed." Still, Wharton makes his final renunciation consistent with his earlier caution as a lover. Once, seeing Ellen at the end of the pier at Newport, he had waited for her to see him first before making himself known, and so had missed a chance for an intimate meeting she was waiting to grant him. Archer lacks the audacity of either Ellen or her grandmother, old Catherine Mingott, who married two of her daughters to Europeans and built a cream-colored stone house ("when brown sandstone seemed as much the only wear as a frock-coat in the afternoon") in "an inaccessible wilderness near Central Park."

Howe, for all his defense of her, criticized Wharton for not being able (unlike James) "to give imaginative embodiment to the human will seeking to resist defeat or move beyond it." As if in reply to him, Wolff presents Newland Archer as a matured person who stays with May because of his "deep-rooted conviction" that "his own moral duty must ultimately be defined by family obligations." If this were true, the terms of his renunciation would be parallel to Isabel's solemn respect for her marriage vows. Yet I believe Wharton does not put her hero on a high plane of moral judgment. She presents him instead in the more mundane context of his half-hearted rebelliousness and detached accommodation to his society. James's story reaches for a more tragic ending, seeking to locate his heroine in the moral consciousness of her situation. In Wharton's novel Isabel's female correlative also has a moral, but less prominent, role to play. Ellen Olenska has the dignity of making a moral decision when she returns Newland Archer's house key to him and accepts the code of decency observed in his society rather than backing her own personal claims. But he only makes his peace with this decision of hers in his final refusal to see her in Paris, when no obligations on either side would have prevented it. There is no moral force by then to his renunciation. It is a matter of realism, of recognizing that too much has flowed under the bridge for him to resume a relationship that had never been consummated.

On closer inspection, James's more tragic conclusion invites our reading it as an ironic commentary on Isabel's romantic predisposition, the motives of her original "fall" recurring in her later renunciation. James relies on the classical idea of a tragic flaw in depicting both the fallen action and her moral response to it. In this respect she is as consistent with her past as her male counterpart is with his history in *The Age of Innocence*. The continuities are symmetrical.

Isabel comes to feel that what she has done deliberately must be accepted because responsibility means accepting the consequences of one's deeds. The obligations of marriage, she believes, are "quite independent of the quality of enjoyment extracted from it." This brave sense of the free act entailing a suffering of its consequences, however unpleasant, is the awesome measure of Isabel's moral grandeur. It is not only her historical distance from our present world, with its devaluation of the permanent marriage bond, that makes her challenging, however; it is also because James has given us an ironic foretaste of her renunciation when he first introduces her. Isabel, he notes, had "a certain nobleness of imagination," but he warns us that she was vulnerable to "the danger of keeping up the flag after the place has surrendered; a sort of behavior so crooked as to be almost a dishonour to the flag." From this point of view Isabel's return to her husband provokes us to ask if her seeming maturity dishonors the flag and reflects her deep-seated fear of passion. In this light Isabel's magnanimity, though magnificent, has a dark side. Three good men (Goodwood, Warburton, and her cousin Ralph) love Isabel, but she will have none of them, for they all entrench on her "freedom." But it finds itself in accepting a miserable marriage as a chosen fate.

Isabel Archer's unconventional marriage had the audacity of her provincial ignorance, as Newland Archer's conventional marriage reflects the timidity of his inhibited pursuit of Ellen. But Isabel has her own timidity. The American businessman, Caspar Goodwood, has the power to move her repeatedly to tears of exasperation and turmoil. When he finally kisses her at Gardencourt, the "white lightning" of the kiss and the intensity of his "hard manhood" almost overwhelm her. She flees for freedom and resolves at that moment to follow "a very straight path" back to her hateful husband. Honoring her promise to return to Pansy, the timid child of her husband's old affair with Madame Merle, is an admirable motive in Isabel's grim decision. Yet the decision itself, while reflecting her feeling for the "tremendous vows" she had made at the altar, is also alloyed with a fear of her own sexuality, not merely Goodwood's. She tells her cousin that she's afraid not of her husband, but of herself. Her defiance of her husband's insistence that she not go to see her dying cousin in England enlists our admiring sympathy. Yet her refusal to consider divorce is partly based on her unwillingness, as she tells her friend, Henrietta Stackpole, to "publish" her mistake to the world. This shame is too much like false pride to earn our full respect, and it surely alerts the irony in James's affection for her.

We can more easily accept Newland Archer's composure at the end of *The Age of Innocence* because he knows what a steep emotional price he has paid for it and what modest but real benefits his compromised life has brought him. There is an emotional ambiguity in Wharton's accounting, but no moral ambiguity. With Isabel the ambiguity is moral because her sacrifice to an ideal is more evident and costly, while its psychological roots are dubious. She is as passionately aware of her need to repudiate Caspar's passion as she is deeply shamed by her merely considering an escape from her marriage vows. Her consciousness is compounded of moral insight and temperamental inclination, which reinforce each other in bringing about her deed of renunciation. What is disturbing about this merger is the suggestion that it has roots Freud has taught us to see as sexually troubled. Howe makes an illuminating remark in comparing Wharton to Freud in being a rationalist who knows how vulnerable reason is, but an analogous point can be made as well about James's treatment of Isabel's "free spirit." His respect for imagination is matched by his awareness of its fallibility. Still, Isabel is more of an exemplar than a resident of Albany, as much an abstract possibility of the romantic imagination as Conrad's Lord Jim. As innocence betrayed, Isabel becomes innocence recovered through experience by insisting on paying the price for her mistaken choice with the same unselfish but dubious idealism that had generated it.

The asceticism of Wharton's heroine is different. It is the result of her realistic aversion to sexual intrigue and her return to her American roots. She affirms them by taking seriously the code of her lover's society. The innocence in question here is no longer hers, for she has seen the Gorgon. It belongs instead to the New York mores in which May Welland's innocence reflects a social standard of what a young woman should be like, frank, "because she had nothing to conceal, assured because she knew of nothing to be on her guard against; and with no better preparation than this, she was to be plunged overnight into what people evasively called 'the facts of life.'" She would lack "the experience, the versatility, the freedom of judgment, which she had been carefully trained not to possess," the very virtues ironically presupposed by Newland Archer's vision of a "passionate and tender comradeship" as his permanent relation to her. Isabel honors her own ideal of free choice when she makes her renunciation. Ellen and her lover honor the stability of a social code by theirs. Edith Wharton has shown us its limitations sharply enough to prevent any indulgence in sentimental nostalgia for its ways.

Quentin Anderson in *The Imperial Self* alerts us to the Emersonian James in which "the compelling character of history, generational order, places and things leaches out, tends to disappear." But Wharton, who does not appear in his book, is one of those for whom "the urgencies and anomalies of a historical moment" do have force. Her novelistic world is a historical one, and it changes before our eyes. Archer's artistic son and athletic daughter are both freer of the old taboos than their parents were. Archer himself recognizes not only some of the decencies in the older, rigidly stratified New York, but also the advantages in the newer, less stable, more fluid way of life. His son can marry a girl born of an extramarital affair, conducted by an unethical businessman, and after 1900 only the older people would remember the scandal of her father's behavior.

It is a tribute to the vicarious imagination that a man created the female Archer and a woman the male Archer, for James is more like Ralph Touchett than any of his other characters and Wharton is more like the Countess

Olenska than anybody else in her story. What their creators have in common, however, is experience of deliberate privation, which enabled them to appreciate renunciation, while feeling its cost. Here too there is a complementary, vital difference. For Wharton the main misery was her twenty-eight year marriage to an unintellectual, unimaginative man, driven to alcohol, drugs, and promiscuity by his own despair at their incompatibility, which was legally recognized in 1913. She had a happy, sensual affair with Morton Fullerton from 1907 to 1910, an episode first revealed in R.W.B. Lewis' biography of her, but sadly it was more serious on her part than on his. For James, on the other hand, it was not sex but work that generated his depressions. He was composed about his bachelorhood for it had been intimated early when he wrote of his cousin Minny Temple's youthful death that "it is the *living* ones that die; the writing ones that survive." (He paid her a survivor's tribute in his portrait of Isabel's spirited charm and its brotherly adoration by her dying cousin.) James was plagued instead by a recurring, doomed wish for a smashing success in the theater, an aspiration which regularly compromised his literary standards, diverted him from his novelistic talent, and plunged him into depressions. Wharton acutely recognized this infirmity as a mark of his "Latin feeling" for "*la gloire*." He had saluted the glory of "history, art, fame, and power" most memorably in his recollection of the Napoleonic gallery of Apollo in the Louvre. (When he suffered a stroke shortly before he died, he even imagined himself as Napoleon, dictating a letter about redecorating the Louvre.) For James, the artist's seeing was his life, but the economic failures of his theatrical career and of the New York Edition of his collected works represented deep deprivation in the crucial area of his self-esteem. (The glib nonsense of Freudianized speculation about his sex life has quite missed the point.)

Though their deprivations were different, the meaning of Wharton's claim that they both belonged to an "old America" is increasingly evident from the perspective of our time with its gluttony for self-fulfillment on every imaginable level. James in 1881 and Wharton in 1920 could turn their stories around the idea of renunciation with a respect for its value as well as for its price. Our current assumption that comparison will be prejudicial to Wharton ought not to keep us from recognizing that the relation between these novels is complementary. The two portraits represent a diptych, having a sort of "inverse similitude," as Melville said about one of his pairings of two short sketches. As we look back and forth from one portrait to the other, we see how the individuality of each is preserved without losing sight of the hinges that firmly connect them.

DAVID HOLBROOK

The Age of Innocence

Newland Archer is another of Edith Wharton's unsatisfactory men. He enters a conventional marriage to one of the old New York families, and the family ensures that the relationship is false, and that he cannot escape it:

> He pulled the sash down and turned back. 'Catch my death!' he echoed; and he felt like adding: 'But I've caught it already. I *am* dead—I've been dead for months and months.'
>
> And suddenly the play of the word flashed up a wild suggestion. What if it were *she* who was dead! If she were going to die—to die soon—and leave him free! The sensation of standing there, in that warm familiar room, and looking at her, and wishing her dead, was so strange, so fascinating and overmastering, that its enormity did not immediately strike him. (*AI*, p. 247)*

By contrast, the Countess Olenska defies the American conventions, and has taken up a European attitude of independence. Yet she has been persuaded to accept the conventional view of the American family that scenes and publicity are better avoided; indeed, Newland Archer himself has persuaded her to this view, as is made plain in the scene in which he first reveals his love for Ellen.

From *Edith Wharton and the Unsatisfactory Man*. © 1991 by David Holbrook.

'May guessed the truth,' he said. 'There is another woman—but not the one she thinks.'

...

'... you are the woman I would have married if it had been possible for either of us.'

'Possible for either of us!' She looked at him with unfeigned astonishment. 'And you say that—when it's you who've made it impossible?'

He stared at her, groping in blackness through which a single arrow of light tore its blinding way.

'*I've* made it impossible—?'

'You, you, you!' she cried, her lip trembling like a child's on the verge of tears. 'Isn't it you who made me give up divorcing—give it up because you showed me how selfish and wicked it was, how one must sacrifice oneself to preserve the dignity of marriage ... and to spare one's family the publicity, the scandal? ... I did what you told me, what you proved to me that I ought to do. Ah ... I've made no secret of having done it for you!' (*AI*, p. 143)

He is crushed by this, but then declares:

'At least I loved you—' he brought out.

On the other side of the hearth from the sofa-corner where he supposed she still crouched, he heard a faint stifled crying like a child's.... (*AI*, p. 144)

He cries, after their kiss, 'Do you see me marrying May after this?'—but that is exactly what he goes on to do.

Ellen Olenska declares that he has given her a new perspective on everything: 'you understood ... you hated happiness bought by disloyalty and cruelty and indifference. That was what I'd never known before—and it's better than anything I've known.' But the logical conclusion of this is her outburst: '"Ah, don't let us undo what you've done!" she cried. "I can't go back now to that other way of thinking. *I can't love you unless I give you up*"' (*AI*, p. 146; my italics). One might say this was Jamesian; but it does represent a dilemma: and this dilemma means that, out of their respect for the values of the traditional rich American family, and through the wiles of May Welland's family, they are prevented from ever consummating their love.

In the end, Ellen promises to allow him to sleep with her once, before she leaves for Europe. But May makes a final plea, and tells Olenska that she is pregnant. Ellen sends him her key, but it is too late. The family believe, however, that Newland and Ellen have been lovers, and draw them into a separation ritual—a dinner especially laid on for Ellen's departure.

> ... then it came over him, in a vast flash made up of many broken gleams, that to all of them he and Madame Olenska were lovers, lovers in the extreme sense peculiar to 'foreign' vocabularies. He guessed himself to have been, for months, the centre of countlessly silently observing eyes and patiently listening ears, he understood that, by means as yet unknown to him, the separation between himself and the partner of his guilt had been achieved, and now that the whole tribe had rallied about his wife on the tacit assumption that nobody knew anything, or had ever imagined anything, and that the occasion of the entertainment was simply May Archer's natural desire to take an affectionate leave of her friend and cousin.
>
> It was the old New York way, of taking life 'without effusion of blood': the way of people who dreaded scandal more than disease, who placed decency above courage, and who considered that nothing was more ill-bred than 'scenes', except the behaviour of those who gave us to them. (*AI*, pp. 279–80)

Archer feels 'like a prisoner in the centre of an armed camp': 'It's to show me ... what would happen to *me*....' '... and a deathly sense of the superiority of implication and analogy over direct action ... closed in on him like the doors of the family vault' (*AI*, p. 280).

'Deathly' it is, and the family vault swallows everything—swallows, especially, the possibilities of sexual passion and that meeting of true minds that can give meaning to lives. This is the 'family' background which surrounded Edith Wharton, through her earlier trials, as with her first engagement to Harry Stevens, which gave her no knowledge of sexual passion, and which led to her disastrous marriage with Teddy.

But yet Newland Archer's romantic attachment to Ellen Olenska remains at the level of fantasy, and he fails dismally to fulfil this hope. Even at the end, when May has died, and Archer is in Paris with his grown-up son, he shrinks from even meeting Ellen:

> 'It's more real to me here than if I went up,' he suddenly heard himself say: and the fear lest that last shadow of reality should lose its edge kept him rooted to his seat as the minutes succeeded each other. (*AI*, p. 301)

'There was nothing now to keep her and Archer apart'—but Archer cannot face the probability. He goes to an art gallery before seeking her out:

> For an hour or more he wandered from gallery to gallery through the dazzle of the afternoon light, and one by one the pictures burst on him in their half-forgotten splendour, filling his soul with the long echoes of beauty. *After all, his life had been too starved....* (*AI*, p. 298; my italics)

He pauses before an 'effulgent Titian':

> ... he found himself saying: 'But I'm only fifty-seven—' and then he turned away. For such summer dreams it was too late; but surely not for a quiet harvest of friendship, of comradeship in the blessed hush of her newness. (*AI*, p. 298)

It is terribly poignant, and yet infuriating—because of the cowardice of the man, in the face of the promptings of his own authenticity. The cowardice may be related to that of Laurence Selden, who could have interposed, again and again, to save Lily Bart's life, but who withdrew into a self-defensive neatness, a studied egocentricity, which shrinks from all the complications of giving (and receiving) in love. Archer's final failure to come up to scratch is logically inevitable, if one traces his reasons for failing in commitment to Ellen throughout the novel.

He is a deplorably unsatisfactory man—but his creation seems appropriate for Edith Wharton, who herself must have felt such bitterness about her own cruel fate. She married Teddy, and, after a thoroughly unsatisfactory introduction to sexuality with him, seems to have given sex up. She loved Walter Berry, but Berry; being a confirmed bachelor, seems to have been incapable of passionate sexual commitment. And then, for three years only, she enjoyed a passionate affair with the strangely uncommitted Morton Fullerton, who was incapable of complete committal and of any relationship lasting any length of time, and who was also bisexual.

Why *The Age of Innocence*? That the latter word is heavily imbued with irony is made clear when Archer is talking to May's mother, who has asked, about Ellen, 'what her fate will be?'

> 'What we've all contrived to make it,' he felt like answering. 'If you'd all of you rather she should be Beaufort's mistress than some decent fellow's wife you've certainly gone the right way about it.'

He wondered what Mrs. Welland would have said if he had uttered the words instead of merely thinking them. He could picture the sudden decomposure of her firm placid features, to which a life-long mastery of trifles had given an air of factitious authority. Traces still lingered on them of fresh beauty like her daughter's, and he asked himself if May's face was doomed to thicken into the same middle-aged image of invincible innocence.

Ah, no, he did not want May to have that kind of innocence, *the innocence that seals the mind against imagination and the heart against experience!* (*AI*, p. 123; my italics)

Newland Archer has imagination, but it is limited to invention. Contemplating May, 'with a thrill of possessiveness' at the beginning of the book, 'in which pride in his own masculine initiation was mingled with a tender reverence for her *abysmal purity*' (my italics), he is 'hazily confusing the scene of his projected honeymoon with the masterpieces of literature which it would be his manly privilege to reveal to his bride' (*AI*, p. 10).

He has had a previous affair—there has been a married lady 'whose charms had held his fancy through two mildly agitated years'; and Edith Wharton hints at 'the frailty which had so nearly marred that unhappy being's life, and had disarranged his own plans for a whole winter' (*AI*, p. 10). Newland may have 'read more, thought more, and even seen a good deal more of the world' than the men surrounding him in the audience of the opera, but

> grouped together they represented 'New York', and the habit of masculine solidarity made him accept their doctrine in all the issues called moral. He instinctively felt that in this respect it would be troublesome—and also rather bad form—to strike out for himself. (*AI*, p. 111)

So, Archer may not subscribe to the lofty moral pronouncements of Mr. Fullerton Jackson, but he is inhibited enough by hard feeling and lethargy from being truly independent. At first he is appalled that his fiancée May should be 'exposed to the influence of a woman so careless of the dictates of taste'.

Ellen is not accepted by New York society, and May, with trained tact, defends her: when Newland asks why she is not coming to the ball, May replies that 'she made up her mind her dress wasn't smart enough.'

> 'Oh, well—' said Archer with happy indifference. Nothing about his betrothed pleased him more than her resolute determination

to carry to its utmost limit that ritual of ignoring the 'unpleasant' in which they had both been brought up. (*AI*, p. 25)

Archer is thus shown to be deeply compromised by the hypocrisy of New York society. Archer seeks to challenge their respectability, but his challenge is only skin deep; when Jackson informs him that the secretary who helped Ellen Olenska to leave her husband was still living with her a year later,

> Newland reddened, 'living together? Well, why not?' Who had the right to make her life over if she hadn't? 'I'm sick of the hypocrisy that would bury alive a woman of her age if her husband prefers to live with harlots.'
> He stopped and turned away angrily to light his cigar.
> 'Women ought to be free—as free as we are,' he declared, making a discovery *of which he was too irritated to measure the terrific consequences*. (*AI*, p. 34; my italics)

The slightly sardonic phrase I have italicized makes plain Edith Wharton's position: she is fully aware of the gulf between Archer's statement and the reality of what this freedom would mean, and of how far short he would fall of his assertion if women became free.

By such subtle placings, she shows Archer and May trapped in the hypocrisy of their social milieu, while Archer (who has had a 'silly business' with Mrs. Rushworth which he once regarded as his 'tragedy') develops a romantic yearning for Ellen Olenska. He looks at the portrait of his fiancée and sees 'the gay innocent mouth of the young creature whose soul's custodian he used to be': 'That terrifying product of the social system he belonged to and believed in, the young girl who knew nothing and expected everything, looked back at him like a stranger' (*AI*, p. 39). He reflects that 'marriage was not the safe anchorage he had been taught to think, but a voyage on uncharted seas.' He sees with a 'shiver of foreboding' his marriage becoming what most of the other marriages about him were: 'a dull association of material and social interests held together by ignorance on the one side and hypocrisy on the other' (*AI*, p. 40). Bitter memories of her mother's evasion of all questions to do with sexuality obviously lie behind Edith Wharton's delineation of Archer's view of his bride-to-be:

> She was frank, poor darling, because she had nothing to conceal, assured because she knew of nothing to be on her guard against; and with no better preparation than this, she was to be plunged

overnight into what people evasively called 'the facts of life'. (*AI*, p. 41)

All this 'frankness' and 'innocence' was an 'artificial product', 'so cunningly manufactured by a conspiracy of mothers and aunts and grandmothers....' These uncomfortable reflections are prompted in Archer by the 'inopportune arrival of the Countess Olenska'.

The latter is the subject of a snub, which she overcomes, and at last the Countess enters the Van der Luyden drawing room, where Archer is impressed by her 'mysterious authority of beauty': 'It frightened him to think what must have gone to the making of her eyes.' Ellen is not conscious of breaking any rules (though she is) when she sits at Newland Archer's side, where she rests with perfect ease. This idiosyncratic poise leads the Countess to behave invitingly to Archer: she touches his knee with her fan, which 'thrilled him like a caress', while she suddenly says, 'Tomorrow, then, after five—I shall expect you'—though there has been no such agreement between them.

Archer is something of a fugitive from his own wedding preparations ('Twelve dozen of everything—hand embroidered') when he enters the mysterious apartment of Ellen Olenska, who returns home there in the brougham of Julius Beaufort. As he tries to urge her to take notice of the Welland mothers and others, she declares suddenly, '... The real loneliness is living among all these kind people who only ask one to pretend ...' (*AI*, p. 68), and is shaken by a sob. In comforting her he calls her 'Ellen!' Calling at a florist, to send his daily bouquet of lilies of the valley to May, he sees a bunch of red roses which he arranges to be sent to the Countess....

Newland continues to believe that 'presently' it would be his task to 'take the bandage from this young woman's eyes' and 'bid her look forth on the world'. But he recalls the Kentucky cave-fish, and how they ceased to develop eyes because they had no use for them: 'What if, when he had bidden May Welland to open hers, they could only look out blankly at blankness?' (*AI*, p. 72). The self-delusion of his confidence in assuming himself to be such a liberator is made clear, step by step, as he hovers between turning sullen about the niceties of whom Ellen Olenska may call on and feeling distress over the possibility of being asked to advise on her divorce: he hates divorce. He feels a 'wave of compassion' for his cousin and believes he must save her 'at all costs from further wounding herself in her mad plunges against fate'.

He ponders his own morality, and asks, 'Are we only Pharisees after all?' He is 'puzzled by the efforts to reconcile his instinctive disgust at human vileness with his equally instinctive pity for human frailty' (*AI*, p. 83). He ponders his affair with 'poor, silly' Mrs. Rushworth, who had been attracted by the secrecy and peril of the liaison as much as by his charm; he had emerged from it 'with an undisturbed belief in *the abysmal distinction between the woman one loved and respected and those one enjoyed—and pitied*' (my italics). In this view he had been abetted by his female relatives who shared the belief that when 'such things happened' it was 'undoubtedly foolish of the man, but *somehow always criminal of the woman*' (my italics).

He is aware of the difference between the Anglo-Saxon, Protestant, position over such matters, and of what tended to happen in 'rich and idle and ornamental societies' such as those in Europe, where a woman might be drawn into 'a tie inexcusable by conventional standards' by 'force of circumstances'.

So, Archer is firmly embedded in conventional (chauvinistic, as we would call them today) views, and when discussing divorce with Ellen, he finds her saying to him, 'But my freedom—is that nothing?' Yet she is pliable, and agrees with him: 'Very well; I will do what you wish.' She is persuaded into the New York view of what is fair and just. Beneath the surface, Newland Archer is more drawn to Ellen Olenska than he is conscious of, while she is attracted to him and aware of the seductive influence she exerts over him: by her sudden reference to the two occasions on which he has sent her roses, she causes in him an 'agitated pleasure'; her colour rises 'reluctantly and duskily' and she asks, 'What do you do while May is away?'—a question that 'faintly annoys' him.

Ellen runs away and sends him a note: he thinks, 'what has Madame Olenska been running away from, and why did she feel the need to be safe?' It seems clear she is falling in love with Archer; she tells him, 'I can't feel unhappy when you're here', and 'I live in the moment when I'm happy': 'The words stole through him like a temptation.... Archer's heart was beating insubordinately. What if it were from him that she had been running away ...' (*AI*, p. 114). She anticipates her 'stealing up behind him to throw her light arms about his neck', but Beaufort arrives—the vulgar rich adventurer who is pursuing Ellen.

Again we may reflect on the degree to which Edith Wharton has the advantage over Henry James. She knows how passionate need can creep up on a man or a woman unawares, as James did not, despite his interest in the morality of passion. She is aware of the subtleties of feminine intuition: for example, when May Welland, by a supreme effort, detects how differently Newland Archer has behaved to her since the announcement of their engagement, which happened to coincide with his interest in Ellen Olenska. May deduces that it is because of his regret over Mrs. Rushworth—and offers him his freedom, with tragic fortitude!

In a later exchange with Ellen, Archer confesses (I have already quoted from the scene) that there is another woman, in his life, but it is she, Ellen. Although she cries, 'Ah, don't make love to me! Too many people have done that ...', she is evidently deeply affected—and admits that she has, through Archer, accepted the New York emphasis on fairness and justice. The scene is one of subtle complexity, since it is clear that Countess Olenska is playing a powerful game, in contradistinction to Archer's betrothed, who is an 'innocent' as she is sophisticated—and Ellen is reckless:

> He had her in his arms, her face like a wet flower at his lips, and all their vain terrors shrivelling up like ghosts at sunrise. The one thing that astonished him now was that he should have stood for five minutes arguing with her across the width of the room, when just touching her made everything so simple. (*AI*, p. 144)

This subtle and intense scene is written from a perception Henry James could not quite have:

> She gave him back all his kiss, but after a moment he felt her stiffening in his arms, and she put him aside and stood up.
>
> 'Ah, my poor Newland—I suppose this had to be. But it doesn't in the least alter things....'
>
> 'It alters the whole of life for me.'
>
> 'No, no—it mustn't, it can't. You're engaged to May Welland; and I'm married.' (*AI*, p. 144)

She looks 'haggard and almost old'.

Archer says, 'It's too late to do anything else' other than to tell May; but she knows—as a woman knows—he is only saying this because it is the easiest thing to say: 'In reality it's too late to do anything but what we've both decided on.' She cannot go back to 'that other way of thinking', and she cannot love (him) unless she gives him up.

She is satisfied, because she loves him, and so possesses him: and this is enough (we may recall Sophy Viner's experience of Darrow):

> I *was* lonely; I *was* afraid. But the emptiness and darkness are gone; when I turn back into myself now I'm like a child going at night into a room where there's always a light. (*AI*, p. 146)

This sense of *having been loved*, and therefore enriched, whatever happens, is something that had happened to Edith Wharton; our only problem is perhaps that we may doubt whether Newland Archer is capable of understanding the subtlety of the woman's view.

Book Two begins with the wedding rite, which Edith Wharton presents with subtle irony:

> All the old ladies in both families had got out their faded sables and yellowing ermines, and the smell of camphor from the front pews almost smothered the faint spring scent of the lilies banking the altar. (*AI*, p. 151)

The panoply of received convention smothers all hope of life; behind it all is the horror indicated by hints: 'concealment of the spot in which the bridal night was to be spent being one of the most sacred taboos of the prehistoric ritual'. The deity is 'Good Form'—and Beaufort is seen among the congregation 'scrutinizing the women with an arrogant stare'. Archer goes through the ceremony with duplicitous reflections: 'he too had once thought such questions important.' (There has been a heated debate on whether the wedding presents should be displayed; there is much discussion as to whether the pews should be dismantled to accommodate the vast form in a bath chair of Mrs. Manson Mingott.) The vision of ceremony is superbly given:

> The music, the scent of the lilies on the altar, the vision of the cloud of tulle and orange-blossoms floating nearer and nearer, the sight of Mrs. Archer's face suddenly convulsed with happy sobs, the low benedictory murmur of the Rector's voice, the ordered evolutions of the eight pink bridesmaids and the eight black ushers: all these sights, sounds and sensations, so familiar in themselves, so unutterably strange and meaningless in his new relationship to them, were confusedly mingled in his brain. (*AI*, p. 156)

Underneath it all 'the same black abyss yawned before him and he felt himself sinking into it, deeper and deeper': the comic portrayal of the social event is based on the author's awareness of the essential utter unauthenticity of the marriage for Archer.

Aware of the approaching defloration, Edith Wharton touches in subtly the essence of May:

> The blood that ran so close to her fair skin might have been a preserving fluid rather than a ravaging element; yet her lack of

indestructible youthfulness made her seem neither hard nor dull, but only primitive and pure. (*AI*, p. 159)

The resonances of the sentence are imbued with Edith Wharton's deep feelings for this girl as the 'terrifying product' of the social system, who is schooled to be in a state in which she 'knew nothing and expected everything'. Archer has now 'reverted to all his old inherited ideas about marriage'; as for new ideas: 'There was no use in trying to emancipate a wife who had not the dimmest notion that she was not free ...' (*AI*, p. 164). 'Whatever happened, he knew she would always be loyal, gallant and unresentful: and that pledged him to the practice of the same virtues' (*AI*, p. 165). May becomes 'the tutelary divinity of all his old traditions and reverences'.

But it is not long before Archer begins to realize that 'in future many problems would be thus negatively solved for him', and that May's pressure was already 'bearing on the very angles whose sharpness he most wanted to keep'. Yet he is contented, 'for she had fulfilled all that he had expected.' 'As for the momentary madness which had fallen upon him on the eve of his marriage, he had trained himself to regard it as the last of his discarded experiments' (*AI*, p. 174). 'The Countess Olenska remained in his memory simply as the most plaintive and poignant of a love of ghosts.'

Chapter 21 begins with an archery contest in which May triumphs; whereupon Archer overhears Beaufort declare, 'Yes, but that's the only kind of target she'll ever hit'—which words send a faint shiver through his heart: 'What if "niceness" carried to that superb degree were only a negation, the curtain dropped before an emptiness?' He feels that he has 'never lifted that curtain' in May.

Edith Wharton's central theme is surely one that concerns individuals like herself who have been cheated of fulfilment by convention, by 'received ideas', by their family training, so that an emptiness remains at the heart of their being. With Newland Archer this problem is never solved.

We have a foretaste of the end when, at this stage, he re-encounters the Countess Olenska.

From the willow walk projected a slight wooden pier hiding in a sort of pagoda-like summer-house; and in the pagoda a lady stood, leaning against the rail, her back to the shore. (*AI*, p. 181)

Archer 'stopped at the sight as if he had waked from sleep'. 'That vision of the past was a dream'; the reality was to return to the house 'which one always knew exactly what is happening at a given hour'.

Ellen Olenska, we learn later, is aware of his presence, but he turns and walks up the hill. May declares she is sorry he did not find Ellen, who, she goes on to declare, might have been better off with her husband. Archer remarks he has never heard May say a cruel thing before. The exchange, and the romantic appearance of Ellen, lead to a 'curious reversal of mood' in Archer:

> The heavy carpets, the watchful servants, the perpetual reminding tick of disciplined clocks, the perpetually renewed stack of cards and invitations on the hall table ... made any less systematized and affluent existence seem unreal and precarious.... But now it was the Welland house, and the life he was expected to lead in it, that had become unreal and irrelevant, and the brief scene of the shore ... was a dose to him as the blood in his veins. (*AI*, p. 183)

In an acutely comic and poignant scene Archer is portrayed as drifting to the house where he believes Ellen Olenska to be; it is not that he is conscious of any wish to speak to her or to hear her voice, but

> she simply felt that if he could carry away the vision of the spot of earth she walked on, and the way the sky and sea enclosed it, the rest of the world might seem less empty. (*AI*, p. 189)

He reaches a summerhouse in the garden, where there is a pink parasol, and lifts the handle of it to his lips: 'He heard the rustle of skirts against the box ... letting the rustle come nearer without lifting his eyes. He had always known that this must happen...' (*AI*, p. 193)—but the woman under the sunshade turns out to be the youngest and largest of the Blenker girls, who prattles at him.

From now on, Archer seems to be sleep-walking, caught up in a dream. Olenska, for her part, when he does catch up with her, seems 'listless'. As soon as Archer appears, her startled look 'gives way to a slow smile of wonder and *contentment*' (my italics). For his part, 'he felt as if he were shouting at her across endless distances, and she might vanish again before he could overtake her' (*AI*, p. 193). When she tells him 'you're not changed', he feels like answering, 'I was, till I saw you again.' Proposing a trip on a steamboat, he suddenly breaks out, 'Haven't we done all we could?' to which she replies, 'You mustn't say things like that to me.' 'Oh, don't calculate!' he exclaims, as she looks at her watch: 'Give me the day!'

Presumably, he means by 'Haven't we done all we could' that they have fallen in as much as they have been able, with what 'society' requires—to overcome their attraction to one another, to meet as beings. It is an extraordinary outburst, and speaks of such a yearning within the man that he falls into a state of drifting abandon, once he re-encounters Ellen. They sit side by side on a bench on the boat, and find

> that they had hardly anything to say to each other, or rather that what they had to say communicated itself best in the blessed silence of their release and their isolation. (*AI*, p. 199)

He feels 'the old familiar world of habit' is receding; surprisingly, we learn:

> There had been days and nights when the memory of their kiss had burned and burned on his lips ... the thought of her had run through him like fire ... they seemed to have reached the kind of deeper nearness that a touch may sunder.... (*AI*, p. 199)

Ellen Olenska, of course, would have been seen by Edith Wharton's readers as behaving with an extraordinary freedom, in so taking such an excursion with a newly-married man. However, 'She seemed to take their adventure as a matter of course, and to be neither in fear of unexpected encounters, nor (what was worse) unduly elated by their possibility' (*AI*, p. 200). (It is possible, I believe, that just as the archery scene comes from *Daniel Deronda*, so the symbolism of drifting here was taken, possibly unconsciously, from *The Mill on the Floss*.)

During lunch he asks her why she has not left New York, and is startled by her reply: 'I believe it's because of you.' What she means is that he has 'made' her. The exchange is very Jamesian and thus difficult to follow, consisting as it does of obliquities. At the centre of it is his confidence:

> '... You sure gave me my first glimpse of a real life, and at the same moment you asked me to go on with a sham one. It's beyond human endearing—that's all.'
>
> 'Oh, don't say that; when I'm enduring it!' she burst out, her eyes filling. (*AI*, p. 203)

She sits with her face abandoned to his gaze 'as if in the recklessness of a desperate peril'.

> The face exposed her as much of it had been her whole person, with the soul behind it....
>
> ...

> 'You too—oh, all this time, you too?' For answer, she let the
> tears on her lids overflow and run slowly down. (*AI*, p. 203)

It is a meeting at a very deep level, and the power to present it surely comes
from Edith Wharton's own most poignant predicament; he remembers once
fixing his eyes on her hand so as not to look at her face:

> ... his imagination spun about the hand as about the edge of a
> vortex.... He had known that love that is fed on caresses and feeds
> them; but this passion that was closer than his bones was not to
> be superficially satisfied. His one terror was to do anything which
> might efface the sand and impression of her words; his one
> thought, that he should never again feel quite alone.
>
>   But after a moment the sense of waste and ruin overcome
> him.... (*AI*, p. 204)

They were 'chained to their separate destinies'. He expresses his wish that she
should not go back to the 'abominations' and the 'temptations you half guess':

> 'What a life for you!—' he groaned.
> 'Oh—as long as it's a part of yours.'
> 'And mine a part of yours?'
> She nodded.
> 'And that's to be all—for either of us.'
> 'Well: it is all: isn't it?' (*AI*, p. 205)

On the boat going back, he feels a 'tranquillity of spirit'. It fills him with a 'tender
awe', although he has not even so much as touched her hand with his lips.

From a meeting with the envoy sent by Ellen's husband, he comes to
realize that his response to May's reference to her being better off with him
has been reported to the family, and in consequence he has been excluded
from family discussions of her future. May is aware that her husband takes a
special interest in Olenska, and is in opposition to her return to her husband;
she is beginning to play a subtle game over the issue. Watching her closely,
Archer thinks:

> 'How young she is! For what endless years this life will have to go
> on!'
>
>   He felt, with a kind of horror, his own strong youth and the
> bounding blood in his veins. (*AI*, p. 222)

Immediately, he announces a trip to Washington, and his wife replies, 'you must be sure to go and see Ellen'—a coded message which Edith Wharton takes half a page to elucidate in full.

When he fetches Ellen from the train to visit 'poor Granny', he declares that '*Each time you happen to me all over again.*' But he is seized by an inability to say anything to her: he could 'only helplessly brood on the mystery of their remoteness and their proximity.' She asks her whether it was M. Rivière who helped her leave her husband, and she admits frankly that it was (we learned earlier that they had been living together). When the carriage lurches, 'suddenly she turned, flung her arms round him and pressed her lips to his.'

He tells her 'a stolen kiss isn't what I want.... What I want of you is much more than an hour or two every now and then....' But she declares, 'we'll look not at visions, but at realities.' '"Is it your idea, then, that I should live with you as your mistress—since I can't be your wife?", she asked' (*AI*, p. 242).

And now the contrast between the imaginative fantasies in which he conceives her and the reality becomes clear:

> 'I want—I want somehow to get away with you into a world where words like that—categories like that—won't exist. Where we shall be simply two human beings who love each other, who are the whole of life to each other; and nothing else on earth will matter.'
>
> She drew a deep sigh that ended in another laugh. 'Oh, my dear—where is that country? Have you ever been there?' (*AI*, p. 242)

She goes on 'I know so many who've tried to find it' ... 'and it wasn't at all different from the old world they'd left, but only rather smaller and dingier and more promiscuous.' She had, one might say, the realism of an Anna Karenina. The Gorgon has opened her eyes:

> ... it's a delusion to say that she blinds people. What she does is just the contrary—she fastens their eyelids open, so that they're never again in the blessed darkness. Isn't there a Chinese torture like that? There ought to be. Ah, believe me, it's a miserable little country. (*AI*, p. 243)

'What is your plan for us?' asks Archer, but she declares there is no 'us'. He proclaims himself 'beyond that'—'trying to be happy behind the backs of the people who trust them'. But she declares: 'No, you're not! You've never been beyond. And I have ... and I know what it looks like there ...' (*AI*, p. 243). He gets out, and walks away. You could say he meets the reality of the situation as Edith Wharton has known it. Though Ellen is in love with him, she is aware they can only have momentary meetings of the soul; theirs is a hard case—and it is his fault, for giving in to the falsifications of the family and Good Form. He has been a coward in the face of life, and there is now no solution, by whatever principles they are guided—least of all, by his, and by what he has taught her. The exchange, again, has a deep bitterness behind its conception, and is drawn from Edith Wharton's own experience of being sacrificed to the conventions and trying to find herself in an adulterous affair.

Newland Archer seems to be groping towards a decision: 'He had so definitely decided on the course he meant to pursue...', 'his path was clear, before him.' He contemplates Japan: 'At any rate she would understand that, wherever she went, he was going.' He was 'not only nerved for this plunge but eager to take it'. But he develops a 'growing distaste for what lay before him'. Now he sees the matter in a new light, and recollects his experience with Mrs. Rushworth and the game she had played to deceive a fond and unperceiving husband.

> ... a smiling, bantering, humouring, watchful and incessant lie. A lie by day, a lie by night, a lie in every touch and every look; a lie in every caress and every quarrel; a lie in every world and every silence. (*AI*, p. 255)

In Archer's little world, a woman's standard of truthfulness was tacitly held to be lower than that of a man; no one, however, laughed at a wife deceived, 'and a certain measure of contempt was attached to one who continued their philandering after marriage.' When he meets Ellen in the street, he feels:

> he had been speaking not to the woman he loved but to another, a woman he was indebted to for pleasure already wearied of: it was hateful to find himself the prisoner of this hackneyed vocabulary. (*AI*, p. 257)

They meet in the Metropolitan Museum and have another Jamesian exchange, trying to determine not to be like all the others. But then she hazards, 'Shall I—once come to you: and then go home?' (*AI*, p. 260). 'It seemed as if he held his heart in his hands, like a full cup that the least motion might overbrim.' She means to go home to her husband; she cannot remain and lie to the people who have been so good to them, or destroy their lives, when they have helped to remake hers. Archer is appalled by the thought of losing her—but agrees:

> for a moment they continued to hold each other's eyes, and he saw that her face, which had grown very pale, was flooded with a deep inner radiance. His heart beat with awe: he felt that he had never before beheld love visible. (*AI*, p. 261)

When he gets home he contemplates the agreement: 'This was what had to be, then ... this is what had to be.' 'What he had dreamed of had been so different that there was a *mortal chill* in his rapture' (*AI*, p. 262; my italics). His wife comes in, with a deep blush on her cheeks, and announces that she has had a 'really good talk' with Ellen. Archer perceives she has been making a great effort to reach out towards something 'beyond the usual range of her vision'. It is a complex scene: at one point Archer almost throws himself on her mercy. But she reports on an error of Ellen's that has outraged the respectability of the family and 'the open door had closed between them again.' His wife's eyes are of 'the same swimming blue' as when he left her to drive to Jersey City; she flings her arms round him, and he feels her tremble in his.

Archer begins to feel pity for his wife, and recalls her remark before they were married, when she alluded to Mrs. Rushworth, 'I couldn't have my happiness made out of a wrong—a wrong to someone else', and he has again an urge to ask her for the freedom he had once refused.

But 'Newland Archer was a quiet and self-controlled young man.' 'Conformity to the discipline of a small society had become almost his second nature' (*AI*, p. 268). He tries to unburden himself to his wife: 'There's something I've got to tell you ... about myself.' In response,

> She was extremely pale, but her face had a curious tranquillity of expression that seemed drawn from some inner source.
> ...
> 'Madame Olenska—' he said: but at the name his wife raised her right hand as if to silence him. (*AI*, p. 270)

May has a note from Ellen to say that Granny has arranged for her to return to Europe, to be independent. She added: 'If any of my friends wish to urge me to change my mind, please tell them it would be utterly useless.' May adds:

I knew you'd been the one friend she could always count on: and I wanted her to know that you and I were the same—in all our feelings ... I think she understands everything. (*AI*, p. 272)

Archer receives a key wrapped in tissue paper, which has been sent to his office. He interprets this as a sign that 'Nothing ... was to prevent his following her' to Europe: 'once he had taken the irrevocable step, and had proved to her that it was irrevocable, he believed she would not send him away.' He believes he still has the trumps in his hands.

But the Archers give a dinner, and Archer perceives this is a ritual *rite de passage*. The Wellands have assumed that he and Ellen have been lovers and the occasion was to mark the end of the *affaire*. He feels 'like a prisoner in the centre of an armed camp', and

all the harmless-looking people engaged upon May's canvasbacks as a band of dumb conspirators, and himself and the pale woman on his right at the centre of their conspiracy. (*AI*, p. 279)

Afterwards, Archer tries again to reveal his problem to his wife: 'There's something I must tell you. I tried to the other night....' He declares he wants to get away from everything. But she declares he cannot, 'unless you take me with you':

And then, as he was silent, she went on, in tones so clear and evenly pitched that each separate syllable tapped like a little hammer on his brain. 'That is, if the doctors will let me go ... but I'm afraid they won't. For you see, Newland, I've been sure since this morning of something I've been so longing and hoping for....' (*AI*, p. 285)

There is a long pause, 'which the inner devils filled with strident laughter'. She then tells him she has told Ellen: 'Did you mind my telling her first, Newland?'

'But that was a fortnight ago, wasn't it? I thought you said you weren't sure till today?'
    Her colour burned deeper, but she held her gaze. 'No, I wasn't sure then—but I told her I was. And you see I was right!' she exclaimed, her blue eyes wet with victory. (*AI*, p. 286)

In the next chapter, May is dead, and Archer is with his grown-up children. Archer has become 'a good citizen', but 'Something he had missed:

the flower of life.' He thought of Ellen Olenska 'as one might think of some imaginary beloved in a book or picture: she had become the composite vision of all that he had missed' (*AI*, p. 289). He has settled for marriage as a 'dull duty': 'this did not so much matter so long as it kept the dignity of a duty'. The thought of Ellen has kept him from unfaithfulness: 'lapsing from that ... it became a mere battle of ugly appetites' (*AI*, p. 289).

Newland Archer feels his heart beating with the confusion and eagerness of youth in Paris. His son announces that 'the Countess Olenska expects us both at half past five.' Fanny Beaumont, to whom the son is engaged, had urged him to look her up. May told her son the day before she died that she had once asked her husband to give up the thing he most wanted: 'She never asked me', is the father's rejoinder.

Ellen never went back to her husband, who has since died. There is nothing now to keep her and Archer apart. When the time comes, however, he prefers to sit outside on a bench and lets his son go up to Ellen's flat alone.

'I believe I'll sit there a moment,' he said. What shall the boy say? 'Say I'm old-fashioned: that's enough.' He imagines the boy going up, and the lady rising to meet him.

> 'It's more real to me here than if I went up,' he suddenly heard himself say; and the fear lest that last shadow of reality should lose its edge to kept him rooted to his seat as the minutes succeeded each other. He sat for a long time on the bench in the thickening dusk, his eyes never turning from the balcony. At length a light shone through the windows, and a moment later a man-servant came out on the balcony, drew up the awnings and closed the shutters.
>
> At that, as if it had been the signal he waited for, Newland Archer got up slowly and walked back alone to his hotel. (*AI*, p. 301)

It is a bitterly sad moment, but perfect in its inevitability: the unsatisfactory man whose opposition to the deathly conventionalities has never been strong enough for him to provoke a crisis is finally exposed: and now it is too late.

The Age of Innocence is a superb novel, spun out of Edith Wharton's own deepest experience. It has greater depths of the understanding of passion than any novel by Henry James, it abounds with profoundly feminine insights, and it possesses the penetration into social *moeurs* of the author of Anna Karenina. We finish reading the novel in a state of miserable ambivalence. We wish that Newland and Ellen could have consummated their love; yet we have to recognize that, since Archer proved unable to extricate himself from his engagement, the only course open to them was one which would deceive and wound others—and involve them in an impossibility of finding harmony within society—with the possibility only of being brought, as with Vronsky and Anna, to increasing despair and frustration. And while the conventions of society are deadening, one cannot but have respect for the dogged courage of May Welland, who defends her marriage with such tact and resolution. But to point out these complexities is only to pay tribute to the life in the art.

* References are to the Penguin Edition of 1981.

KATHY MILLER HADLEY

Ironic Structure and Untold Stories in
The Age of Innocence

In her 1920 *The Age of Innocence*, Edith Wharton presents a story which, on
the surface, is a man's story, and which in many ways appears to be a
conventional nineteenth-century romance. These things *appear* to be so
because Wharton tells the story from Newland Archer's point of view,
focusing on his consciousness and the way he deals with the potential love
triangle in which he finds himself. But as Rachel Blau DuPlessis argues, while
nineteenth-century authors made certain "that *Bildung* and romance could
not coexist and be integrated for the heroine at the resolution," twentieth-
century women writers are "writing beyond" such endings, breaking the
narrative structure which says that women must ultimately sacrifice their
questing to marriage, or die.[1] In *The Age of Innocence*, Wharton writes beyond
a traditional nineteenth-century ending by ironically undermining the
structure of the novel and its focus on Newland Archer, a would-be
American hero. and by drawing the reader's attention to the untold stories of
Ellen Olenska and May Welland.

Wharton's careful structuring of *The Age of Innocence* is evidenced by
the three different plans she outlined for the novel.[2] In the first version, May
and Archer break their engagement. Archer is shocked when Ellen responds
to his proposal by suggesting that they spend a few weeks together to make
sure of their feelings for each other. Ellen and Newland marry despite

From *Studies in the Novel 23*, no. 2 (Summer 1991): 262–272. © 1991 by the University of North
Texas.

Archer's misgivings but eventually separate because Ellen's soul "recoils" from the prospect of an old New York marriage. Ellen returns to Europe, where "She is very poor, & very lonely, but she has a real life"; Archer returns to his mother's house. Apparently this version of the novel would have emphasized Ellen's ability to act and to cause extensive changes in the lives of others.

Wharton's second plan calls for a much more conventional novel: Archer marries May and has a brief affair with Ellen, who then returns to Europe. Discussing these plans, Alan Price concludes that Wharton shifted the focus from Ellen to Archer in the second version partly because: "she could not be confident [in her first plan] that her readers would share her sympathy for a woman who broke up the engagement of a nice girl, suggested a trial marriage, and then abandoned her husband because she thought New York's seasonal social life was dull" (p. 24).

The third plan again has Archer marrying May but having an affair with Ellen. Although everyone else surmises that Newland and Ellen are lovers, May "suspects nothing." As a Catholic, Ellen cannot divorce, so she could not marry Newland even if he left May. But Ellen again grows tired of New York and her affair with Archer and returns to "the freedom and variety of her European existence." The final dinner for Ellen in versions two and three is simply a good-bye, not the ritual of ostracism it becomes in the finished novel.

By the time she had completed *The Age of Innocence* in its published form, Wharton had made Ellen Olenska an ostensibly minor character, while Newland Archer became the novel's central figure. As Wharton's chosen center of consciousness, Newland appears to be a traditional American hero: the American male whose search for a new frontier, according to such critics as Henry Nash Smith and Richard Chase, makes this country's literature distinctly American.[3] Discussing the way the myth of the American hero has displaced women writers from the canon and has trivialized women characters in fiction, Nina Baym says that the myth entails "the pure American self" confronting "the promise offered by the idea of America ... that in this new land, untrammeled by history and social accident, a person will be able to achieve complete self-definition." Society becomes "something artificial and secondary to human nature" which "exerts an unmitigatedly destructive pressure on individuality." Because both society and landscape are "depicted in unmistakably feminine terms," the American hero is realized as the opposite of the feminine, and the myth becomes exclusively male (pp. 131–33).

The American hero's story becomes, in effect, a male *bildungsroman*; thus Archer, whose first name refers to the American hero's quest for a *new land*, struggles with his romantic triangle and his need for self-definition. Newland persistently fails to define himself, however. Married to May for a year, he contrasts his present life with his "vision of the past" and muses, "What am I? A son-in-law—."[4] At the end of the novel, Newland reminisces about having "risen up at the call" to politics (dropping "thankfully" into obscurity when not re-elected), and of having been "a good citizen" and "what was called a faithful husband" (pp. 349–50). To the end, Wharton emphasizes that Newland is defined by his social roles.

May is originally the frontier on which Newland plans to exercise his selfhood. She is to be a "miracle of fire and ice," both passion and purity, which he will create by his "enlightening companionship" (p. 5). But Newland relinquishes this goal after his wedding, concluding that "There was no use in trying to emancipate a wife who had not the dimmest notion that she was not free," an assumption based largely on the "most tranquil unawareness" Newland believes he sees in May's eyes (pp. 195–98, 188).

Ellen is the promising landscape; for Newland, this quite *unfree* woman comes to represent the freedom of a world different from his own. Sitting beside Ellen in his wife's carriage, Newland tells her, "The only reality to me is this." When Ellen asks if he wants her to be his mistress, the flustered Newland replies:

> I want somehow to get away with you into a world where words
> like that—categories like that—won't exist. Where we shall be
> simply two human beings who love each other, who are the whole
> of life to each other; and nothing else on earth will matter. (pp.
> 292–93)

This is the new-land of Archer's name. What he really wants is the ability to move between May's and Ellen's worlds without any cost to himself, and without deciding between the two worlds. That Newland seeks a dream world rather than an actual place is suggested by the fact that he had previously rejected the possibility of a physical quest. When Ned Winsett had spoken of emigrating, Newland had thought, "Emigrate! As if a gentleman could abandon his own country!" (p. 124). Ironically, one of the few physical journeys Newland does make is his flight from Ellen to Florida, where he begs May to hasten their wedding—with the result that Ellen can be, at most, his mistress.[5] Ellen sees through his romanticized longing for another world and responds, "Oh, my dear—where is that country?" (p. 293).

Wharton undermines her own form throughout the novel, writing beyond the story about Newland Archer to convey a sense of the women characters that her attention to her audience and to acceptable forms removed from center stage. Beside Newland's *bildungsroman* is that of Ellen Olenska, whose search *is* manifested by a physical journey—"home" to New York, then back again to Europe.[6] Wharton makes it clear that Ellen's return to New York is a type of quest. At the van der Luydens' dinner, Newland assures Ellen that she is "among friends." She answers. "Yes—I know. Wherever I go I have that feeling. *That's why I came home*. I want to forget everything else, to become a complete American again" (p. 62, my emphasis).

Not that Ellen's journey to New York involves a wholesale acceptance of its ways. She refuses to live with her grandmother because she "had to be free," and she moves away from the social center of New York to be surrounded by artists, as she was in France (pp. 74, 72). When Archer tells her that her house is in an unfashionable quarter, she says, "Why not make one's own fashions? But," she concedes, "I suppose I've lived too independently: at any rate, I want to do what you all do—I want to feel cared for and safe." She continues, "Being here is like—like—being taken on a holiday when one has been a good little girl and done all one's lessons" (p. 72). She appeals to Newland for help with learning how to fit in: "But you'll explain these things to me—you'll tell me all I ought to know." Newland responds, "It's you who are telling me: opening my eyes to things I'd looked at so long that I'd ceased to see them." He has turned Ellen's appeal for help around, thus re-focusing her energies, and the reader's, on *his* quest (p. 73). Newland is unable to truly help Ellen because he is so self-absorbed.

Ellen's respect for the ways of old New York becomes increasingly tinged with skepticism.[7] She soon begins to see New York differently: it is no longer a haven. Ellen's early ability to see through the van der Luydens' reclusiveness anticipates her increasing ability to make her own informed judgments about New York and to decide whether or not her quest should end there (p. 73). Newland, trying to steer Ellen away from the influence of Julius Beaufort, assures her that the older women "want to help you." Ellen answers, "on condition that they don't hear anything unpleasant ... Does no one want to know the truth here, Mr. Archer? The real loneliness is living among all these kind people who only ask one to pretend!" (p. 75). Ellen has already discovered that she must continue to be a "good little girl" if she is to get along in New York; her success there depends on behaving to please others, as children must do, and stifling her adult views and feelings. If she fails to do so, Ellen may, like a bad little girl, lose her allowance.

In a later scene, Newland (not yet married) confesses his love for Ellen and speaks of their freeing themselves for each other (p. 171). But Ellen rejects Newland's plan because of the sense of loyalty he has made her feel: "you hated happiness bought by disloyalty and cruelty and indifference. That was what I'd never known before—and it's better than anything I've known" (p. 172). Ellen's words suggest that Wharton wants the reader to view Newland positively, as a champion of loyalty, kindness, and concern. But while Ellen sees his advice that she give up her divorce suit as evidence of Newland's strong moral character, Newland was simply representing the family's view when he gave her that advice (pp. 96–98). By speaking for the family and urging Ellen not to divorce, Newland has, in effect, sabotaged his own quest. Finding that they are now inconvenient to him, he is willing to overthrow the principles for which he had stood. Ellen, however, refuses to do so.

In this scene, Ellen also tells of Granny's revealing how New York sees her.

> I was perfectly unconscious at first that people here were shy of me—that they thought I was a dreadful sort of person ... New York simply meant peace and freedom to me: it was coming home. (p. 172)

She tries to explain to Archer the way this realization has affected her: "I *was* lonely; I *was* afraid. But the emptiness and the darkness are gone: when I turn back into myself now I'm like a child going at night into a room where there's always a light" (p. 173). This is a critical stage in Ellen's quest. She has learned to find comfort and strength within herself, rather than seeking them in the external world.[8] She is now able to leave New York (returning only when her grandmother has a stroke), so that she does not disrupt Newland's and May's wedding. But Archer responds, "I don't understand you!" He still assumes that a woman needs a man to sustain her; earlier in their confrontation, when she cried "I can't love you unless I give you up," he had retorted, "And Beaufort? Is he to replace me?" (p. 173). Newland, unable to comprehend Ellen's psychological self-reliance, continues to think that she is simply rejecting him in favor of another man.

Because she is seen through Newland's eyes and appears primarily as a factor in his quest, much of Ellen's story is untold. Discussing the politics of the untold story, DuPlessis says: "To compose a work is to negotiate with these questions: What stories can be told? How can plots be resolved? What is felt to be narratable by both literary and social conventions? Indeed, these are issues very acute to certain feminist critics and women writers, with their senses of the untold story, the other side of a well-known tale" (p. 3). Wharton negotiates such questions by constantly *reminding* us that Ellen's is an untold story. She ironically invites the reader to speculate about Ellen's story by focusing on Newland's obsessive curiosity about it—a curiosity that is fed by Ellen's own willingness to leave her story untold. In this way, Newland's quest becomes largely a search for information about *Ellen's*.

In Ellen's legal file, Newland finds a letter from her husband which he tells himself contains "the vague charge of an angry blackguard"—that Ellen had an affair with his secretary, Yet Newland wonders, "how much truth was behind it? Only Count Olenski's wife could tell" (p. 108). Many of Newland's subsequent conversations with Ellen involve attempts to answer this question. Initially, he gropes for a denial, but Ellen does not give one. When he asks what she thinks she can gain by divorcing her distant husband. Ellen says, "But my freedom—is that nothing?" Newland concludes that "the charge in the letter was true, and that she hoped to marry the partner of her guilt" (pp. 109–10). For Newland, apparently, Ellen's freedom *does* mean nothing; he assumes that she would only want to be free from one man in order to marry (i.e., relinquish her freedom to) another.

Unsettled by Ellen's failure to deny having an affair, Newland "rambled on" in "his intense desire to cover over the ugly reality which her silence seemed to have laid bare" (p. 110). Newland needs to know whether or not Ellen has had an affair because for him it is important to keep women in categories: he remembers how young men make an "abysmal distinction between the women one loved and respected and those one enjoyed—and pitied" (p. 95). He tries to tell himself that in Europe, there might arise situations "in which a woman naturally sensitive and aloof would yet, from the force of circumstances ... be drawn into a tie inexcusable by conventional standards" (p. 95). Newland is clearly uncomfortable with such a scenario, however; only when Ellen implicitly denies her husband's accusation, saying "I had nothing to fear from that letter," is Newland ready to commit himself to her (p. 170).

Contrasted with Ellen's *bildungsroman* is May's seemingly conventional romance. But Wharton undermines May's romance plot, as well. One of the more obvious ways in which Wharton wrote beyond a traditional nineteenth-century novel ending was her handling of Newland's and May's wedding. Rather than concluding the novel with Archer's feelings for Ellen resolved beforehand, as it would have a conventional novel, the wedding begins Book II of *The Age of Innocence*. Structurally, placing the wedding here suggests a new beginning, but in fact Newland's conflict continues—and intensifies—once he is married.

The wedding itself is an extremely ironic occasion. It takes place the Tuesday after Easter, a holiday that symbolizes regeneration, new life, hope: yet, as Virginia Blum notes, the service is "cast in funereal language."[9] Newland compares his wedding with an Opera night and wonders if, "when the Last Trump sounded, Mrs. Selfridge Merry would be there with the same towering ostrich feathers in her bonnet, and Mrs. Beaufort with the same diamond earrings and the same smile—and whether suitable proscenium seats were already prepared for them in another world" (p. 181). With this imagery. Wharton juxtaposes the two traditional nineteenth-century novel endings: marriage and death become one. Newland cannot concentrate on the ceremony: he looks for Ellen, and misses half of the bridal procession (pp. 184–85).

Placing the wedding in the center of the novel suggests that *The Age of Innocence* will fit another pattern that developed early in the twentieth-century: novels "which either begin with [the heroine's] marriage or launch her rapidly into it, and concern a working out of her identity within or against the context of the marriage."[10] Wharton does not work out May's identity, however; May's story, like Ellen's, remains untold. The difference is that, while Newland becomes obsessed with Ellen's story, he has almost no curiosity about his wife's. He prefers the potentially scandalous past of another woman even to the present of his own wife who, he assumes, has no past worth his notice.

Newland discounts May's experience because he perceives her as completely innocent.[11] In fact, we see May only through his eyes; Newland projects his ideal of innocence onto May (just as he projects an aura of secrecy onto Ellen). May appears to be the innocent of the novel's title, but she is not, and Newland must misinterpret his interactions with May in order to continue viewing her as innocent. When May questions his reason for wanting to hasten their wedding, Newland recognizes her insight. But when she "flushed with joy" at his assurance that "There is no pledge—no obligation whatever—of the kind you think," May "seemed to have descended from her womanly eminence to helpless and timorous girlhood" (pp. 147–49). Ironically, he is disappointed with May for believing that he is telling the truth.

This scene also indicates May's "potential for growth and change."[12] This potential is what Archer does not see, One of the few times in the novel that he really looks at his wife is near the end, when he "was struck by something languid and inelastic in her attitude" and briefly "wondered if the deadly monotony of their lives had laid its weight on her also" (p. 296). He does not consider that she may suspect his feelings for Ellen, much less that she may be pregnant. Newland then trivializes what he sees by attributing May's languid demeanor to the fact that he had forgotten to meet her at her grandmother's that day (p. 296).

Only in the novel's penultimate chapter, at the dinner for Ellen, does Archer realize how much his wife has suspected and how often she has acted. "And then it came over him, in a vast flash made up of many broken gleams, that to all of them he and Madame Olenska were lovers ... he understood that, by means as yet unknown to him, the separation between himself and the partner of his guilt had been achieved, and that now the whole tribe had rallied about his wife on the tacit assumption that nobody knew anything" (p. 338). The "means" had culminated in May's telling Ellen she was pregnant, before she knew for certain: and in telling this lie, May was "acting with the knowledge and approval of the family," as Judith Fryer notes.[13] Fryer says that *Because of the way we are used to reading novels*, the romance of Newland and Ellen at first obscures the force of the countersubject: the inexorableness of the offensive launched by the women" against Ellen (p. 138, my emphasis). Wharton gives us what appears to be a traditional novel and then surprises us with this most powerful glimpse of May's untold story. In fact, it has been Newland's lack of attention to May's story that has enabled her to destroy his hope of "escape": while he fell asleep exhausted after arranging for Ellen to come to him once, May was having the "really good talk" with Ellen that causes her to finally decide to return to Europe (pp. 316–17).

May's careful, knowing control of her situation—contrasted with Newland's ignorance—makes the title of *The Age of Innocence* especially ironic. Wharton appears to have intended this effect. Her working title for this novel was *Old New York*. In both of the plans in which Newland and May marry, Newland has an affair with Ellen which his wife never suspects.[14] Only in the final version, when she changed the title to *The Age of Innocence*, did Wharton invert the relationship between suspicion and truth, changing May into a woman who assumes that her husband has had an affair when he has not.

Also ironic is the way Wharton treats May as domesticator. This role, like that of May's innocence, is largely projected onto her by Newland. Early in the novel, Newland had "thanked heaven that he was a New Yorker, and about to ally himself with one of his own kind" (p. 29). But as he becomes enamored with Ellen, "there were moments when he felt as if he were being buried alive under his future." His response is to rush to May, to encourage her, in effect, to seal his future before he risks involvement with Ellen (p. 139). Much later, at the dinner which is "the tribal rally around a kinswoman about to be eliminated from the tribe," Newland "felt like a prisoner in the center of an armed camp" (pp. 337–38). These and other references to Newland's feeling trapped are juxtaposed with the fact that he begged that his wedding be hastened, and that May offered to break their engagement when she sensed that he loved another woman.

As Wharton takes care to describe it. May's house represents all the negative aspects of domesticity; here Newland also feels trapped, as the following scene indicates. One winter evening in his library, watching May as she sews, Newland opens the window because "The room is stifling: I want a little air." Leaning out the window, "The mere fact of not looking at May, seated beside his table, under his lamp, the fact of seeing other houses, roofs, chimneys, of getting the sense of other lives outside his own, other cities beyond New York, and a whole world beyond his world, cleared his brain and made it easier to breathe" (p. 298). May is infringing on Newland's space; this is *his* table, *his* lamp, *his* library—the only room in the house he has decorated as he likes. He looks out the window to "a whole world beyond," much as the traditional American hero looks to the landscape and the frontier for escape from a domesticated world.

But Wharton undermines Newland's perception in two ways. In this scene, Newland is frustrated because Ellen has just refused to become his mistress. And Newland's sense of May as entrapper is ironic because he has considerably misunderstood her character. Before opening the window, "he said to himself with a secret dismay that he would always know the thoughts behind [her clear brow], that never, in all the years to come, would she surprise him by an unexpected mood, by a new idea, a weakness, a cruelty or an emotion" (p. 298). Yet Wharton makes it clear that Archer does *not* know May's thoughts: he not only hasn't realized that she suspects his feelings for Ellen, he does not yet know that May and the rest of the family have determined to exclude him from their discussions of Ellen (p. 299). When May says. "Do shut the window. You'll catch your death." he wants to tell her, "I am dead—I've been dead for months and months." But any sympathy we may feel for him wanes when he thinks. "What if it were *she* who was dead! ... [May] might die, and set him suddenly free" (pp. 298–99). Having failed to take control of his own life, Newland now passively hopes for a catastrophe to change his life for him.

If May represents domesticity and her house, that domesticating force, Ellen's house represents escape for Newland. Ellen's drawing room is "unlike any room he had known"; it contains pictures that "bewildered him, for they were like nothing that he was accustomed to look at (and therefore able to see) when he travelled in Italy" (pp. 67–68). In the same way, Newland is "unable to see" Ellen herself; she will remain, for him, wrapped in an aura of European mystique. Newland had contrasted Ellen's drawing room, with its "vague pervading perfume ... like the scent of some far-off bazaar," with the stuffy, conventional house that awaited him after his conventional honeymoon with May (pp. 69–70). As Fryer notes, Ellen "offers the possibilities of individual freedom and experience, instinct and variety, cultural and sexual richness ... [so] Newland sends her not lilies-of-the-valley, but yellow roses."[15]

Unlike the typical nineteenth-century woman's *bildungsroman*, Ellen's story ends in neither death nor marriage. Her quest has not been sacrificed to romance, as far as we know; she rejects the novel's two major romance possibilities: an affair with Newland and return to her husband.[16] At the end of the novel, twenty-six years after Ellen is banished from New York, Newland has an opportunity to see her again. May has died, and Newland, in Paris with his son Dallas, has received an invitation to Ellen's. But upon reaching her apartment building, Newland decides not to go in. Critics have offered several convincing reasons for this ending: Newland may be afraid to take the risk of a real relationship, or that Ellen will have changed too much; or, he may be so struck with Dallas' revelation that May had understood what it meant for him to give up Ellen, that he does not want to disturb his memory of May, who had "guessed and pitied" (p. 360).[17]

However we choose to interpret Newland's declining to see Ellen at the end, the fact is that with this ending, Wharton leaves the resolution of Ellen's *bildungsroman* open, and once again invites us to speculate about her untold story. Like Newland, we can only imagine whether or not quest and romance coexist for Ellen, just as we can only imagine what it was like for May to live at the center of "a kind of innocent family hypocrisy" in which her husband and children treated her as one "so lacking in imagination, so incapable of growth" that she saw nothing that happened around her (p. 351). Wharton does invite us to imagine the best for Ellen, however, by suggesting that she has kept herself free all these years.

So the novel ends with the bittersweet denouement of Newland Archer's quest in which, because his son touches on what he and May had never spoken of, "He had to deal all at once with the packed regrets and stifled memories of an inarticulate lifetime," a life which "had been too starved" (pp. 360–61). And in the same city where his quest comes to an end is Ellen, who so far as we can tell, enjoys the "freedom and variety of her European existence" on the same street in Paris where the divorced Wharton lived for many years, surrounding herself with "a quiet harvest of friendship" (p. 361).

NOTES

1. Rachel Blau DuPlessis, *Writing Beyond the Ending: Narrative Strategies of Twentieth-Century Women Writers* (Bloomington: Indiana Univ. Press. 1985), pp. 3–4. Subsequent references are cited within the text.

2. Alan Price, "The Composition of Edith Wharton's *The Age of Innocence*," *The Yale University Library Gazette* 55 (1981): 23–28. Subsequent references are cited within the text. See Price for Wharton's three plans for *The Age of Innocence* and for further discussion of those plans.

3. Nina Baym, "Melodramas of Beset Manhood: How Theories of American Fiction Exclude Women Authors," *American Quarterly* 33 (1981): 131–32. Subsequent references are cited within the text.

4. Edith Wharton, *The Age of Innocence* (New York: Appleton, 1920), p. 217. Subsequent references are cited within the text.

5. Cynthia Griffin Wolff reads the novel this way, noting that unlike most *bildungsromans*, Newland's is an "entirely internal" search: "He cannot flee the provincial world of old New York; he must learn to transmute it into something valuable." What his search leads to, Wolff argues, is Newland's "dedication to generativity," the same commitment to the future that May and the other mothers in the novel share. See *A Feast of Words: The Triumph of Edith Wharton* (New York: Oxford Univ. Press, 1977), pp. 314–15.

6. Wendy Gimbel also discusses Ellen's *bildungsroman*, in *Edith Wharton: Orphancy and Survival*, ed. Annette Baxter (Landmark Dissertations in Women's Studies Series, New York: Praeger, 1984), pp. 127–30, 144. But Gimbel considers this primarily an "interior quest" manifested by Ellen's movement among houses. She also argues that in returning to New York, Ellen initially seeks oblivion and regression. Similarly, in *The Female Intruder in the Novels of Edith Wharton* (Rutherford, NJ: Fairleigh Dickinson Univ. Press 1982), Carol Wershoven discusses R. W. B. Lewis' criteria for an American hero and says "Wharton's novels with their intruder heroines are a variation of the American theme." with the heroines working "toward their own autonomy" (p. 17). Subsequent references to Gimbel and Wershoven are cited within the text.

7. In *Female Intruder*, Wershoven discusses the way that, in Wharton's novels, a woman who becomes an outsider often "begins to form her own, new values, and to act and to grow independently" (p. 16). In "Purity and Power in *The Age of Innocence*," *American Literary Realism* 17 (1984), Judith Fryer also discusses Ellen's place as a "marginal" character who "threatens to engulf the little world of order and purity in a world of sexual and cultural richness that would destroy it" (p. 164).

8. Gimbel, in contrast, interprets this scene as evidence that Ellen is still acting and thinking as a child (*Orphancy and Survival*, p. 147).

9. Virginia L. Blum, "Edith Wharton's Erotic Other-World," *Literature and Psychology* 33 (1987): 25.

10. Sally Allen McNall, *Who is in the House? A Psychological Study of Two Centuries of Women's Fiction in America, 1795 to the Present* (New York: Elsevier, 1981), pp. 76–77.

11. Elizabeth Ammons discusses the "American girl" idealized in late nineteenth-century novels—"adventurous, ignorant, virtuous, self-assured"—and says that "Wharton was attacking an entire tradition when she entered May Welland in the lists of nineteenth-century American girls," because this ideal of innocence is so negative and destructive. See "Cool Diana and the Blood-Red Muse: Edith Wharton on Innocence and Art," *American Novelists Revisited: Essays in Feminist Criticism*, ed. Fritz Fleischmann (Boston: G. K. Hall, 1982), pp. 213–15.

12. Weishover, p. 87.

13. Judith Fryer, *Felicitous Space: The Imaginative Structures of Edith Wharton and Willa Cather* (Chapel Hill: Univ. of North Carolina Press 1986), p. 138. Subsequent references are cited within the text.

14. Price, pp. 24–27.

15. "Purity and Power." p. 161.

16. DuPlessis discusses the way that, in traditional nineteenth-century novels, "any plot of self-realization was at the service of the marriage plot" (*Writing Beyond the Ending*, p. 6).

17. See Fryer ("Purity and Power") p. 156; Gimbel, p. 162: and Ammons, pp. 210–11 for these three major interpretations of the ending.

JOHN J. MURPHY

Filters, Portraits, and History's Mixed Bag:
A Lost Lady *and* The Age of Innocence

It has always been surprising to me that Willa Cather's and Edith Wharton's lives failed to touch. They were born eleven years apart (1862 and 1873); their careers in fiction overlapped for more than three decades; two years separated their Pulitzer Prizes (Wharton's for *The Age of Innocence* in 1921, and Cather's for *One of Ours* in 1923); they both were Jamesians, Francophiles, shared acquaintance with fellow writers like Sinclair Lewis and Scott Fitzgerald; and they died a decade apart—Wharton in 1937, Cather in 1947. In a 1931 Colophon piece Cather admits trying to imitate Wharton's fashionable fiction before discovering her own home pasture in *O Pioneers!* (1913) (*On Writing* 93), and in a *New York Times* interview in 1924 she mentioned reading a Wharton article on France (*WC in Person* 70), but I find no other recognition. Neither in the R.W.B. Lewis biography nor in the collection of Wharton letters does the index include Cather; the exhaustive James Woodress biography of Cather includes only three entries under Wharton, and these refer to inclusions in lists of Cather contemporaries. Surely Cather must have read the 1921 Pulitzer Prize-winning *The Age of Innocence*, which appeared when she was concluding *One of Ours* and before she began *A Lost Lady*. I begin with a question I can't answer: How much did Cather's reading of Wharton's masterpiece influence *A Lost Lady*? Questions like this can seldom be answered satisfactorily; however, the comparisons

From *Twentieth Century Literature* 38, no. 4 (Winter 1992): 476–485. © 1992 by Hofstra University.

45

they generate do contribute understanding of the subjects, and placing these two novels side by side indicates significant similarities, if not influence.

Cynthia Wolff's labeling Wharton's writing *The Age of Innocence* "a nostalgic act" (310) could easily be applied to Cather's writing *A Lost Lady*. Both novelists observe their subjects over the chasm left by the war in France. Wharton laments the losses of these years in her autobiography: "The brief rapture that came with the cessation of the war ... soon gave way to a growing sense of the waste and loss wrought by these irreparable years.... I myself had lost a charming young cousin, Newbold Rhinelander, shot down in an aeroplane battle in September 1917" (*Backward* 363–64). She then mentions the untimely death of a young American officer friend, Ronald Simmons, for whom she commissioned a vault in a Marseilles cemetery, and also the passing of older intimates Howard Sturgis and Henry James. In a spirit heavy with these losses she began writing about the war "with a new intensity of vision," she says. "A study of the world at the rear [she had lived in Paris during the war] seemed to me worth doing, and I pondered over it till it took shape in *A Son at the Front*" (368–69), a novel "intended as another wreath on Simmons' grave" (Lewis 457), which appeared, to mixed reviews, only in 1923. "Meanwhile," Wharton continues, "I found a momentary escape in going back to my childhood memories of a long vanished America, and wrote *The Age of Innocence*" (*Backward* 369). Lewis bluntly says that disillusionment with the contemporary American cad of the type she saw overrunning Paris after the war led her back to the world of her growing up and young womanhood, a nineteenth-century world she defined to Sara Norton as "a blessed refuge from the turmoil and mediocrity of today—like taking sanctuary in a mighty temple" (Lewis 423–24). But the writing was more than a refuge, notes Lewis; it helped her rediscover a vital continuity in herself after experiencing a cleavage from everything she had known and been—became, in effect, an "act of reconciliation. In *The Age of Innocence* Edith Wharton sought to come back to herself" (424–25).

At this point we are able to approach Willa Cather. In a brief prefatory statement in her 1936 essay collection, *Not Under Forty*, Cather wrote, "The world broke in two in 1922 or thereabouts, and the persons [like Flaubert's niece, and Mrs. Fields, Sarah Orne Jewett, Katherine Mansfield, and Thomas Mann] and prejudices recalled in these sketches slide back into yesterday's seven thousand years.... It is for the backward, and by one of their number, that these sketches were written." Woodress notes Cather's increasingly valetudinarian attitude from 1922 on, her disillusionment with the postwar Jazz Age, the callousness of prosperity—stingy, grasping, extravagant—and the lazy descendants of earlier generations (335–36). *A Lost Lady* is a product of this watershed year and of nostalgia. The idea for the novel came to Cather during a Toronto stay with Isabelle and Jan Hambourg in the middle of the exhausting writing stint of her 1922 war novel, *One of Ours*, triggered by the death of her soldier cousin, G.P. Cather, and inspired too by the killing of talented young violinist David Hochstein. While in Toronto Cather read the obituary of Lyra Garber, former wife of early Nebraska Governor Silas Garber, personages from Red Cloud childhood days. Once *One of Ours* was finished, the new novel went quickly, was written in five months, and Cather returned to Red Cloud for her parents' golden anniversary and a family reunion, to reconnect with many friends among the immigrant settlers, and to be confirmed in the local Episcopal church. *A Lost Lady*, set "thirty or forty years ago, in one of those gray towns along the Burlington railroad, which are so much grayer today [in 1922] than they were then" (9), recaptures the pioneer past of the 1880s and betrays a nostalgia for that past while continuing the harsh attack on American materialism evident in the more contemporary *One of Ours*.

The postwar, pro-pioneer attitudes in *A Lost Lady* can best be gauged by reading it alongside Cather's 1923 lament for the old days in the "These United States" series in Mencken's *The Nation*, "Nebraska: The End of the First Cycle." The novel offers a summary of Captain Forrester's autobiographical narrative:

> ... a concise account of how he came West ... and took a job as driver for a freighting company that carried supplies across the plains from Nebraska City to Cherry Creek, as Denver was then called. The freighters, after embarking in that sea of grass six hundred miles in width, lost all count of the days of the week and the month. One day was like another, and all were glorious, good hunting, plenty of antelope and buffalo, boundless sunny sky, boundless plains of waving grass, long fresh-water lagoons, yellow with lagoon flowers, where the bison in their periodic migrations stopped to drink and bathe and wallow.   (52)

This passage serves as a concise account of "Nebraska; The End of the First Cycle":

> When silver ore was discovered in the mountains of Colorado near Cherry Creek—afterward ... the city of Denver—a picturesque form of commerce developed across the great plain of Nebraska.... One of the largest freighting companies, operating out of Nebraska City, in ... 1860 carried nearly three million pounds of freight across Nebraska.... The oxen made

from ten to twenty miles a day. I have heard the old freighters say
that, after embarking on their six-hundred-mile trail ... out in that
sea of waving grass, one day was like another; and ... all the days
were glorious.... Along these trails were the buffalo "wallows"—
shallow depressions where the rain water gathered when it ran off
the tough prairie sod.... The freighters lived on game and shot
the buffalo for their hides. The grass was full of quail and prairie
chickens, and flocks of wild ducks swam about on the lagoons.
These lagoons have long since disappeared, but they were
beautiful things in their time.   (236)

But, like *The Age of Innocence*, *A Lost Lady* is more than nostalgia. Woodress
sees in it "a new note ... Cather's implicit message that one must learn to live
with change, adapt to new conditions, accept the inevitable" (348). Survival
tactics, then, fuse with the reworking of historical periods in *A Lost Lady* and
The Age of Innocence, as portraits of exceptional women of the past are
managed from vantage points of less than exceptional, if sympathetic, men in
their lives.

Cather confessed that her initial hurdle in *A Lost Lady* was point of
view: "I discarded ever so many drafts, and in the beginning wrote it in the
first person, speaking as the boy [Niel Herbert] himself. The question was,
by what medium could I present her [Marian Forrester] the most vividly, and
that, of course, meant the most truly. There was no fun in it unless I could
get her [Mrs. Garber/Mrs. Forrester] just as I remembered her and produce
the effect she had on me and the many others who knew her" (Woodress
340). The task was to accomplish "a portrait like a thin miniature painted in
ivory." Wharton, too, made point of view the key; her "narrative vantage is
carefully chosen," observes Wolff. "The narrator may step outside of
Newland Archer's mind to make judgments or draw conclusions; but ... the
[old New York] world ... becomes ... a mirror of Newland's mind and the very
condition of his being" (314). Merrill Skaggs's contention that in Cather's
portrait of Marian we are given angles of vision on a woman who chooses to
be a sex object (47–48) can be applied to Wharton's Ellen Olenska. And
Hermione Lee's observation that Cather's novel involves "a sense of betrayal
felt by and about the central figure" (193) can be applied helpfully to
Wharton's. Indeed, Lee's definition of Marian Forrester and Myra Henshaw
(*My Mortal Enemy*) as feminine rather than heroic is more applicable to Mrs.
Forrester and Madame Olenska: "They have no children, they are separated
from their family roots, they have no independent occupations, and they
define themselves in terms of their relation to men. They are confined and
thwarted, not expansive and self-fulfilling. Their energies are poured, not

into something impersonal and bigger than themselves—the shaping of the land, the making of an art—but into personal feelings and self-expression" (193–94).

Like John Singer Sargent's "Madame X" (Madame Pierre Gautreau), the portraits titillate while idealizing, a combination that leads the point-of-view males to feel betrayed by and then betray the reality of their fascinating women. What is satirized in each case is a young man shaped by the ideals of a society he views flatly and fails to understand. Wolff notes that Newland Archer's literary dabbling merely contributes, due to his lack of occupation, to his fantasies and that his conformity prevents him from measuring his own society against his reading (315–16). This is also true of Niel Herbert, who condemns Marian Forrester vehemently five pages after we are told how in his reading "he was eavesdropping upon the past, being let into the great world that had plunged and glittered and sumptuously sinned long before little Western towns were dreamed of" (81–82). Newland's reading prepares him as little for marriage as Niel's prepares him for the shock of Frank Ellinger's yawning laughter from Marian's bedroom window. Newland's contemplation of his bride-to-be, May Welland, from across the Academy of Music during a performance of *Faust* is a clear example of his shallowness as well as its undercutting by Wharton's narrator: "'The darling! She doesn't even guess what it's all about. We'll read *Faust* together ... by the Italian lakes ...' he thought, somewhat hazily confusing the scene of his projected honeymoon with the masterpieces of literature which it would be his manly privilege to reveal to his bride" (7). The ambivalence of all this is evident in Newland's expectations in a wife of lily-of-the-valley innocence combined with the worldly wisdom of his ex-mistress. "How this miracle of fire and ice was to be created, and to sustain itself in a harsh world," comments the narrator, "he had never taken the time to think out" (7). Similarly, after insisting on Ellen Olenska's right to freedom and a divorce, he reflects that "nice" women "would never claim the kind of freedom he meant, and generous-minded men were therefore ... the more chivalrously ready to concede it to them.... But here he was pledged to defend, on the part of his betrothed cousin, conduct that, on his own wife's part, would justify him in calling down on her all the thunders of Church and State" (44). The same contradiction surfaces in Niel's reflections on Marian before his discovery of her affair with Ellinger, in his recognition that his interest in her is, curiously, in relation to her husband, in her capacity for the sexual exploits she chooses not to have:

> He rather liked the stories, even the spiteful ones, about the gay life she led in Colorado, and the young men she kept dangling

about her every winter. He sometimes thought of the life she might have been living ever since he had known her,—and the one she had chosen to live. From that disparity, he believed came the subtlest thrill of her fascination. She mocked outrageously at the proprieties she observed, and inherited the magic of contradictions.   (78–79)

Fascination is the bedfellow of suspicion at the dramatic heart of each novel, as their comparable winter scenes illustrate. In *The Age of Innocence* Newland follows Ellen to Skuytercliff, the van der Luydens' Hudson River estate, intercepting her on a snowy footpath returning from church. He has by this time compromised his belief in women's freedom by siding with the Mingott family against Ellen's divorce because he fears that her husband's charges concerning her infidelity, which she has failed to deny, might be true. At the same time his feelings for her are deepening, and he is excited, his gaze "delighted" by her red-cloaked figure, a "red meteor against the snow" (132). The scene is a brilliant Jamesian combination of picture, action, character, as, amid spurts of dialogue about her flight from New York, Ellen breaks into a race and Newland follows, meeting her panting and laughing at a park gate. The conversation that ensues, about her need to escape, he only partially fathoms. Then in the Patroon cottage, soon to be the setting of his honeymoon with May, their talk turns intimate, and his heart beats "insubordinately. What if it were from him that she had been running away, and if she had waited to tell him so till they were here alone in this secret room? ... If the thing [declaration of love] was to happen, it was to happen in this way, with the ... width of the room between them, and his eyes ... fixed on the outer snow" (135). But as he waits, "soul and body throbbing with the miracle to come," the image of heavily-coated Julius Beaufort, a notorious rake later ostracized for financial dishonesty, appears in the window. Was Ellen running from Beaufort, or planning to meet Beaufort at the cottage? Newland's disgust propels him to St. Augustine to have May move up their wedding date because he mistrusts his feelings for her suspicious cousin. In *A Lost Lady* Marian takes Niel on a run down a snowy hill one night in the middle of her first winter confined to Sweet Water after the Captain's stroke. She tells Niel of her frustration and fear: "Suppose we should have to stay here all next winter, too, ... and the next! What will become of me, Niel?" (77). Niel sympathizes, for this woman is the ideal he has worshiped since boyhood, and follows her down the drifts to the frozen creek as the clouds thin to reveal a new moon. But her exclamation that she has seen the moon over the wrong shoulders, shoulders not broad enough, hurts her self-appointed champion, who immediately recalls Frank Ellinger, about whose sexuality Niel "felt something evil" (46): "Instantly before his eyes rose the image of a pair of shoulders that were very broad, objectionably broad, clad in a frogged overcoat with an astrachan collar. The intrusion of this third person annoyed him as they went slowly back up the hill" (78).

Disillusionment puts an end to suspicion in both cases. For Niel it comes on the June morning when Captain Forrester is away in Denver heroically saving the poor depositors from ruin by ruining himself. Ellinger has come to Sweet Water, and Niel attempts to inspire distaste in Marian for this man by leaving roses outside her bedroom window:

> As he bent to place the flowers on the sill, he heard from within a woman's soft laughter; impatient, indulgent, teasing eager. Then another laugh, very different, a man's. And it was fat and lazy—ended in something like a yawn.
>
> Niel found himself at the foot of the hill on a wooden bridge, his face hot, his temples beating, his eyes blind with anger.... In that instant between stooping to the window sill and rising, he had lost one of the most beautiful things in his life.   (86)

Newland's disillusionment results in a fixed gaze at the Gorgon, the reality of Ellen and their situation. He pressures her at the train after her grandmother's stroke, and she bluntly asks if he would have her live with him as his mistress behind the backs of the people who trust them. Protesting that he wants to escape to a place beyond categories like mistress, she insists such places prove "little" and "miserable": "You've never been beyond. And I have, and I know what it looks like there" (290–91). Here is the confession of infidelity he has so long feared. After struggling out of May's brougham, the ironic setting of this conversation, Newland watches it roll away, noticing that his tears have frozen stiff on his eyelashes—he has had to look unblinkingly at the Gorgon. Disillusionment in this case causes recklessness rather than anger, merely increases Newland's compulsion to escape with Ellen. It is Ellen herself, May, and the clan that force his self-confrontation, his submission to the old New York values essentially defining him. According to Wolff, his reaction to May's craftily manipulated announcement of her pregnancy reveals his firm moral commitment: "Newland is restrained from leaving not by any objective and external force—but by the deep-rooted conviction that his own moral duty must ultimately be defined by family obligations" (327).

The lesson of both novels involves the complexity of history and society. Newland Archer's judgment of his society as he sits at the farewell dinner for Ellen, that it "dreaded scandal more than disease, ... placed decency above courage" (335) is one-sided and superficial, and liberated Ellen herself replaces him as spokesperson for it: "It was you who made me understand that under the dullness there are things so fine and sensitive and delicate that even those I most cared for in my other life looked cheap in comparison" (241). Newland's disgust at the dinner recalls Niel's during his last dinner at the Forresters', where the young men look puny to him in the chairs of the pioneers. His simplification about dreamers losing the West to his "generation of shrewd young men, trained to petty economies by hard times," "who had never dared anything, never risked anything" (106–07), is the same kind of half-truth. Mrs. Beasley, Molly Tucker, and most of the folks who invade the Forrester place near the end are not the younger generation, and the affair with Ellinger that Niel discovered before he developed his theory on the decline of the West was not unknown or unacceptable to Captain Forrester. Financial dishonesty might not have been tolerated among the pioneer aristocracy or in old New York, but other immoralities were. "Morals were different in those days" (49), says Cather's narrator before describing Ellinger's scandalous activities with Nell Emerald and then his devotion to his invalid mother. Societies and generations are complex, contradictory.

As younger writers, Cather and Wharton might have simplified, positively or negatively, their generations and past generations, including the so-called heroic ones. Heroic decline in *A Lost Lady* is represented in the physical decline and heaviness of Captain Forrester, whose "features were running into each other, as when a wax face melts in the heat" (109), and whose "ruggedness had changed to an almost Asiatic smoothness. He looked like a wise old Chinese mandarin" (136–37). In *The Age of Innocence* matriarch Catherine Mingott's transformation "from a plump active little woman with a neatly turned foot and ankle into something as vast and august as a natural phenomenon" (28) represents a similar passing. As one looked back over the chasm of the war, the terrain wrinkled into complexity and the expectations of youth seemed as elusive and illusive as they were precious. In Wharton's epilogue a mellow Newland Archer, widowed now after twenty-five years of faithful marriage to May, views the flower of life he had associated with Ellen as "so unattainable and improbable that to have repined [about missing it] would have been like despairing because one had not drawn the first prize in a lottery" (347). In the final coda of Cather's novel, a mature Niel, now "very glad that he had known [Marian Forrester] and that she had had a hand in breaking him into life," reflects on her laughing eyes, that

> seemed to promise a wild delight that he has not found in life. "I know where it is," they seemed to say, "I could show you!" He

would like to call up the shade of the young Mrs. Forrester, as the witch of Endor called up Samuel's, and challenge it, demand the secret of that ardour; ask her whether she had really found some ever-blooming, ever-burning, ever-piercing joy, or whether it was all fine play-acting. Probably she had found no more than another; but she had always the power of suggesting things much lovelier than herself, as the perfume of a single flower may call up the whole sweetness of spring.   (171–72)

Mature views have replaced green, resentful ones. Niel takes comfort in learning that Marian Forrester, the woman he had fled with "contempt for ... in his heart" (*Lost* 169), had been well cared for during her last days; and he shares that comfort with Ed Elliot, now a mining engineer but previously one of those upstart boys Niel had associated with decline. Newland had long ago grown to recognize that the dull duty symbolized by old, innocent New York had preserved dignity and prevented life from becoming "a mere battle of ugly appetites" (347), yet he now concedes that "trenchant divisions between right and wrong, honest and dishonest, respectable and the reverse, had left so little scope for the unforeseen" (351), that "there was good in the new [turn of the century] order too" (349). *The Age of Innocence* and *A Lost Lady* are relatively brief novels, but they are big books and, I think, important ones in communicating the complexities of history, society, and human relationships. Comparing them at least makes this clearer.

WORKS CITED

Cather, Willa. *A Lost Lady*. New York: Vintage, 1972.
———. "Nebraska: The End of the First Cycle." *The Nation* 117 (5 Sept. 1923): 236–38.
———. *Not Under Forty*. New York: Knopf, 1936.
———. *On Writing*. New York: Knopf, 1962.
———. *Willa Cather in Person: Interviews, Speeches, and Letters*. Ed. L. Brent Bohlke. Lincoln: U of Nebraska P, 1986.
Lee, Hermione. *Willa Cather: Double Lives*. New York: Pantheon, 1989.
Lewis, R. W. B. *Edith Wharton: A Biography*. New York: Harper, 1977.
Skaggs, Merrill. *After the World Broke in Two: The Later Novels of Willa Cather*. Charlottesville: UP of Virginia, 1990.
Wharton, Edith. *The Age of Innocence*. New York: Scribners, 1968.
———. *A Backward Glance*. New York: Appleton, 1934.
Wolff, Cynthia Griffin. *A Feast of Words: The Triumph of Edith Wharton*. New York: Oxford, 1977.
Woodress, James. *Willa Cather: A Literary Life*. Lincoln: U of Nebraska P, 1987.

CLARE VIRGINIA EBY

Silencing Women in Edith Wharton's
The Age of Innocence

The most respectable women are the most oppressed.
                                        —Mary Wollstonecraft

Silence has been designated "a category of intelligence of the twentieth century," a response to the modern experience of "alienation from reason, society, and history." Silence has also been called a feminist issue, one not confined to any historical moment but "a form of imposed repression" enforcing the traditional view of the "appropriate condition for women."[1] Edith Wharton's *The Age of Innocence* (1920), a novel poised between the Victorian and modern eras which provocatively examines the potential for women's freedom through a male center of consciousness, encourages a reading of its many silences.[2] The most momentous conversations never become articulated in the text: the plot pivots on May Welland Archer's telling the Countess Ellen Mingott Olenska that she is pregnant, and is sealed by the tribe's decision to cast off the recalcitrant Countess. The novel also illustrates the tragic consequences of evasion and under-specification for the three principal characters. But after recognizing the importance of silences, the interpretive question remains: does Wharton's own rhetorical reticence align her with old New York's last stand as a unified, cohesive society before it is splintered by twentieth century anomie, or does she

From *Colby Quarterly* 28, no. 2. © 1992 by Colby College.

expose the reticence of old New York, showing its cohesiveness to be maintained only by silencing dissent? Reading the silences in *The Age of Innocence* provides an approach into the debate over Wharton's feminism, itself part of a larger debate over her politics.[3] I will argue that Wharton depicts silence and silencing as old New York's means of social control, particularly for maintaining a constricting definition of "the feminine." Contrasting New York's responses to the subversive words spoken by Newland and Ellen, Wharton exposes a sexual double standard. She indicts Newland Archer for his failure to shatter silences and to live by his words. Wharton's treatment of silences calls for a modification in the dominant interpretations of the novel which overstate both her sympathy for Newland and the power of New York women.[4]

Old New York's capacity for silent communication indisputably reflects its cohesiveness as recognized even by a representative of the younger generation, Dallas Archer, in the coda. When Ellen falls from grace, "The Mingotts had not proclaimed their disapproval aloud: their sense of solidarity was too strong."[5] As Cynthia Griffin Wolff rightly says about *The Age of Innocence*, one of New York's "great strengths ... lay in its powerful, unspoken capacity for complex communication." Wolff finds New York's silences "rich with communication," suggesting a "totality of understanding" that the twentieth century will make obsolete. But strength is not necessarily benevolent, and Wolff's premise that Wharton depicts the New York of her youth in *The Age of Innocence* as "prelapsarian"[6] obscures the novelist's critique of the politics of silence. The unity of old New York is that of a police state—its silences resonant, yes, but used as a means of surveillance and control. This can be seen by examining two arbiters of silence and speech, the van der Luydens and Sillerton Jackson.

Wharton's description of the couple at the top of New York's "small and slippery pyramid," Mr. and Mrs. Henry van der Luyden, to whom other New Yorkers turn for the "Court of Last Appeal" (49, 56), illustrates the use of silence for social control. Judge as well as jury, the van der Luydens are "mouthpieces of some remote ancestral authority,"a phrase which aligns sanctioned discourse, power, and maintenance of the status quo. Their position as official "mouthpieces" permits their determination of what can be said and what must he silenced. Firmly aligned with "authority," the van der Luydens literally speak the law. That this law sustains a "remote ancestral authority" underscores the antique roots of the status quo. Significantly, a private conversation offstage always precedes a van der Luyden verdict (56, 53). The power they wield over the rest of New York, kept "remote" by withholding its operation from public view, is the prototype for maintaining hegemony in this small world.

Wharton's reference to the van der Luydens' "remote ancestral authority" participates in the archaeological and anthropological imagery that helps to define her attitude toward her subject. As R. W. B. Lewis has demonstrated, *The Age of Innocence* shows Wharton's "entirely new consciousness of history" brought about by World War I. This new historical consciousness accounts for Wharton's bifurcated perspective.[7] Old New York emerges both as a singular historical moment (one which, as the ticking clocks in the novel remind us, will soon end) and as a manifestation of an institution that stretches back through a succession of like moments to the "dawn of history" (179). *The Age of Innocence* seems both ancient and well-preserved, like the braided hairs in the locket of my Civil War ancestress. But Wharton felt her own ancestresses to be anonymous. Even the constrained and conservative *A Backward Glance* (1934) suggests the difference between male history (visible, voluble, and accessible) and female history (invisible, silent, and buried):

> I know less than nothing of the particular virtues, gifts and modest accomplishments of the young women with pearls in their looped hair or cambric is ruffs round their slim necks. who prepared the way for my generation. A few shreds of anecdote, no more than the faded flowers between the leaves of a great-grandmother's Bible, are all that remains to me.[8]

Wharton is as conscious of her matrilineage as she is of its muteness. *The Age of Innocence* suggests why Wharton's ancestresses left no verbal record. Like her contemporary, Thorstein Veblen, Wharton adopts an anthropological stance to examine critically the origins and continuity of patriarchal power.[9] From the "inscrutable totem terrors that had ruled the destinies of [Newland's] forefathers thousands of years ago" mentioned in the novel's first chapter to the "tribal rally around a kinswoman" occurring in the penultimate (4, 334), nothing changes. The source of this immutable tribal power extends back to the hieroglyphs and pyramids associated with old New York (45, 49). Like Veblen's alignment of leisure-class institutions with barbaric rituals, Wharton's descriptions of New York make the familiar and hegemonic seem like a queer anachronism. Institutions, whether marriage, social calls, or going to the opera, come to seem less inspired by God or "nature" than a product of, as Veblen says, a "habitual frame of mind which experience and tradition have enforced upon [one]."[10] An anthropological perspective on powerful institutions tends to erode their credibility. No wonder that the one archaeologist in the novel, Professor Emerson Sillerton, is considered "revolutionary" and dangerous. The Professor "filled [his] house with long-haired men and short-haired women" (220) who, like Ellen, resist tribal categorization.

A second arbiter of speech and silence is the gossip monger, Sillerton Jackson. As much as the van der Luydens, Jackson helps to sustain the status quo by surveillance and control. By carrying a mental (that is, an unspoken and unwritten) "register of most of the scandals and mysteries that had smoldered under the unruffled surface of New York society" (10), Jackson provides a sanctioned context for speaking the unspeakable, a steam valve that helps to sustain the illusion of an unchanging, unruffled surface. Any action, presumed action, or speech labelled scandalous is publicly suppressed and privately processed by Jackson.[11] Wharton ironically remarks that he "was fully aware that his reputation for discretion increased his opportunities of finding out what he needed to know" (10). If the van der Luydens provide the Court of Last Appeal, Jackson functions as a secular priest hearing confessions. His predictable reticence ensures that actions the community deems sinful will be confessed and thereby can be checked. Sillerton Jackson co-opts the potentially subversive.

Old New York does not rely entirely on the van der Luydens and Jackson to sustain its hegemony. The ability to silence dissent is a communal power, and New York silences whatever it designates "unpleasant": scandal, authentic suffering, anything "foreign," any harbinger of change. Thus they "ignore[d social transitions] till they were well over, and then, in all good faith, imagin[ed] that they had taken place in a preceding age" (259). Like silencing, ignoring is not the absence of actions or speech but their active suppression and denial. Consequently, ignoring permits what Wharton ironically terms "good faith," lying to one's self as well as harming others. The insidious use of silence and silencing culminates in the expulsion of Ellen and subsequent cover-up. At the climactic dinner party Archer, facing "a band of dumb conspirators" and "silently observing eyes," suddenly finds "a deathly sense of the superiority of implication and analogy over direct action, and of silence over rash words, clos[ing] in on him like the doors of the family vault" (335–36).[12] Newland apprehends the undeniable, the "superior" power of his community's silence. But the pervasive death imagery makes clear that this silence is not benign, much less prelapsarian. New York's unspoken communication is a power that kills. Because it does not need to speak, New York can erase the trace of its own sentence. Right after the verdict comes the "obliteration": "The silent organization ... was determined to put itself on record as never for a moment having questioned the propriety of Madame Olenska's conduct, or the completeness of Archer's domestic felicity" (339). So successful a masking of power accounts for its persistence.

New York reacts so violently against Ellen because she says subversive things that challenge its hegemony. Even as a girl, she "asked disconcerting questions [and] made precocious comments" (60). Ellen repeatedly speaks the truth about New York: that the van der Luydens' house is "'gloomy'" (a comment giving Newland "an electric shock"); that New York studiously avoids the truth and fears privacy (73, 78, 133). But it is less what Ellen says than her assumption of free speech that must be silenced. Early in the novel, when the van der Luydens invite Ellen to dinner, she shocks everyone by "plung[ing] into animated talk" with the visiting Duke of St. Austrey. Wharton makes clear that this plunging into talk defies protocol, the very protocol celebrated by the first of two ritualistic dinner parties:

> Neither seemed aware that the Duke should first have paid his respects to Mrs. Lovell Mingott and Mrs. Headley Chivers, and the Countess have conversed with that amiable hypochondriac, Mr. Urban Dagonet of Washington Square, ... (63)

It is telling—and prophetic—that although Ellen and another man speak improperly at this first dinner party, it is the woman who will pay for it. This is because the Countess' uninhibited speech challenges the socially constructed category of "the feminine." After twenty minutes with the Duke, Ellen walks over to Archer. The movement is considered unfeminine and defiant, for:

> It was not the custom in New York drawing rooms for a lady to get up and walk away from one gentleman in order to seek the company of another .... She should wait, immovable as an idol, while the men who wished to converse with her succeeded each other at her side. But the Countess was apparently unaware of having broken any rule. (64)

Ellen's assumption of free speech breaks a rule, so it is dangerous. As Janis P. Stout notes in her study of four women writers' uses of silence, "the woman is no more expected to 'lead' in conversation than she is in ballroom dancing."[13] Ellen's oblivion to her lawlessness means she must be cast out. That she should choose her conversational partner seems to suggest, to the minds of the van der Luydens' guests, that she might be capable of breaking other rules—perhaps even choosing her sexual partner. No wonder that Newland is titillated by this "undeniably exciting" woman (64).[14]

Readers who contend that women wield the power in this novel need to scrutinize the narrow boundaries within which these "idols" function.

R.W.B. Lewis is one of the more authoritative voices to see May "thwart[ing] her husband and cousin's illicit affair"; James W. Tuttleton is one of the more recent to declare that the women "dictate the constraining forms and terms and conditions of ... New York". It would be more accurate to say that the women *take* dictation.[15] How actions that predictably, even monotonously, uphold a hegemonic code are "free" is difficult to see. Wharton illustrates the circumscription of female power through her treatment of May's relationship to language and silence. May is, it is true, adept at silencing the distasteful, a characteristic trait of powerful figures in the novel. Early in their courtship, Newland celebrates his betrothed's "resolute determination to carry to its utmost limit that ritual of ignoring the 'unpleasant' in which they had both been brought up" (26). But as Newland soon grows to resent May, he "wonder[s] at what age 'nice' women began to speak for themselves" (82). The answer, of course, is never. It is May's "duty" neither to speak nor to think for herself; her duty is to wait until men speak to her, to "have no past" and to acquire no experience (44), to remain an undefiled, indeed an untouched, idol. That the category of the "nice" woman is as much a social construct as the "unpleasant," Wharton emphasizes by enclosing each word in quotations marks. These social fabrications, indeed, are mutually reenforcing. May's silencing others' "unpleasant" behavior leads, as Newland quickly discovers, to her self-censorship. This self-regulation is the ultimate goal of institutionalized silencing.

One of the primary social uses of silence in the world of this novel is to contain women within the category of "nice."[16] That Wharton makes this point most strongly through Newland's consciousness has caused many readers to bewail the plight of sensitive, oppressed males with alarming and uncritical haste. Wharton deserves more credit for using Newland, not projecting herself onto him, in this subtle and convoluted novel. In a moment of rebellion that is adolescent in its predictability and inefficacy, Newland articulates *what no female character in this novel could possibly say*: "'Women ought to be free—as free as we are'" (42). The syntax indicates why only a man can speak it: men comprise the "we" who are, relatively, "free." The non-freedom of the second sex is visible only indirectly, by contrast. That is precisely why Newland's statement is so subversive: it "struck to the root of a problem it was agreed in his world to regard as non-existent."[17] The real conspiracy in this novel, not to control men but to declare women's enslavement a non-issue, reveals the terrible power of silence. That the social construct of the "nice" woman rests on perpetuating silence about alternative behaviors Wharton makes clear by following Newland's revelation with: "'Nice' women ... would never claim the kind of freedom he meant" (44).

What kind of freedom does Newland mean? In this novel constructed out of contrasts, "freedom" means individual freedom from social labels, "strik[ing] out for [one's] self," to use Newland's phrase (8). The antinomy resonates soundly in Wharton's life. As a young woman she felt herself "a failure in Boston ... because they thought I was too fashionable to be intelligent, and a failure in New York because they were afraid I was too intelligent to be fashionable" (*Backward*, 119). Although phrased to provoke laughter more than serious reflection, the implication is that the actual person, Edith Wharton, transcends the labels of small social worlds. A greater antinomy Wharton expressed, one that some of her critics have sought to canonize, is that of "male" versus "female" roles. The much-quoted designation of Wharton as a "self-made man" suggests less, it seems to me, her alliance with male values or distrust of women than her impatience with gender categories altogether.[18] The contrast Wharton establishes between her two leading female characters in *The Age of Innocence* illustrates both the meaning of individual freedom and the price that society will extract for it. The narrator's description of May's face as "representative of a type rather than a person; as if she might have been chosen to pose for a Civic Virtue or a Greek goddess" (188) brings Ellen's individuality into focus. Ellen refuses to act as part of the tribe; one cannot conceive of her posing as a statue for Civic Virtue or going to the "Ladies Room" *en masse*. Like her fashionable *and* intelligent author, Ellen cannot be contained by a label like "nice" or "representative" woman. That Ellen had been living in France before the novel begins points to *French Ways and Their Meaning* (1919), in which Wharton contrasts American and French women. The American "disappears from sight upon marriage and withers away" while the French woman remains a free individual.[19]

May once behaved like a free individual, not a part of the tribe, before her marriage. Since so much has been made of May's power to enforce conventions, her "superhuman" and "unorthodox" (150) moment deserves emphasis. Beginning "'Let us talk frankly,'" May shatters the code of silence and steps outside the boundary of the "feminine" when she offers to free her fiance from their engagement (148). Newland refuses, no more able to live with the implications of honest speech with May than with Ellen. May's moment of independent drought and free speech is silenced by that "sacred tabo[o] of the prehistoric ritual," her marriage (180). Once a tribal bride, May's status as representative rather than individual woman is sealed and her husband gives up "trying to disengage her real self from the shape into which tradition and training had moulded her" (327). Maintaining the status quo means silencing the free woman, whether she flits through Newland's stray musings or takes shape in Ellen's behavior. "Nice" women behave like Mrs. Beaufort, "who always preferred to look beautiful and not have to talk" (117).

In the pivotal scene when Newland approaches Ellen as her legal counsel, the narrator show his betrayal of the ideal of the free woman with his conversational style and silences. His speech is marked by the hesitations and the unfinished sentences characteristic of old New York, he cannot get more than the first four letters of the word "unpleasant" out of his mouth (110). He counsels Ellen against divorce on the grounds that it would open her up to "'a lot of beastly talk,'" which now strikes him as unendurable. Ellen significantly counters *his* tribal worries with, "'But my freedom—is that nothing?'" (111). Newland seems conveniently to have forgotten about the free woman. This conversation illustrates his decision to privilege tribal labels over Ellen's self-assertion. No wonder that Newland speaks in "stock phrases ... to cover over the ugly reality which her silence seemed to have laid bare" (112). Newland misinterprets Ellen's silence as would the rest of old New York: rather than consider that she has nothing to say about her putative adultery because it never happened, Newland construes it as a confession.[20] As Lily Bart remarks in *The House of Mirth* (1905), "'What is truth? Where a woman is concerned, it's the story that's easiest to believe.'"[21] Newland adopts the New York strategies of silence, surveillance, and evasion so completely that he reads Ellen's innocent silence as an admission of guilt.

Despite Wharton's alliance of Ellen with "experience" throughout the novel, she is innocent of sin. Later conversations between the would-be lovers align Newland with an insidious silence and Ellen with honest speech. Many of her comments later in the novel shock the now-tribal husband. When Ellen says the word "secretary" Newland blushes, for "She had pronounced the word as if it had no more significance than any other in her vocabulary" (232). More shockingly to Newland, Ellen asks, "'is it your idea, then, that I should live with you as your mistress ...?'" That Newland is "startled" by "the crudeness of the question" (289) illustrates his retreat to the New York science of evasion. He is assuming a role like that of the van der Luydens' shocked guests. Unwilling to forego the titillation that is his prerogative as a male, Newland resorts to a romantically banal language which functions like New York's silences in its disingenuousness and evasion of reality. "'I want,'" he stammers, "'I want somehow to get away with you into a world where words like that—categories like that—won't exist'" (290). Like many another male character in American literature, Newland opts to avoid social commitment and light out for new territory. But in the context of Wharton's socially dense novel, the idea is, as Ellen's response indicates, laughable. Knowing that silence has already begun to condemn her, the idea of avoiding labels by fleeing into silence strikes Ellen as absurd. Newland's utopian fantasy shows him still unwilling to accept responsibility for his contraband desires. In Wharton's terms, there is no freedom without responsibility. Appropriately, Newland soon "find[s] himself prisoner of this hackneyed vocabulary" (309), the bars made out of the words like "mistress" he had tried to avoid.

The irony of *The Age of Innocence* is that Ellen is labelled his mistress. Notably, there is no corresponding term for a sexually delinquent male. Even the women characters believe that when, as they euphemistically put it, "'such things happened,'" the unspeakable act marks the man merely "foolish" but the woman "criminal" (97). According to the sexual double standard, in other words, only a woman can break the law. This only makes sense if we concede that Wharton is writing about a world in which men wield the power. That Ellen is expelled while Newland is reclaimed into the tribe illustrates the double standard at the heart of patriarchy.

The preservation of society—at the expense of a woman silently charged with a crime but not permitted to speak in her defense—suggests that adultery is a social, not a moral issue. As R.W.B. Lewis has shown, Wharton agonized over her own adulterous affair with Morton Fullerton, fearing the violation "not [of] some abstract morality but rather [of] the civilized order of life."[22] In *The Age of Innocence* Wharton criticizes the double standard that holds women responsible for maintaining the civilized order, then stands prepared to condemn them when anything goes awry. The "traitor in the citadel" is "generally," Wharton dryly remarks, thought to be a woman (259). Nice women uphold the status quo. A conservative statement published in 1879 on "The Woman Question" unintentionally illustrates what Wharton exposes in 1870s sexual politics. According to historian Francis Parkman:

> Nations less barbarous have tried to secure the object [of "the integrity of the family and the truth of succession"] by constant watching and restriction, sometimes amounting to actual slavery. European civilization uses better and more effective means. It establishes a standard of honor, and trusts women to conform to it.

What May so zealously guards, after all, is her woman's honor and, behind that, the integrity of the patriarchal family. The remarkably effective "standard of honor" that Parkman refers to *is* nineteenth-century woman's "slavery."[23] As Wharton puts it, "she was the subject creature, and versed in the arts of the enslaved" (*Age*, 305). Perversely, woman's slavery then becomes the grounds for holding her accountable for all sexual transgressions: "A woman's standard of truthfulness was tacitly held to be lower" (305), a conclusion that follows from the premise of women's inferiority. For that reason, a Lawrence Lefferts can conveniently divert attention from his own liaisons by spreading rumors about Ellen (55–56). His lies are valued far more highly than her silence. Newland comes to realize that the social construction of female honor rests on his own "precautions and prevarication, concealments and compliances" (305). Women's honor is a matter of lies and silences, spoken and withheld by men.[24]

The expulsion of Ellen so that Archer can remain one of the tribe provides an exaggerated illustration of the fact that women must sacrifice themselves to maintain the social order. Nancy Cott's description of the expected role for women in the early nineteenth century clearly persists in Wharton's old New York: "constant orientation toward the needs of others, especially men."[25] Behind the differences between Ellen and May that Wharton so painstakingly articulates is their fundamental similarity: both resort to self-sacrifice at moments of crisis. As Ellen tells Newland, "'You showed me ... how one must sacrifice one's self to preserve the dignity of marriage .... I did what you told me .... I've made no secret of having done it for you!'" (169). May, similarly, after her unorthodox moment of promising to free her fiance (not herself), reverts to type, "and he understood that her courage and initiative were all for others, and that site had none for herself" (150–51). The capacity for self-erasure that Ellen and May both exhibit shows old New York's triumph in silencing the free woman.

One of the things Newland confronts in the final chapter of *The Age of Innocence* is his "inarticulate lifetime." As his son Dallas characterizes the Archer marriage, "'You never told each other anything. You just sat and watched ... and guessed .... A deaf-and-dumb asylum, in fact'" (356). That Wharton valued communication can be inferred not only from her prolific writing career; it has been confirmed by her biographers and critics. Wolff, for instance, emphasizes Wharton's "striving for communication" from childhood. As an adult, argues Wolff, "Wharton was obsessed by the need to be able to talk to sympathetic and understanding friends.... Nothing is worse than to be 'mute.'" It is difficult to reconcile this view of Wharton, valuing "the open and spontaneous expression of emotion," claiming her mother's reticence "did more than anything else to falsify and misdirect my whole life,"[26] with Wharton's nostalgia for the deaf-and-dumb asylum.

But we need not resort to general biographical speculations. The first chapter of *A Backward Glance* concludes with a scene that provides the model for Wharton's treatment of silences in *The Age of Innocence*. Recalling a mysterious cousin from her father's side of the family, George Alfred, Wharton says he "vanished ... out of society, out of respectability" after allegedly breaking old New York's sexual code. Although Wharton's family, like Ellen's, effectively silences the transgressor by "ceas[ing] even to be aware of his existence," Wharton's mother Lucretia occasionally evoked him, always with an altered expression and in a lowered voice appropriate to the offense. Wharton attributes her mother's calling up the pariah to "malice" and in a courageous moment "drove her [mother] to the wall" by demanding to know, "'But, Mamma, *what did he do?*'" Wharton's request that the unpleasant be stated, taken out of the closet and faced, reduces her mother to mutterings. At first glance what stands out from this scene is that a woman presides over the reputation of George Alfred. Lucretia's silences and strategic breaches of silence illustrate her control: she makes the cousin vanish and appear at will, presumably embarrasses her husband, and certainly trains her daughter to fear the results of sexual license. Edith's portrayal of George Alfred, however, paints a more complex portrait than can be reduced to the scenario of rampant matriarchal power. By retelling the story herself, Wharton shows she hears and understands the unspeakable. She fashions her youthful musings about a recalcitrant cousin into a general principle: "in those simple days it was always a case of 'the woman tempted me.'"

The same principle, that the woman is always at fault, clearly operates in *The Age of Innocence*. George Alfred remains individual enough to retain his name while his companion in crime is reduced, like both May and Ellen, to type: "some woman," a "siren." Wharton closes the memory with evocations of "regions perilous ... outside the world of copy-book axioms, and the old obediences that were in my blood; and the hint was useful—for a novelist" (25). The copybook suggests doing things by rote—being, as Wharton says, "obedien[t]" to hereditary rules—but the novelist takes a different "hint" from the once subversive, now silent, cousin. Asking questions, probing silences, not telling stories by rote, Wharton exposes old New York. She probably considered George Alfred's story important enough for the first chapter of her autobiography because her relatives responded to her writing as they did to his adultery:

> None of my relations ever spoke to me of my books, either to praise or blame—they simply ignored them, and among the immense tribe of my New York cousins ... the subject was avoided as though it were a kind of family disgrace. (*Backward*, 144)

In *The Age Of Innocence*, Wharton speaks out against New York silence.

NOTES

1. Ihab Hassan, *The Dismemberment of Orpheus: Toward a Postmodern Literature* (New York: Oxford Univ. Press, 1971), 15, 13; Janis P. Stout, *Strategies of Reticence: Silence and*

Meaning in the Works of Jane Austen, Willa Cather, Katherine Anne Porter, and Joan Didion (Charlottesville: Univ. Press of Virginia, 1990), vii. Cf. Susan Sontag, "The Aesthetics of Silence," rpt. in *Styles of Radical Will* (New York: Farrar, Strauss and Giroux, 1976), 19: "Silence is often employed as a magical or mimetic procedure in repressive social relationships, as in the Jesuit regulations about speaking to superiors and in the disciplining of children."

2. Stout, *Strategies*, 19, emphasizes the collusion between narrator and reader, the "use [of] silence rhetorically as an invitation to the reader to perceive more than is said or to perceive the fact of the imposition of silence." Jean Frantz Blackall's "Edith Wharton's Art of Ellipsis," *Journal of Narrative Technique* 17.2 (Spring 1987): 145, 156, similarly focuses on the role of the implied reader: "Most important, Wharton uses ellipses to entice the reader into imaginative collaboration with the writer." Blackall declares "Whartonian silence ... an obtrusive presence," demanding to be read. Judith Fryer notes in *Felicitous Space: The Imaginative Structures of Edith Wharton and Willa Cather* (Chapel Hill: Univ. of North Carolina Press, 1986). 117, 139, that in *The Age Of Innocence* "spoken language often fails as a means of communication; the common language in this world is that of sign and gesture." But Fryer's conclusion, that women "command without speaking," locates the power of silence in a different social place than I do. Carol Wershoven finds in *The Female Intruder in the Novels of Edith Wharton* (Rutherford, N.J.: Fairleigh. Dickinson Univ. Press, 1982), 82, 78, 92, that Ellen "speaks openly of the evasion of New York" and "exposes New York as a fortress of evasion." Although seeing the Countess as the "most obvious victim of the cruelty of evasion," Wershoven does not analyze how New York transforms passive evasion into active silencing. In *No Man's Land: The Place of the Woman Writer in the Twentieth Century*, Vol. 2: *Sexchanges* (New Haven: Yale Univ. Press, 1989), 157, 158, Sandra M. Gilbert and Susan Gubar note that "Wharton's imaginings of change or at least of (momentary) freedom from institutions that may be changeless, are almost always mediated through allusions to what is literally or figuratively *unsayable*: through evocations of what is illicit, what is secret, what is silent," but develop their argument in a different direction than my own. Gilbert and Gubar focus on Wharton's messages "from beyond the grave," her ghost stories, and her affair with Morton Fullerton.

3. That the current debate over Wharton's feminism participates in the larger question of her political allegiances is evident in James W. Tuttleton's "The Feminist Takeover of Edith Wharton," *The New Criterion* 7.7 (March 1989): 6–14.

4. My reading of *The Age of Innocence* is most in line with Elizabeth Ammons, *Edith Wharton's Argument with America* (Athens: Univ. of Georgia Press, 1980), 126, 131. She finds all of Wharton's "long fiction from *The House of Mirth* to *The Age of Innocence* tak[ing] up the woman question." She sees through the nostalgic veneer of the latter novel to locate a "severe and radical criti[que ... of] underlying social structures and ancient taboos that buttress patriarchal attitudes and prohibit freedom for women."

Patriarchy is an unfortunately vague concept, its meaning best understood by analysis of power relations in a specific community, factual or fictional. Patriarchy is also a *necessarily* vague concept, for its continuance is most assured when its existence is masked. As Adrienne Rich remarks in *Of Woman Born: Motherhood as Experience and Institution* (New York: Norton, 1986), 57–8: "The power of the fathers has been difficult to grasp because it permeates everything, even the language in which we try describe it."

According to Wharton's friend, Henry Adams, in "Primitive Rights of Women" (1891: rpt. in *The Great Secession Winter of 1860–61 and Other Essays*, ed. George E. Hochfield [New York: A.S. Barnes and Co., 1963]), 360, who dates the subjection of women to the growth of the Church, "patriarchal theory" derives from "a curious conglomeration of Old Testament history and pure hypothesis.

5. *The Age of Innocence* (1920; New York: Scribners, 1965), 260. Subsequent references will be cited parenthetically.

6. *A Feast of Words: The Triumph of Edith Wharton* (New York: Oxford Univ. Press, 1977), 331, 321, 313.

7. *Edith Wharton: A Biography* (New York: Harper & Row, 1975), 423. On changing views of history in nineteenth- and early twentieth-century America and the impact on literature, see Susan L. Mizruchi, *The Power of Historical Knowledge: Narrating the Pact in Hawthorne, James, and Dreiser* (Princeton: Princeton Univ. Press. 1988).

8. *A Backward Glance* (1934; New York: Scribners, 1964), 15. Subsequent references will be cited parenthetically.

9. Lewis, 432, notes that Wharton. "always addicted to anthropology," drew upon her readings of *The Golden Bough* in *The Age of Innocence*. Ammons describes Wharton's anthropological posture as enabling a "laboratory study of the fundamental, primitive attitudes that mold patriarchal aversion to the mature female" (144), whereas Fryer argues that women "transcend domestic limits ... by creating their own society and sustaining it by rituals (131). Thorstein Veblen's *The Instinct of Workmanship and the State of the Industrial Arts* (1914; New York: Norton, 1964), 94, theorizes that women initially occupied the "chief place in the technological scheme" during what he terms the "primitive phase" of human evolution. But, as he reasons in *The Theory of the Leisure Class* (1899; New York: Modern Library, 1934), 23, 83, the "ownership of women" dates back to "the lower barbarian stages of culture" and marks the beginning of the institution of ownership: "The original reason for the seizure and appropriation of women seems to have been their usefulness as trophies." Veblen finds "as the latter-day outcome of this evolution of an archaic institution, the wife, who was at the outset the drudge and chattel of the man, both in fact and in theory,—the producer of goods for him to consume,—has become the ceremonial consumer of goods which he produces. But she still quite unmistakably remains his chattel in theory." An 1894 essay, "The Economic Theory of Woman's Dress" (rpt. in *Essays in Our Changing Order*, ed. Leon Ardzrooni [New York: Augustus M. Kelley, 1964]), 67, provides an example of the continuation of patriarchal ownership of women especially relevant to the fashionable world depicted in Wharton's novels: "Still even today, in spite of the nominal and somewhat celebrated demise of the patriarchal idea, there is that about the dress of women which suggests that the wearer is something in the nature of a chattel." Veblen's comment in "The Barbarian Status of Women" (rpt. in *Essays*), 56, that "the masterless, unattached woman ... loses caste" concisely describes Ellen Olenska's fate.

10. "Barbarian Status," 54.

11. Old New York's dread of scandal also determines the plot of *The Custom of The Country* (1913; New York: Scribners, 1941), 437, 436. Ralph Marvell's breakdown results from internalizing the family code: "For Paul's sake! And it was because, for Paul's sake, there must be no scandal, that he, Paul's father, had tamely abstained from defending his rights and contesting his wife's charges, and had thus handed the child over to her keeping!" Immediately thereafter Marvell recognizes his "innate" "weakness." His maintenance of "all the old family catchwords, the full and elaborate vocabulary of evasion: 'delicacy,' 'pride,' 'personal dignity,' 'preferring not to know about such things,'" associates rhetorical evasion wish destruction, as in *The Age of Innocence*. Ralph's suicide marks a terrifying silence.

12. The deathly possibilities of silence are foretold by Newland's and Ellen's tête-à-tête at the end of Book I when "the silence that followed lay on them with the weight of

things final and irrevocable. It seemed to Archer to be crushing him down like his own grave-stone" (170).

13. On women who speak out, Stout comments: "'impertinent' speech that challenges the male's 'sentence' of perpetual self-denial and subservience had better be squelched unless one is prepared to pay a very high price indeed" (*Strategies*, 110, 13).

14. Martha Banta makes an interesting distinction in *Imaging American Women: Ideas and Ideals in Cultural History* (New York: Columbia Univ. Press, 1987), 449, while explaining why Newland is continually titillated by Ellen yet hesitates to press for sexual consummation. He does not go to Ellen even after May's death because then he "would have to love her, while putting aside the bittersweet pleasures of his desire."

15. *Edith Wharton*, 430: "Feminist Takeover," 11. Nina Baym explains in "Melodramas of Beset Manhood: How Theories of American Fiction Exclude Women Authors," rpt. in *The New Feminist Criticism*, ed. Elaine Showalter (New York: Pantheon, 1985), 73, 72, how "although women are not the source of social power, they are experienced as such." Both women and men "experience social conventions and responsibilities and obligations first in the persons of women, since women are entrusted by society with the task of rearing young children."

16. Gilbert and Gubar's reading of Wharton as criticizing America's insistence on "a debilitating feminization" (126) is on this count similar to mine. They argue that "despite all [the] evidence that Edith Wharton was neither in theory nor in practice a feminist, her major fictions ... constitute perhaps the most searching—and searing—feminist analysis of the construction of 'femininity'" (128). But Gilbert and Gubar are, like most critics, more sympathetic to Newland than I am. I would argue that the problem with Newland is not that he "realizes too late the hollowness" (151) of his life, but that he realizes it at the beginning of the novel and lacks the courage of his convictions. Similarly, Gilbert and Gubar's criticisms of May do not sufficiently consider the extent to which her "feminization" makes her not only a product but a victim of the system. Looking at what individual characters can and cannot speak provides a mechanism for analyzing the power dynamics in the novel.

17. This articulation of supposedly nonexistent problems is at the heart of feminist challenges. As Rich remarks in *Of Woman Born*, 62, "women are beginning to ask certain questions which, as the feminist philosopher Mary Daly observes, patriarchal method has declared nonquestions." That only a *man* in Wharton's novel can ask the nonquestion illustrates the extent to which the women characters are bound and gagged.

18. On Wharton's striving to move beyond the category of "feminine" in her writing, see Amy Kaplan, *The Social Construction of American Realism* (Chicago: Univ. of Chicago Press, 1988). 67 ff. Taking issue with the tendency of feminist criticism to locate women's writing in a "separate sphere," Kaplan finds Wharton's writing "undermin[ing] those boundaries between feminine and masculine, private and public, home and business."

19. In "Fashion," *International Quarterly* 10 (October 1904): 143, Georg Simmel associates female passivity, non-individuality, and maintenance of the status quo: "the weakness of [woman's] social position ... explains her strict regard for custom, for the generally accepted and approved forms of life, for all that is proper. A weak person steers clear of individualization; he [sic] avoids dependence upon self."

20. It is surprising that so little has been said of Newland's repeated nastiness to Ellen, for instance his insinuations that she is having an affair with Beaufort.

21. *The House of Mirth* (1905; New York: Signet, 1964), 233–34.

22. *Edith Wharton*, 221.

23. Parkman, "The Woman Question." *North American Review* 129.275 (October

1879): 309, 307. As Nancy Cott says in *The Bonds of Womanhood: "Woman's Sphere" in New England, 1780–1835* (New Haven: Yale Univ. Press, 1977). 22–23: "In its strictly economic aspect the traditional marriage contract resembled all indenture between master and servant.... This economic skeleton of marriage supported a broader cultural body of meaning."

24. On the relationship between women's honor and silence see Adrienne Rich's "Women and Honor: Some Notes on Lying," rpt. in *On Lies, Secrets, and Silence* (New York: Norton, 1979), 186: "Women's honor, something altogether else: virginity, chastity, fidelity to a husband. Honesty in women has not been considered important. We have been depicted as generically whimsical, deceitful, subtle, vacillating. And we have been rewarded for lying" and "Lying is done with words, and also with silence."

25. *Bonds*, 22.

26. *Feast*, 14, 24–25; *Female Intruder*, 16; Wharton quoted in Lewis, *Edith Wharton*, 54.

DALE M. BAUER

"Edith Agonistes"

Poor Billy Carlton's taste for cocaine was as nothing to mine for your conversation ...
 —Wharton to Gaillard Lapsley, 21 May 1920 (Beinecke Library)

Wharton's ability to "think against herself," to resist all of her conservative impulses, is revealed nowhere more clearly than in her ironic confession of an "addiction" to intellectual exchange. She likens her need for that stimulation to an acquaintance's addiction to cocaine, a very popular drug during the twenties. Indeed, Wharton's craving for intelligent conversation with her cohort of friends increased in the twenties and thirties, when both her money and her mobility decreased. As she reports in her autobiography, *A Backward Glance* (1933), Wharton loved to be among her intimate friends more than anything else in her life. By the thirties, when many of her companions, like Henry James and Walter Berry, had died, and when her longtime maid, Catharine Gross, had spent her last years growing increasingly feeble and senile, Wharton's signature on a 25 May 1937 letter, "Edith Agonistes," was a telling phrase for her sense of a lonely struggle (see Letter 3, Lilly Library). While Wharton and her friends had once confronted a disintegrating culture and an increasing cultural conservatism, she now imagines that she fights, like Samson, alone and figuratively in the dark. With

From *Edith Wharton's Brave New Politics*. © 1994 by the Board of Regents of the University of Wisconsin System.

characteristic self-parody, this letter's sign-off humor suggests, in 1937, Wharton's both ironic and sympathetic stance toward the issues that had engaged her ever since her 1917 *Summer*. Irony and sympathy characterized the twin features of her imagination throughout her career and, in her loneliness, they also marked her response to a world irrevocably changed.

Both her Pulitzer-Prize winning *Age of Innocence* and her last novel, *The Buccaneers*, unfinished at the time of her death, converge on the political issues of assimilation and social exclusion. In the 1920 novel, Wharton figures these "trends" in the presence of the gipsy-like Ellen Olenska, whose associations with the foreign are treated as a perceived threat to American social standards. By her last work, published posthumously in 1938 with a Note by Lapsley explaining Wharton's progress on the novel, the racial and class amalgamation that dominated the previous generation—sounded in the fears of degeneration by sociologists such as Edward A. Ross—is figured as a comedic cultural invasion, when two American families "invade" London aristocracy as the "buccaneers" of Wharton's title. Both of these novels are historical romances, representing Wharton's fantasy of cultural history and crystallizing anxieties of dangerous social trends and foreign ideas. In the seventeen years between them, as we have seen in *The Mother's Recompense*, *Twilight Sleep*, *The Children*, and "Roman Fever," Wharton argued more strenuously than ever that the international audience she envisioned for her novels—American, French, and British readers—had less to fear from foreign intruders and their alien ideas or from indigenous "cultural invasions" like bohemianism and sexual revolutions than it did from internalized fears and projections of dominance over others. *The Buccaneers*, then, establishes the limits of dominance and ascertains the value of cultural assimilation.

We might remember here Wharton's "lesson" in *The Mother's Recompense*, concerning Kate Clephane's desire to transcend the past even as the novel confirms that the past cannot be transcended. Like Alice Haskett-Varick-Waythorn in "The Other Two," Kate Clephane cannot shed her past the way a man, like Chris Fenno—Kate's old lover, can and does. The new America of the twenties holds out this false utopia of new tolerance, while Wharton's novel refuses the terms by which such a new tolerance could help her heroine Kate create a new identity. For Wharton, identities are predicated on past actions and decisions, just as they are on traditional class and race categories. The novel is at once both sympathetic to the new spirit of tolerance and its loosening hold on the social scene and, at the same time, is deeply split, especially with respect to the threat of unchecked sexual desires, in which Wharton sees social anarchy such as the kind she envisioned in the Harlem Renaissance.

Wharton's ambivalence about heredity, race, and personal change is revealed in these character studies. This ambivalence is especially apparent in the fear of exposure Wharton plots as the novel's theme. Chris's fear of exposure is intertwined with Kate's fear of her past sexual relation with Chris. Yet, as we have seen, only when Kate realizes that a black woman, Phemia, might guess Kate's secret does Wharton reveal the limits of the "new tolerance." To Kate's amazement, Phemia informs Kate's daughter Anne about her mother's furtive visit to Chris in Baltimore. That revelation sets the second half of the narrative going, since Anne's discovery of her mother's interference causes her to break with her mother and reconcile with Chris. The novel turns on the fear of exposure and revelation—and, what is worse for Kate, exposure because of a black woman, a maid. Here Wharton's repressed racial unconscious returns with a vengeance.

In the bleak light of this subsequent novel, it is interesting that *The Age of Innocence* invokes the familiar and often-repeated fears that Americans needed in order to hold the line against both immigrants and their influence.[1] The kind of anti-social behavior associated with the "lower" cultures of Eastern Europeans could be discovered in Ellen's refusal to return to her husband and in the inherited madness of the Chivers family, two examples of the ways in which the popular belief in Darwinian and neo-Lamarckian theories about instinct and heredity made familial aberrations all the more threatening as a sign of the danger within rather than outside the family. The fear of hereditary madness reinforced the greater modern inclination for social engineering and control. As Carl Degler notes, "Charles Loring Brace in his influential book *The Dangerous Classes of New York and Twenty Years' Work Among Them*, published in 1872, warned that the pathological character traits of drunken or criminal parents might well be inherited by their offspring. Medical men, Brace pointed out, were convinced that children could inherit insanity, criminal habits, and even a tendency toward prostitution" (35). Julius Beaufort—also a foreigner—commits bank default, thereby reinforcing the popular sense of crime as hereditary. That Ellen seems to be able to associate with foreigners and with radicals, like her bohemian neighbor Ned Winsett, suggests just how potentially contaminating such associations were understood to be. Reading Ellen through Mary Douglas's anthropology, Judith Fryer argues in *Felicitous Space* that Ellen's danger arises from her potentially polluting presence (Fryer 138–39). Her presence portends a sexual transgression, further complicated by a symbolic alliance with her Eastern European married name as well as her mixing with other bohemians.

Elizabeth Ammons's claims in *Edith Wharton's Argument with America* are important in this respect, contending as she does that Wharton focused on motherhood—and The Mothers—as women's ways to establish authority in light of increased attention to cultural purity through maternal (genetic) influence. Ammons writes: "[Wharton's] new argument is fundamentally emotional and conservative and says that women must sublimate their desires for freedom to the higher duty of serving their families and the culture as mothers" (185). Ammons sees this move as "reactionary" and faults the writer for not creating "fully dimensioned" mothers and instead imagining "maternal characters to argue a thesis about American culture" (186). In a time when American societies offered women political propaganda about motherhood, however, it is possible to say that Wharton offered her own. Referring to Bachofen's *Das Mutterrecht* ("The Mother Right") as Wharton's source, Ammons concludes that the matriarchal theories of the nineteenth century shape Wharton's sense of mothering and power (192). Yet we know that Wharton came to distrust those matriarchal theories which were the very same as had fueled the totalitarian eugenic politics she most feared. Wharton trained her hatred of radicalism in general and bolshevism in particular on such domestic policies, and she also denounces American anti-foreign activity for its ritualistic and totemic bloodshed. In fact, Wharton discredited this vision of cultural formation in favor of a sociological one, a vision meant to defeat the rising tide of xenophobia, immigration restriction, and 100%-Americanism as social bywords.

As Claudia Koonz argues in "Genocide and Eugenics," the prevailing sentiment after World War I was inspired by the wide support for the 1926 law stipulating forced sterilization laws: "Oliver Wendell Holmes wrote the majority decision—declaring that after so many of the nation's finest had sacrificed their lives in World War I, it would not represent a great sacrifice if the least qualified gave up their potential to reproduce" (156). Such a bio-political dimension of modern science was central to the theory behind Nazism in particular, and modern culture in general. Marked by instability in established religious, familial, and communal life, the culture sought radical bio-political solutions, like sterilization of the "unfit," while growing nostalgic for the past. Wharton's solutions, however, did not take a reactionary form. Instead, she tried to divest authoritative mass-produced culture of its alienating control over individuals. Whether the threat was a standardized beauty (as it was in *The Children*) or the more blatant class argument for twilight sleep and eugenic legislation, Wharton blasted the simplification in such measures and the state regulation of the individual. As Nancy Stepan and Sander Gilman argue in "Appropriating the Idioms of Science: The Rejection of Scientific Racism," the rhetorical power of late nineteenth-century science rested in its claims of objectivity, neutrality, and universality; in order to present an intellectual resistance to these claims, one had to appropriate scientific idioms to subvert them. "From 1870 to 1920, science became more specialized and authoritative as a cultural resource and language of interpretation.... The outcome was a narrowing of the cultural space within which, and the cultural forms by which, the claims of biological determinism could be effectively challenged" (80). In *The Age of Innocence*, Wharton begins to revise the ethical and political claims of the new sciences and their explanatory force. In doing so, she posits fiction's moral force against the determinism of science by subverting science's own terms and theories. In taking up the contradictions of human nature, she suggested that desire is more variegated than the movements for birth control, marriage, or family studies policy were allowing for.

Ultimately, Wharton sought to unravel the implicit ties between the early twentieth-century campaign for racial purity and the cult of feminine purity she herself inherited as a legacy of nineteenth-century domestic life. Almost every Wharton novel of the twenties centers on divorce (engineered by a New Woman), with divorce serving as Wharton's dominant trope for the disruption of the bourgeois family. Unlike contemporary writers such as Charlotte Perkins Gilman and Gertrude Atherton, Wharton resisted the call of eugenics schemes as a bulwark against changes in the social "trend."[2]

Appearing in 1920, the year that saw a great wave of anti-foreign incidents culminating in the second wave of the KKK and the Anti-Immigration Act of 1924, but set in the 1870s, Wharton's *Age of Innocence* links two central preoccupations, women's purity and hereditary purity—concerns that come unnervingly together in the person of Ellen Olenska. What critics have called May Wellandism is less nostalgia for the cult of true womanhood and more the fantasy of women's freedom from such demands. Throughout the novel, Wharton links Ellen to the fears of racial impurity and even to the anti-immigrationist sentiment contemporaneous to this novel. May Welland, on the other hand, is associated with a no less disquieting social blindness. Newland Archer contemplates May's ambiguous "abysmal purity" (7) and what marriage to "that terrifying product of the social system he belonged to and believed in" might mean: "the young girl who knew nothing and expected everything, looked back at him like a stranger through May Welland's familiar features; and once more it was borne in on him that marriage was not the safe anchorage he had been taught to think, but a voyage on uncharted seas" (43). As much as anything, Archer's "readings in anthropology" affect his view of this situation (69). Indeed, the 1870s witnessed a passion for social science, especially anthropology, matched only in Wharton's time by the twenties' consequent fascination for the primitive. The anthropology that people would have been reading in the 1870s was hereditarianist in kind, drawing on theories of instinct to describe human nature, and Archer himself is learning to see the world through his new anthropological framework.

Marriage becomes more complicated for Archer precisely because he interprets it as a ritual function, exorcising impure and threatening social elements. Newland's rumored adultery with Ellen is also much more complex than it appears, in that, for him, their love affair threatens the ritual transmission of American cultural values. The anxiety over foreign contamination and amalgamation guarantees the ritual exclusion of Ellen from the family. Not only is she married to a foreigner, but she is also likened to gipsies and aligned with Mediterranean stock, and with an Eastern European stock as embodied in the Polish Count Olenski.

Archer's worry merely renders small the novel's claims about intermarriage and how its dangers clarify the perceived threat to cultural transmission: the Albany Chiverses had "insanity recurring in every second generation" (10) and Ellen Olenska's Uncle Thorley Chivers dies in a madhouse (60). The lessons of intermarriage and eugenics are clear: marriage is much less an affair of the heart and more a social cement, one which could be used to yield "blameless stock" (12). The "family," as the critical backdrop of Wharton's novel, is something to be investigated and guarded to preserve its purity. When Newland Archer's mother worries that the "trend" was changing Old New York, she sees it embodied not only in Ellen's bohemianism but also in that professor of archeology, Emerson Sillerton, a member of "a venerable and venerated family tree" (219). Mrs. Welland especially objects to the professor's giving a party for a "black man," but it is impossible to tell whether she objects to the guest of honor or the party's timing, since the party coincides with Julia Mingott's *thé dansant* (220). For the Wellands, blacks appear only as a supply of house servants in St. Augustine or as Mrs. Mingott's maid. Mrs. Welland expects the professor to know that her *kind* does not mix socially in the black man's society: "No one in the Mingott set could understand why Amy Sillerton had submitted so tamely to the eccentricities of a husband who filled the house with long-haired men and short-haired women, and, when he traveled, took her to explore tombs in Yucatan instead of going to Paris or Italy. But there they were, set in their ways, and apparently unaware that they were different from other people" (220).

At every turn, Wharton parodies the good breeding of her characters, whose genetic lines are assumed to assure "congenital" supremacy. When describing Lawrence Lefferts, she trivializes the character traits phrenology was once assumed to reveal: "One had only to look at him, from the slant of his bald forehead and the curve of his beautiful fair moustache to the long patent-leather feet at the other end of his lean and elegant person, to feel that the knowledge of 'form' must be congenital in any one who knew how to wear such good clothes so carelessly and carry such height with so much lounging grace" (8). With little more than a knowledge of form to promote himself, Lefferts gossips and snipes. Personal qualities seemed to have been purged from the leisure classes, and Archer wonders about May whether "'niceness' carried to that supreme degree were only a negation, the curtain dropped before an emptiness?" (211). Repeating a fear she had first expressed in *French Ways and Their Meaning*, Wharton has Archer liken May Welland to the Kentucky cave-fish, blind and able only to "look out blankly at blankness" (83). In this way, Archer comes to realize that the good breeding he once believed in is little more than "factitious purity" (46).

Arguably the most famous passage from *The Age of Innocence*, as I have suggested in the Introduction, concerns the "arbitrary signs" of the "hieroglyphic world" Wharton depicts. Following that passage is another which suggests how anthropology, one of the new social sciences popularized in the late nineteenth century, had begun to influence "advanced culture": one of those arbitrary signs is Mrs. Welland's "air of having had her hand forced [in the announcement of her daughter's engagement], quite as, in the books on Primitive Man that people of advanced culture were beginning to read, the savage bride is dragged with shrieks from her parents' tent" (45). Books about Primitive Man were the rage; they kindled in Wharton the sense that the line between primitive and advanced was as arbitrary, but no less powerful, than any other sign in culture. Preserved in the rite of marriage is the "elaborate system of mystification" Newland Archer recognizes as cultural lore about the exchange of the young girl in marriage, which is the subject of at least one of Malinowski's books and of several other contemporaneous anthropological texts, and of the new sexology that Havelock Ellis and Sam Schmalhausen codified. Here Archer fears that May cannot survive in his world, since social purity demands that women become blind to passion and that the power of "insight" be bred out of them (83).

To this extent the commonly-held functionalist view of the family as regulatory force is the object of Wharton's criticism. The family's irregularities and permutations interested the writer as important human and familial variations. In this regard, a key word in *The Age of Innocence* is "bohemianism" with which Ellen is associated: even as a child she is dressed as a "gipsy foundling" instead of in black American mourning clothes for her parents (60); she is linked to the "gipsy-looking people" Wharton had first discussed in Charity's lineage in *Summer*. Katherine Joslin reads "the Bohemian Peril" embodied in Ellen as a threat to Old New York and to Newland, since bohemia is "a world of independent ideas and artistic expression" (Joslin 106–7). Yet the reference to the bohemian in this novel is not to the artistic world of the 1920s but to the influx of Bohemian immigrants of the 1870s. The "Bohemian" in the novel refers first to the largely peasant immigrants from Eastern Europe, not the few spirited inhabitants of the social and sexual enclaves of New York. This confusion may well be deliberate, significantly so because it illustrates the connections Wharton makes between European immigration and the artistic and intellectual freedom that followed. Reading the "Bohemian" in the novel simply as a sexual threat, then, ignores the 1870s anthropological influence. That Wharton creates an amalgam of 1870s and 1920s cultures is telling: the bohemian life represented a threat to culture not because of its sexual permissiveness per se but because of what it suggested about heredity and radical thought. Remember that the "Bohemian" is associated with Mediterranean stock: Marchioness Manson's Spanish shawls, Nastasia's Sicilian accent and "swarthy foreign-looking" demeanor (70), and Ned Winsett's radical intellectualism are all distrusted as expressions of inferior ancestry compared to Nordic roots, not to mention the failed European revolutions of 1848–49: "Archer, who dressed in the evening because he thought it cleaner and more comfortable to do so, and who had never stopped to consider that cleanliness and comfort are two of the costliest items in a modest budget, regarded Winsett's attitude as part of the boring 'Bohemian' pose that always made fashionable people who changed their clothes without talking about it, and were not forever harping on the number of servants one kept, seem so much simpler and less self-conscious than the others. Nevertheless, he was always stimulated by Winsett ..." (124). Winsett's greatest wish is to emigrate, and he addresses his radical bent to a sympathetic but ironic Archer: "You'll never amount to anything, any of you, till you roll up your sleeves and get right down into the muck" (126). Winsett implies that Archer might end up like the social gadfly Larry Lefferts, shallow and smug, unless he commits himself to radical change, namely politics. Where Winsett fails, Ellen succeeds in compelling Archer to be "once more conscious of the curious way in which she reversed his values" (104).

Ned Winsett lives in the same bohemian neighborhood as Ellen, which Ellen's family dislikes. It was "not the peril but the poverty" to which her family objected, the relative squalor of "a 'Bohemian' quarter given over to 'people who wrote'" (104). "People who wrote" as the neighborhood's principle of inclusion suggests that intellect and inclination, and temperament and talent, would presumably distinguish who belonged and who didn't much better than heredity or money—and this was a situation not to be abided. Yet its poverty is explicitly linked to a self-consciousness, to the extent that writing and privation were closely associated with peril, both in politics and waning culture. Wharton is quick to undermine this danger, however, since Winsett's and Ellen's lives are intertwined by an act of kindness Ellen does for Ned's little boy, whose leg she bandages when she sees him hurt in the street outside her house. Here Ellen's foreign threat is domesticated by one democratic act of kindness. The subtler impact of the scene is also part of Wharton's strategy: the maternal instinct, seen as a universal trait binding all women together, served to show how all women held the same values of family and home that Americans did. By appealing to a kind of universal motherhood, Ellen Olenska—"bare-headed, carrying [the son] in her arms, with his knee all beautifully bandaged, and ... so sympathetic and beautiful"—represents the "better" sort of immigrant, the maternal symbol of the universal family (123).

Or does she? This image of Ellen is almost immediately reversed when she appears out of the "armor" ladies usually wore in the evening. Wharton's ambivalence about Ellen is never so clear as when Ellen appears as the *Venus in Furs*, the figure for whom Leopold von Sacher-Masoch named his 1870 novel. Wharton's depiction of Ellen's attire—"heedless of tradition"—closely recalls Sacher-Masoch's icon of masochism: "But Madame Olenska ... was attired in a long robe of red velvet bordered about the chin and down the front with glossy black fur. Archer remembered, on his last visit to Paris, seeing a portrait by the new painter, Carolus Duran, whose pictures were the sensation of the Salon, in which the lady wore one of these bold sheath-like robes with her chin nestling in fur. There was something perverse and provocative in the notion of fur worn in the evening in a heated drawing room, and in the combination of a muffled throat and bare arms; but the effect was undeniably pleasing" (105–6). Sacher-Masoch's hero Severin, who becomes the love slave of the masochist Wanda in the 1870 novel, feels the same about seeing his mistress draped in furs: at various points, Severin (whom Wanda renames Gregor) associates the furs with cruelty, despotism, and tyranny (108). Their symbolic meaning is tied to masochistic love, as Severin declares: "I have repeatedly told you that suffering has a peculiar attraction for me. Nothing can intensify my passion more than tyranny, cruelty, and especially the faithlessness of a beautiful woman" (75).

Why does Wharton identify her heroine with the sensational confessions of the masochist? One could argue that she merely employs this reference as a cultural marker for the historical setting, just as she refers to *Middlemarch* and books by Herbert Spencer and Alphonse Daudet (Archer's impatiently awaited books from London) to give her novel the social texture that the realist novel required. Yet the comparison is more deliberate since the novel concerns Ellen's erotic control over Archer, with one lover as the hammer, the other as the anvil, as Sacher-Masoch has it. Drawing as it does on the contemporaneous images of sadomasochism, Ellen's appearance as the *Venus in Furs* gives the lie to Wharton's ironic title, "age of innocence," since the age was not innocent but embroiled in new sexological debates about sadomasochism and perversion. The "age" of the novel is not innocent; rather, it is the "age" that lost the struggle to preserve innocence and that set in motion the corruptions to come. In this context, Wharton's matriarch, Catherine the Great, the nickname of old Catherine Mingott, is also ironic: as Sacher-Masoch, among others, suggests, she was history's first sadist. The heroine of *Venus in Furs*, Wanda, instructs her slave Severin about the moral of his punishment: "I may confess to you that I loved you deeply. You yourself, however, stifled my love by your fantastic devotion and your insane passion. From the moment that you became my slave, I knew it would be impossible for you ever to become my husband ..." (238). Ellen's lesson to Archer is no different: Archer is willing to abandon himself to his ideal of Ellen, without making her his equal. He wants to be her slave, to be dominated by her worldliness. Archer's abjection at Ellen's hands supplants the fantasy of cultural purity underwriting the age's pretense of innocence and taste, in a novel where divorce and default are the most popular topics of conversation.

If passion is instinctual and inherited, as some sociologists argued, then those who would give themselves over to it—like Ellen and like Archer—must be disciplined from within the familial ranks. May's pregnancy proves to be just such a retaliatory function, reining in Archer just as he is about to stray. May prematurely assures Ellen that the Newland Archers are about to have a baby, an announcement that in clinching Ellen's allegiance to familial order proves to be an internally motivated regulation by the family. As a weapon against Ellen, May's intimation of her pregnancy takes on an unethical cast; in miniature, this act harbingers the state regulation of families through eugenics, which was portentous for Wharton. Nevertheless, that Newland and May's three children are studies in human variation and heredity—Mary and Bill like their mother, but Dallas ready to marry the exiled Julius Beaufort's daughter, Fanny—suggests that these human variations are necessary to revitalize culture and to establish "more tolerant views. There was good in the new order too" (349), Archer reflects.

At the end of the novel, Archer contemplates the scientific changes of technological modernity in this new order: "There would one day be a tunnel under the Hudson through which the trains of the Pennsylvania railway would run straight into New York. They were of the brotherhood of visionaries who likewise predicted the building of ships that would cross the Atlantic in five days, the invention of a flying machine, lighting by electricity, telephonic communication without wires, and other Arabian Night marvels"

(284). He conjectures that these modern inventions would propel changes in social behavior and compel human adaptability to them. Yet Wharton represents the antimodern impulse, too, in *The Age of Innocence*, in a group whose nostalgia for simpler, less self-conscious life leads them to recreate it. A brotherhood of visionaries, Dr. Carver's Community offered spiritual antidotes to the general fears of a disintegrating society. While Archer fosters his alienation as his refuge from Family, Carver's meetings try to combat such feelings in their outward search for meaning and simplification of life. At the same time, one response to the new anthropology is suggested by the vague transcendentalism of Dr. Carver's "Valley of Love Community," his theories of "Direct Contact," and his "Inner Thought" meetings (158–60, 184, 208). These are antidotes to the general sense of cultural decline the Wellands name the "trend." But they are also, as Jackson Lears suggests, ballast for antimodernism. For Lears these communities arose in opposition to the new ethnic and class-divided laborer societies in urban centers. What the "overcivilized bourgeoisie" needed was a self-improvement community of their own, derived from the Protestant evangelical tradition and with a certain antimodern appeal (see Lears 1981, 71–73).

Even so, Wharton distances herself—and Archer—from these radical antimodernists in that she returns to Ned Winsett's claim for sustained, however tentative, political engagement. Archer's own refusal as a "gentleman" to enter politics early in life is drawn from his indifference to collective politics and a belief—as his above rumination suggests—in technological and scientific progress. That he later enters politics under the mentorship of Teddy Roosevelt suggests how shaken his vision of innocence has been. For Archer, the new society has courage, but he has no conviction in it: "The young men nowadays were emancipating themselves from the law and business and taking up all sorts of new things. If they were not absorbed in state politics or municipal reform, the chances were that they were going in for Central American archaeology" (345). Once again, South America serves as Wharton's dystopia of political evasion, as it had in *The Reef* and *The Children* in particular.

The contradiction between Wharton's professed interest in the new anthropology and her hatred of the so-called primitive such as Harlem life— or, here, her scorn for antimodern primitives—cannot be overemphasized. She writes approvingly of the discoveries of anthropology at the same time that she relegates blacks to "the local African supply" of servants (143). Franz Boas's 1911 *The Mind of Primitive Man* changed social science in its insistence on the complexity of the "primitive," arguing for the equality of mind between primitive and civilized—a tack Wharton also seems to take in *The Age of Innocence* by showing how primitive the rituals of bloodshedding, potlatch, and fetishism were in New York society. On the other hand, while Wharton launches an attack on the neo-primitivism of the Simple Lifers in Dr. Carver's communities and brotherhoods, she objects to the representation of the primitive as Van Vechten celebrates it in *Nigger Heaven*, since its simplifications seem to her to glorify primitive over civilized consciousness. Wharton knew that civilization could not return to such profound "innocence," and saw in the worship of the primitive in modern jazz the same distorted and misguided resistances to the enervation and commercialization of modern life that she did in Carver's Valley of Love Communities. The way to salvation and happiness, for Wharton, led through the much more complex terrain of cultural contradictions, by embracing the ambivalence that was so much a part of modern life for her. To see the "beyondness of things" (137), as her heroine Nan St. George in *The Buccaneers* later expresses it, was the goal of the "inner life" and the focus of Wharton's last novel (see Hoffman 269).

NOTES

1. Immigration had virtually stopped during World War I, but increased soon after the war's end.

2. For instance, on Sinclair Lewis's advice, she refused to join the Literary Council of the Authors' League of America (see letter to Minnie of 29 January 1929, Beinecke Library).

PAMELA KNIGHTS

Forms of Disembodiment: The Social Subject in The Age of Innocence

"Everything may be labelled—but everybody is not."[1]

In 1921, excited by news of a plan to stage *The Age of Innocence*, Edith Wharton responded immediately with proprietarial advice about getting the 1870s right—the moustaches ("not tooth brush ones, but curved & slightly twisted at the ends"), the clothes and the buttonhole flowers (violets by day, gardenias by night), the manners and the language (no slang, no Americanisms—"English was then the language spoken by American ladies & gentlemen").[2] Since she had insisted that she did not want the novel taken as a "costume piece" (*Letters*, 433), this punctiliousness might seem surprising. But in *The Age of Innocence*, social details matter: "As Mrs. Archer remarked, the Roman punch made all the difference: not in itself but by its manifold implications" (1276). Reconstructing knowledge of half a century earlier, Wharton writes as if she has forgotten nothing. Social forms, her letters explain, are imprinted young and are impossible to erase. Her story, she tells one friend, was about "two people trying to live up to something ... still 'felt in the blood'" (*Letters*, 433); anxious about the dramatization, she exclaims, "I could do every stick of furniture & every rag of clothing myself, for every detail of that far-off scene was indelibly stamped on my infant brain" (*Letters*, 439).

From *The Cambridge Companion to Edith Wharton*, edited by Millicent Bell. © 1995 by Cambridge University Press.

For some readers, the interest of the novel is psychological: some ask what the act of returning to that childhood scene meant to Edith Wharton in 1919. Others, abetted by Newland Archer, speculate about the nature of "real" experience (passion, perhaps, or art?) as something apart from the "tyrannical trifles" (1188) which bind one hour to the next and tie the self firmly into the everyday social world. But the text makes it hard to sustain readings that dismiss cultural furnishings as "background" (whether picturesque or oppressive) or that see characters as discrete beings, with an independent "selfhood" separate and intact from any social inscriptions. Wharton was critical of modern fiction that took its bearings entirely within the flux of the subconscious; for her, the novel had found its form when it became aware "that the bounds of a personality were not reproducible by a sharp black line, but that each of us flows imperceptibly into adjacent people and things."[3] *The Age of Innocence* lives up to her paradigm. Readers soon discover that any observation about an individual character—about his or her consciousness, emotions, body, history, or language—also entangles us in the collective experience of the group, expressed in the welter of trifles, the matrix of social knowledge, within and out of which Wharton's subjects are composed.

Where and how far that entanglement extends is one of the novel's questions. Its hero, Archer, raises the inquiry, but by the time we hear that he "had long given up trying to disengage her [May's] real self from the shape into which tradition and training had moulded her" (1276), we realize his limits. Though acknowledging social formation, he still assumes that somewhere a "real" self survives. The suggestion of the unfolding narrative is, more radically, that without the shape, the social mold, there may be no self at all.

Wharton was always interested in what happens to the self when separated, by will or circumstance, from the world that has formed it. Archer is her specimen rather than her spokesman. In examining him, *The Age of Innocence* goes beyond his brand of analysis to parallel, in its own terms, contemporary debates about the social basis of consciousness. In turn-of-the-century writings by, for example, William James, Charles Horton Cooley, or (slightly later) George Herbert Mead, we find early explorations of the idea that, to use Ian Burkitt's helpful summary, "personality develops within discourse," that is ... "self" and "mind" are formed within the "communicative activity of the group."[4] For Mead, the self developed through language, above all, in the very processes of thinking, grounded in an inner dialogue with the social group. Wharton, in *French Ways and Their Meaning* (1919), essays that she assembled for publication as she was working on *The Age of Innocence*, suggested that looking at a race's preponderant words is one of the best ways of getting at its nature. *The Age of Innocence* contains a glossary to old New York. The quoted terms ("nice," what was "not the thing," and the rest) take us a long way into what Society feels in its blood, and in reading it becomes hard to think outside their limits—or to know whose words they are. Frequently we meet objective narrative commentary, often at the start of a chapter, which suddenly relocates itself in Archer's focalizing vision: "These things passed through Newland Archer's mind" (1063); "Newland Archer had been aware of these things ever since he could remember" (1097). As we continue, then, public and private, personality and surroundings, begin to fuse, as New York's consciousness and Archer's emerge in the text together.

Archer is a thoroughly middle-of-the-road subject. *The Age of Innocence* begins with him solidly the gentleman, brushed and white-waistcoated, his coordinates clear. Everything about him proclaims his firm insertion within the symbolic order, from his secret satisfaction in his mastery in the home to his work as legal caretaker of the large estates and "conservative" investments (1115) of New York gentility. Putting Archer in the office of a Mr. Letterblair, with a roll of dead names on the letterheads and a senior partner who "was, professionally speaking, his own grandson" (1089), the text could not have inscribed him in a more patrilineal institution—worlds away from the "real" life of letters that tempts him in imagination.

Despite his intellectual pretensions to be a person of "advanced culture" (1051), Archer's reading, too, confirms him in the assumptions of his class and gender. He consumes science and literature in his upper-floor quarters, while his mother and sister squeeze themselves into the narrower space below. Later he uses history as a shield against his wife (1249). He chooses Michelet, a historian, so Ludmilla Jordanova tells us, "obsessed with sexual difference."[5] He pursues his beloved through the pages of Rossetti. Even his anthropology is far from radical. Archer's London bookseller sends him Herbert Spencer and, we suppose, other dominant thinkers of the decade (Sir Edwin Tylor, Sir John Lubbock, or John F. McLennan, for instance) who could supply him with the templates for marriage by capture, the service of the prospective son-in-law, the parental feints of reluctance, and so on, through which he characterizes his own experiences. According to the historian Elizabeth Fee,[6] these writers were conservatives to a man, lawyers and amateurs like Archer himself. (One of them, McLennan, shared Archer's taste for pre-Raphaelite verse and, under the pseudonym of "Iconoclast," even wrote a volume himself.)

Viewing the sheltered reserve around Washington Square through their terminology of "inscrutable totem terrors" (1018), "sacred taboos," and savage practices, Archer shapes the 1870s for us into the customs and ceremonies of a vanishing tribe. There is no denying the extent to which his model pervades the text. But against the more sophisticated ethnological eye of the novel as a whole, Archer's anthropology has a distinctly old-fashioned air. By the 1900s, the evolutionary discourse of "survivals" was being replaced by an interest (which the narrative shares) in "functions," the interpretation of social features in terms of their contemporary meanings. From the vantage point of 1920, then, we see farther than Archer does. (We shall find that while Archer gazes smugly on archaisms, the text shows us an active system.) *The Age of Innocence* asks us to explore questions of social process; the "books on Primitive Man" (1051), in contrast, assure Archer of the hazardousness of women and the primacy of the patriarchal modern family. As McLennan was certain, "With the advance of society ... the superiority of the male sex must have everywhere tended to establish that system."[7]

So, far from being the enlightened ethnologist, Archer himself is structured by the discourse of Family. At every step, his life embodies the family design, and the novel takes form around it. In the narrative of engagement, marriage, and fatherhood, Archer's identity is always positional: he is a son, brother, part of an affianced couple, caught in the "bridegroom's convulsive gesture" (1162), unable to break free even when he realizes his own condition ("'What I am? A son-in-law,'" 1186), trapped, finally, by May's victorious news of his forthcoming paternity. His role is compounded by his casting as the official voice, the spokesman for Firm and Family, who has to represent the word of all the tribal fathers in the containment of the woman who threatens them, until he even hears himself talking of "our ideas" in a voice that sounded like Mr. Letterblair's (1103).

As the novel proceeds, Archer begins to try to talk his way out of these words (the "categories like that" [1245] that make his world. In his anguished (and much-quoted) discussions with Ellen Olenska, he always comes up against Ellen's paradoxical certainties that they cannot exist beyond their social roles; for her, there can be no new entity ("no us in that sense!," 1246), except in a disembodied, romantic union, possible only if they never meet. Otherwise Archer will always be "the husband of Ellen Olenska's cousin" and she "the cousin of Newland Archer's wife" (1246), involved in shabby liaisons.

Ellen's parodic genealogy holds Archer (and us) firmly within the tidy structures of New York. If Archer remains a social agent stuck inside his culture, we must read his story in the broader context of class survival. *The Age of Innocence* looks back to the New York of Wharton's parents, a place Wharton located on the edges of history or myth, like Schliemann's Troy or the vanished Atlantis.[8] In the Metropolitan Museum, we see the newly recovered fragments of Ilium first through Ellen's sympathetic eyes, as small domestic objects, poignantly broken and labeled "Use unknown" (1262); then, in the final chapter, as scientifically catalogued treasures. Either view offers a possible approach (*The Age of Innocence* has been seen as both a sentimental and a dispassionate record), but the narrative also enables more active readings. Its pace and chronology (the leisurely scenic presentation of two years in the 1870s, the precipitate switch in the last pages to two days in the early 1900s, all read with hindsight from the immediate postwar years) allow us to see the items both labeled and successfully in use, and encountering the pressures of change. When the novel opens, the old New York families seem secure but are already under threat. Although the Academy still keeps the "new people" out, a new Opera House (with boxes for anyone who can afford them) is already being talked of, and from 1920, the concealed narrative standpoint, we know its building is imminent and that we are watching the rituals of an imperiled class. *The Age of Innocence* maps its field with the air of a textbook in systematic social observation. As Elsie Clews Parsons, a near contemporary, advised students in 1906, it was important, as a base for more advanced social analysis, to consolidate one's data: "The bounds and nature of the inhabited territory, the size of the group, its modes of subsistence, its economic and political classes, and its general social organisation, tribal, monarchical, democratic, etc.... In particular, the prevailing means in general of enforcing custom should be noted."[9] (And all this in one's first report.) We can try out her scheme against Archer's New York: details of territory (the streets, houses, rooms, furnishings, clothes, ornaments), subsistence (the menus? or the pastimes?— the Chivers's house parties, the van der Luyden's perfect lawns, or the Archer women's ferns in Wardian cases), hierarchies (a guest list ticked off with Mrs. Archer's sharp gold pen, precedence at table, a silent butler), or the invitations, visits, dinners, opera going, dances, and weddings that keep it all in place. All these take us into the language and being of the 1870s leisure class and together make up the cultural capital through which it maintains and reproduces itself, and, as critics demonstrate, any might do as an opening into the world of the novel.

For an example here, we might as well remain with the Roman punch and the dinner table (as ethnology knows, always a cultural minefield). There is a lot of dining in *The Age of Innocence*. In the 1870s, when the Newland Archers inaugurate themselves as a married couple, the punch, unambiguously, signified exclusiveness and accompanied "either canvas-backs or terrapin, two soups, a hot and cold sweet, full *décolletage* with short sleeves, and guests of a proportionate importance" (1276). By 1922, Emily Post was warning, "To eat extra entrees, Roman punch, or hot dessert is to be in the dining-room of a parvenu."[10] New York, as the novel's first paragraph tells us, is drawn to the new people, even as it dreads them: meanings are in contest and will shift as society changes.

To help us read the hieroglyphs, to know just who is an acceptable guest and why, *The Age of Innocence* supplies experts, who come confidently equipped with opera glasses and innuendo, axioms, long memories, and forests of family trees, to instruct us in social placing. We learn to read gesture and to listen to the unspoken. In polite voices, even gaps between syllables ("'Anyhow, he—eventually—married her'") teach "volumes" (1044). At dinner in a room which speaks loudly of social purity, Mrs. Archer and Mr. Jackson securely query others' origins. Family portraits guarantee their own. Dark frames on dark walls oppose the crude glossiness that marks the upstart. (Here, real ladies put their Paris dresses away for at least two seasons to rebuke the vulgarity of fashion.) The grandfathers still rule the table: Grandfather Newland's voice giving advice about how to keep the dynasty pure ("Don't let that fellow Beaufort be introduced to the girls," 1043), and Grandfather Archer's picture, in front of his white-columned country seat, giving an ever-present reminder of social stability and family property in the face of the socially suspect. Mr. Jackson's "sniff" at the mushroom sauce is "scarcely perceptible" but is enough to suggest that he "would probably finish his meal on Ellen Olenska" (1045). Women and mushrooms are hard to label, might well be poisonous, grow in dubious places, and it may be unwise to admit them to the table.[11] In the next chapter New York refuses a dinner invitation to meet her and, at the end of the novel, stages the final party to expel her permanently from society.

The dinner-table topics are central to the novel. *The Age of Innocence* is transfixed, as the speakers are, by outsiders and by the problems of classification. In a world where mobility is dangerous, to define is to begin to control. The Archer voice declares itself the social norm; its social distinctions, Mrs. Archer claims, have "nothing to do with rank or class" (1054); it lies somewhere between the "plain people" and the aristocracy, and its wealth and its morality are the standard. Mrs. Archer makes clear that her family fortune came from good clean stock. With this world view, everyone else embodies deviant forms. Extreme wealth and sexual excess are displaced elsewhere—Mrs. Struthers's saloon in the West, the Tuileries or Count Olenksi's acres of roses, historic pearls and Sobieski emeralds in Europe. Extreme poverty appears only obliquely in a passing simile: the specter of killing time haunted Mrs. Welland "as the spectre of the unemployed haunts the philanthropist" (1190). Here rises up the ghost of what lies beyond the farthest boundaries of the Family's territory: the persistent depressions of the

1870s and the thousands of homeless on the streets of New York. From within the heart of the citadel, Archer, we learn, feels caught between "the bosses and the emigrant" (1115), who, he believes, possess the country. His worries are those of his class, afraid of new forms of money, civic expansion, ethnic and social fluidity. To maintain the "middle way" requires constant vigilance. Afraid of politics, "decent people" (1115), the elite, intent on keeping their place and their privileges, need other means of social control. The discourse of social categories provides it: the pervasive nineteenth-century rhetoric of "types" that, through indexing faces, features, temperamental and intellectual qualities, identified the "right" people and could eject the socially dubious—or, in this novel, anyone outside the slippery pyramid of leisure-class New York. (Archer is a quick reader. He sees in an instant that Monsieur Rivière is a misfit in a crowd of "American hotel" faces, 1212.)

In a society that sees itself as beleaguered, desire follows cultural conformity. In Edward Westermarck's summary (of 1894), "Men find beauty in the full development of the visible characteristics belonging to the human organism in general; of those peculiar to the sex; of those peculiar to the race"; and, we might also add, of those peculiar to the class.[12] For New York in *The Age of Innocence*, replication seems everything. In domestic space, we frequently hear of characters growing into copies of their parents; May Archer, we are told, dies content, leaving a daughter of whom she is as sure as of her own self. In the larger public scenes, we see heritage made visible. The opera repeats itself season after season; the wedding places Archer in a rite going back to the dawn of history; and even an archery match produces a diamond arrow to be passed on to the eldest daughter.

The spectacle is self-confirming, but it also aims outward.[13] At Archer's wedding, the family row over whether the presents should be "shown" is not childish, as he imagines, but highlights the problem of how to exhibit the class to a wider audience. Mrs. Welland would as soon "turn the reporters loose" (1159) in her house; her fears are picked up in the reference to "the mob of dressmakers and newspaper reporters ... outside fighting to get near the joints of the canvas" (1160). The family finds "painful" the idea of the "monstrous exposure" of Granny Mingott's person, compounded with the menace that "'they might take a photograph of her [May] *and put it in the papers!*'" (1160). But though Mrs. Archer claims that the "aristocracy" is a journalistic invention (1054), wealthy society needs the press to represent its exclusivity to the outer world. We hear on the novel's first page that the newspapers have already learned the appropriate discourse. The Assembly at the opera is seen by "an exceptionally brilliant audience" (1017); the "most brilliant wedding of the year" (1164) will presumably attract a glowing paragraph. Mr. van der Luyden can read about his own important guests in the list of ship arrivals in the *Times*. But society does not want to meet cheap copies of itself in every carriage in the street. A photograph of May is for a bridegroom's desk, not for the fashion pages of *Hearth-fires*, next to New England love stories and advertisements for temperance drinks. By the turn of the century, if we remember the van Osbrugh wedding in *The House of Mirth*, the press are already through the canvas and at large in the house, and the leisure class has been reproduced in cinematograph throughout the land. By the 1920s, showing the presents was well established, and etiquette books were warning of more mundane burglaries: "When valuable presents are on view, one or more detectives should be engaged, and if the wedding is a large one the police should be informed, for pocket-picking often takes place on such occasions in the church porch," enjoined Lady Troubridge.[14]

Occasions like this reinforce images of exclusiveness, of a class reproducing itself without contamination. The novel's formal structure underlines the pattern, as scenes reenact themselves in a closed number of variants and the family names reappear in everlasting permutations, filling the text with the paper dolls and stenciled patterns that haunt Newland Archer (and the reader) with sameness (1082). Nevertheless, the rituals allow us the measure of change. At Grace Church, Julius Beaufort sits inside the white ribbon that marks the preserve of the family, and on summer afternoons his lawns host the archery contest and his wealth upgrades the prize. The leisure class is caught in a dilemma of wanting sameness but needing difference. Outsiders may mean disintegration or renewed strength. The accommodations operate in a very narrow realm. If artists will not decorate the salon, they are kept at a distance. Radical groups remain at the edges of the novel, and, Ellen's voice aside, the tone of high comedy in which Mrs. Welland reads out Professor Emerson Sillerton's invitation is used by the text of most of its agents of political or intellectual difference. We never join the Wednesday Afternoon Club, where, presumably, as Julia Ward Howe remembered, ideas, literature, and talk of reform "made it possible to be sensible even at Newport and during the summer"),[15] and we never enter the dissident house of "long-haired men and short-haired women" where the Sillertons once gave "a party for a black man" on the day of a *thé dansant* (1189–90).

But even limited transitions must be carefully managed, to maintain the boundaries against the outside as class identity alters. When it suits the group, society can relabel, forget origins, and assimilate. Despite Mrs. Struthers's beginnings in the dirt of western expansion and industrial manufacture (the "pit," for Mr. Jackson, 1044), society digests her before the end of the novel: "Once people had tasted of Mrs. Struthers' easy Sunday hospitality, they were not likely to sit at home remembering her champagne was transmuted Shoe-Polish" (1222). Good looks, a spell in Europe, the support of a duke, a famous pianist, dull Sunday evenings, and an outbreak of chicken pox smooth the process. (It was thus that New York "managed its transitions," 1222.) In the same way, when the novel opens, it has accepted Julius Beaufort. Deploying all the tactics Thorstein Veblen would itemize in his *Theory of the Leisure Class* (1899), Beaufort has thrown a screen over his shady past, married an impoverished beauty from "one of America's most honoured families" (1030), set her up for display in his brownstone palace ("dressed like an idol, hung with pearls," 1031), designed her smile and her drawing room, and kept all his work behind the scenes, to turn himself into the portrait of a gentleman: "and two years after young Mrs. Beaufort's marriage it was admitted that she had the most distinguished house in New York" (1031). Society preserves its health and its definitions by attributing the inclusion of Beaufort to "miracle" (1031), a sudden and inexplicable transformation in nature. But miracle masks corporate self-interest. The glitter of the Beauforts' ballroom, the "hot canvas-back ducks and vintage wines" (1031) at their dinners, and the careful exhibition of Mrs. Beaufort's perfect profile to the admiring stalls at the opera (1109) all contribute conspicuous evidence of New York's prosperity: "The Beaufort house was one that New Yorkers were proud to show to foreigners" (1032).

Old Mrs. Mingott sums up the process: "we need new blood and new money" (1039). Having heard this near the start of the novel, from a speaker described as "carnivorous," we soon begin to sense, more generally, that a social body with its own collective, even physical, identity is at large in the text. Some of the effect is built up by the rhetoric which speaks of "tribe" and "clan" but more substantially by a myriad of small references to an entity which can recoil with a collective shudder at the unthinkable, draw a breath of relief when it retreats, assume one voice on what "was generally agreed," and assemble in a "silent organisation" (1285) to act on it. Its interests, reactions, and mechanisms of survival go beyond those of any single member of the group but are variously focused for us in vivid individual figures.

Old Catherine's vast body is society's weightiest incarnation and holds its liveliest blood, energized by the Spicer past, life at the Tuileries, the pioneering house, and the goddesses on her ceiling. Change comes from this quarter, as Catherine recognizes more diverse ways of surviving than do most of the clan. This self-preserving dynamic of "Family" has one of its most cautious embodiments in Mr. Welland, whose careful attention to his bronchial tubes and, by extension, to the perfect plumbing of his daughter's married home, is only an extreme manifestation of the economies of self-conservation. Other family Elders consolidate the image of social purity and power successfully preserved. Mr. van der Luyden's patriarchal hand may be "bloodless" but, "weighed down by the Patroon's great signet-ring," it knows its authority (1087). His houses suggest a society kept on ice; his wife is the perfect replica of her aristocratic ancestress and of her own younger self, striking Archer as something "rather gruesomely preserved ... as bodies caught in glaciers keep for years a rosy life-in-death" (1056). If Mrs. van der Luyden is deep-frozen, Mrs. Manson Mingott is petrified, her body submerged in accreted flesh "like a flood of lava on a doomed city," within which "traces" of her face "survived as if awaiting excavation" (1036). At the center of the family nervous system, mystery protects them: they keep their influence, as Ellen knows, by making themselves so rare.

On a first reading, we may miss the signs of active life in all these images and see New York through Archer's eyes as tame and unsurprising at best, a paralyzing Gorgon at its deadliest. But (as Archer finds out) the social body is a highly alert and powerful working system, with "countless silently observing eyes and patiently listening ears" (1282), alive to what will advantage it and prompt to respond to danger. No experience is private. The family gaze marks Archer's entire narrative. From the first, it sees the signals—the conversation pursued too long, Archer's thrill at the touch of Ellen's fan. The weight of an "admonitory glance" (1067), the look "from the pure eminence of black velvet and the family diamonds" (1068), warn and correct; and delicate asides gain a double edge: "As Mrs. Archer remarked: when the van der Luydens chose, they knew how to give a lesson" (1068). Others take up the task: Mrs. Welland's "reproachful eyebrows" (1069) that pin Archer to a long engagement or, when he seems on the point of flight, the glint of more dangerous weapons—Old Catherine's "round eyes suddenly sharp as penknives" (1255), or Mr. Jackson's "tranquil gaze" hardening into a trap, which "held Archer's face as if in a spring of steel" (1225).

For this highly tuned organism, women are an obvious site of danger. As Elsie Clews Parsons knew, "The more thoroughly a woman is classified the more easily is she controlled."[16] The "Egyptian style" of Mrs. Struthers (1044) or the golden beauty of Fanny Ring (like the intellectual ambition of Elsie Clews) make the signs unreliable and send shudders through the family. (When Mrs. Archer was a girl, "only the people one knew had carriages," 1097.) Anyone outside the usual range of types is hard for those at the center even to see: just as May thinks Monsieur Rivière common, so Ellen knows that in America she is not thought handsome. An extreme case of downward mobility shows us the strength of the system. Medora Manson never stays long in any one social category, and her body seems to have lost its form accordingly. She is "long, lean and loosely put together ..., clad in raiment intricately looped and fringed, with plaids and stripes and bands of plain colour disposed in a design to which the clue seemed missing" (1140). What is the "clue"? a tinct of the Rushworth imprudence? or of friends and marriages in foreign places? or, as some critics think, of transgressive energy—her introductions of outsiders to New York and her forays into various utopian cults? (When we meet her, she is poised on the edge of plunging into the Valley of Love with the ominously named Dr. Carver.) Though it is tempting to admire Medora under a New Woman label, she has other, contradictory shapes ("Marchioness" and Count Olenski's envoy, for example), as tradition bound as any in the text. To New York she remains unreadable; her narrative takes her farther and farther away from acceptable spaces, as she resettles "each time in a less expensive house" (1062), until she loses her fortune in the Beaufort crash, finishing in Paris with Ellen.

If Medora is the "disastrous exception" (1022), the novel is full of women who have been more consistently formed by New York: among them, Janey as Old Maid, complete with suppressed springs of romance in slackening virgin body, or Mrs. Welland as Dutiful Wife, clad in an "automatic" "armour of cheerfulness" (1190, 1238). The text, like society itself, outlines its categories through the extended binary set of May and Ellen, inserting them in the structural slots they occupy in Archer's desires.

In New York's eyes, May is the "Nice Girl," the Angel and Diana of public statuary.[17] Seen from the male club box, everything about her signals purity—an "innocence" which licenses her appeal and guarantees the survival of the family. As Mrs. van der Luyden reminds Archer, at their dinner May is thought the handsomest girl in the room (1068). Archer recognizes marriage as an "association of material and social interests" (1050), and family councils legitimate his own: "There was no better match in New York than May Welland" (1044). The contract is hedged round with sanctions, "'Twelve dozen of everything—hand-embroidered'" (1069), to ensure that "Form" prevails. Safely married, May exults that no horrors "ever *can* happen now" (1163). To her new husband, she looks like "a type rather than a person," a model for "a Civic Virtue or a Greek goddess," with "preserving fluid" for blood (1164). Family blood and property are safe for another generation: May is not a foolish Rushworth, an insane Albany Chivers, a widow, one of Archer's "clever people" (1112), a "foreigner" of doubtful origins, or an unnamed hazard from the "Siren Isle" (1044).

"Innocence" is a powerful force in the narrative. Enacting "blameless domesticity" (1044) and social stability, May writes Archer back into class and family. Her telegrams to and talks with Ellen close down the novel's two main sections, blocking Archer's attempted flights outward. (Even the Miss du Lacs' leaky water tank conspires to ensure that the correct couple honeymoons in the Patroon's house.) May can detect a household menace in Ellen and utter her challenge in an exchange about a smoking lamp: "'They smell less if one blows them out,' she explained, with her bright housekeeping air" (1228). After this, her timely pregnancy almost seems self-generated, an affirmation of the community's claims as well as her own.

Seen through Archer's eyes, innocence is altogether simpler. Once again, although he believes himself detached from his cultural preferences, he embodies them in basic forms. At the opera, his version is comically disposed of in Madame Nilsson's caricature of the blonde ingenue in the garden of love, but his "thrill of possessorship" makes it plain that at this point Archer wholly approves of May's blushing ignorance, as he dreams of a honeymoon initiation via the "masterpieces of literature which it would be his manly privilege to reveal to his bride" (1020). As he begins to question these gendered patterns of power and passivity, the text produces what many readers find its most disturbing reflections: May is an "image made of snow," designed to flatter the "lordly pleasure" of the husband who smashes it (1051); a horribly adapted Kentucky cave fish (1081); a curtain dropped before an emptiness (1182). Archer decodes male gratification (at least to a degree) but never escapes it. Few critics, certainly, rush to congratulate him on his feminism. His similes (the flip side of his opera-box fantasies?) hardly go farther than dissatisfaction with the sexual temperature of a New York marriage. Before the honeymoon has ended, he has reverted to "all his old inherited ideas about marriage" (1170) and, though May is excited by seeing Parisian *cocottes* in the *cafés chantants*, he censors the words of the songs.

Archer locks May in the virginal script he criticizes. So do some readers; for at least one critic, May "fades out" in the latter part of the novel. For others, she has her own story as an unappreciated victim (of husband, patriarchy, or convention), or as the lovers' malign and implacable enemy.[18] If her blushes are a "red flag," signaling the knowledge for which a lady is permitted no language, then May speaks volumes: "Good gracious, look at her blushing again all over her blushes" (1184). The blushes, like the blue dazzle in May's eyes, witness to the interior self, the imagination, blood, and feeling that Archer prefers to overlook. Before their marriage, he credits her with a single "effort of speaking" (1134) but otherwise construes her only in the rhetoric approved by his society. He makes her eyes transparent, blind, and bandaged, and stops trying to read meaning in her silences. She remains a vacuum and a blank for him, the white page of convention, asexual, infantile, boyish, solid, cold, and suffocatingly present. ("'The room is stifling: I want a little air,'" 1250).

Ellen, in contrast, seems cast as the Woman of Experience, presented in typical postures from melodrama.[19] In Archer's scheme, set against May's emptiness, Ellen represents unattainable plenitude. From the start, he fills her with "suggestion" (1021)—of enigma, passion, womanliness, Europe, mysterious joys, appalling suffering, conversations, art, music, literature, expressed in the exoticism of her room, the authority in her beauty, and the expression in her eyes. He imagines her as a shrine and a relic, a traveler in Samarkand and a vision in Rossetti, and sees her in terms of images of candle beams, butterflies, flickering fires, summer lightning, pre-Raphaelite haziness, the effulgence of Titian, and the golden light of Paris, "too dense and yet too stimulating for his lungs" (1300).

With yellow roses heading Ellen's column, as lilies of the valley do May's, the lists could lengthen indefinitely. Archer's terms are conventional ones: though he romanticizes Ellen and society fears her, she remains the unsettling Other. New York, like Archer, is clear about May but cannot decide about Ellen: born a Mingott, she has been fashioned in other circumstances that make her radically unstable. Fleeing her husband, she leaves a trail in different places and companies—Lausanne, West Twenty-third Street, "diplomatic society" (1185), the female house of the Blenkers. Entering the Mingott box in the first chapter, she is introduced in a paragraph framed by astonished exclamations from the arbiters of "form" and "family," while the men wait in "visible suspense" (1023) for a judgment. Like Mrs. Archer, society prefers young women to be "simple" (1136). Ellen has only to walk alone across a drawing room to offend its definitions. A lady should be an "idol," all surface, inert, an ornament meant to rest the gentlemen's eyes after their talk. Ellen's "animated" talk and relaxed posture are alarming signs of self-will and vitality (1065), and, faced with her documents, the lawyer, Mr. Letterblair looks "like the Family Physician annoyed with a patient whose symptoms refuse to be classified" (1089). If the symptoms are what he suspects, "unpleasantness" threatens the health of the family. Accordingly, much of the narrative is spent in trying to put Ellen in her place, whether by reabsorbing her into the clan, finding her a little house, sending her back to her husband, brooding endlessly about her intentions, or consecrating her in a small dim chapel in the memory.

Readers find Ellen even less simple than New York does. She is an endlessly variable text, impossible to read with any certainty. Though she has experienced other forms of existence, the novel leaves them mysterious. Her husband's letter is a "grimacing ... spectre" that we are never allowed to see (1102); her secrets remain in a locked drawer at Mr. Letterblair's. Her European life (with Count Olenski or with Monsieur Rivière) is, in both New York and the narrative, literally unspeakable. Though readers can try to shape it out of the gaps of her story, to represent it would need a different kind of novel altogether: a turn-of-the-century feminist one, for example, or a genre outside of realism. Ellen's past, after all, lies in the fantastic realm of Dracula: "a kind of sulphurous apotheosis" of marriage to a "white sneering" count with "many square miles of shooting in Transylvania" (1063, 1027).

Unreadability is part of the standard construction of the enigmatic woman, but beyond this stereotypical vision we may be seeing a more interesting figure, who writes her scripts herself. Ellen knows how to manipulate signs or to confound them. She is astute about men's use of women as badges of respectability: she saves her aunt from being exploited by Dr. Carver, refuses to lend herself to head her husband's table, and, when Regina Beaufort has no more value than an out-of-date banknote, restores her credit by driving the Mingott carriage to her door. As a girl, she looked like a gypsy child, in crimson; as a debutante, she wore black. Her room is an oriental mystery, and the litany of her fabrics and her furs (which begins to look to the 1990s like a list of endangered species, including green monkey, sealskin, eagle feathers in her fan, a heron wing in her cap) codes the erotic for everyone who sees her. (Ellen is as "romantic"-seeming for Miss Blenker, Medora, and Janey as she is for Archer.) Presenting herself as the image of sexuality (in a "sheath-like" robe of "red velvet bordered about the chin and down the front with glossy black fur" (1099), she seems unequivocally the type of the sensual. In a draft, she even advocates what is in effect a trial marriage, but she leaves Archer because she has "eaten of the Pomegranate seed and can never live without it."[20] But if we can find *Ur*-images of sexuality in the manuscripts, the text as published never confirms them. Behind Ellen's veils and screens might equally be self-containment and chasteness, just as unthinkable to the family. The clan holds that a woman can be defined only in relation to men; even Medora preaches the ideology of marriage as sacrifice, and old Catherine believes a married countess better than a single Mingott: whatever the source of Ellen's energies, unclassifiable or "'classed' ... irretrievably" (1124), she remains an embarrassment.

If unregulated women trouble New York, so does unregulated capital. Perhaps because the novel makes its points so succinctly, some readers have felt that *The Age of Innocence* is less interested in the dynamics of money than is some of Wharton's earlier fiction. But from start to finish, the text has money on its mind: its sources, legitimacy, and limits. Whereas it distributes different aspects of femininity between a set of different characters, it largely concentrates finance into one: that of Julius Beaufort. Like Ellen, he is a perpetual riddle in the narrative: any answers only produce the same question: "Who was Beaufort?" (1030). We meet him as a New Yorker by custom, but at every appearance in the text he sets up currents of disquiet. Like Simon Rosedale in *The House of Mirth*, he is an outsider, possibly Jewish (he "passed for an Englishman" [1030],[21] whose rumored excesses set whispers murmuring "not only in Fifth Avenue but in Wall Street" (1181). Whether in monetary or sexual versions, Beaufort is viewed in terms of spending, with all its suggestion of fluidity, bleeding, giving out too much, being used up: "Some people said he had speculated unfortunately in railways, others that he was being bled by one of the most insatiable members of her profession; and to every report of threatened insolvency Beaufort replied by a fresh extravagance" (1181).

Lavish outgoings, speculation, risky investments, tainted capital, all run counter to the image of the self as constituted in leisure-class New York. Good form restrains other men. (Lefferts's mistresses do not drive bright-yellow carriages at the fashionable hour.) Cautious, conservative, resistant to indiscreet expenditure, New York reigns in passions and capital; the self remains solvent, its moral and its business consciences sound, and its identity clear. While Beaufort simulates integrity, he is acceptable. Once he overreaches, his smash threatens the whole of New York: "'Everybody we know will be hit one way or another'" (1230). As both sexual and financial disasters rise to a crisis, shock waves pass through society. Mr. Letterblair, the family's legal conscience, is left "white and incapacitated" (1230), and in the body blow to "Family," Mrs. Mingott suffers a stroke. Less "mysterious" (1231, 1236) to readers than to her relations, Beaufort's fall registers the worst that can happen—an intolerable rupture at the center of New York that lays it open shamefully to the world: "That afternoon the announcement of the Beaufort failure was in all the papers.... The whole of New York was darkened by the tale of Beaufort's dishonour" (1236).

This is the place to return to Archer. A novel's central character, as Wharton suggested in *The Writing of Fiction*, often seems the emptiest. Archer is no exception. The other figures represent social power, in concentrated and vivid forms. Archer, for most of the novel, is a subject in the process of disintegration: "Absent—that was what he was: so absent from everything most densely real and near to those about him that it sometimes startled him to find they still imagined he was there" (1224). Given his formation in the society we have been looking at, it is hardly surprising that the two figures who most disturb him are the two who most trouble his class. Both Ellen Olenska and Julius Beaufort set up vibrations that threaten his very structure. At Ellen's name, his heart stops; he wonders "if, whenever he heard those two syllables, all his carefully built-up world would tumble about him like a house of cards" (1165); in Beaufort's presence, he feels "an odd sense of disembodiment" (1123) and angry perplexity. In this state, Archer fights to maintain his ground and, contradictorily, to escape from the words and role that trap him.

But if social role seems constriction, declassification is loss of being. At his wedding, as he waits at the chancel step in the part of the eager bridegroom, signs come adrift from their meanings:

> The music, the scent of lilies on the altar, the vision of the cloud of tulle and orange-blossoms floating nearer and nearer, the sight of Mrs. Archer's face suddenly convulsed with happy sobs, the low benedictory murmur of the Rector's voice, the ordered evolutions of the eight pink bridesmaids and the eight black ushers: all these sights, sounds and sensations, so familiar in themselves, so unutterably strange and meaningless in his new relation to them, were confusedly mingled in his brain. (1162)

The structure of the paragraph is familiar: the catalogue of effects, followed by its location in Archer's consciousness; but this time, the scene consists of disconnected sense data, with no unifying narratorial exposition, and when we join Archer it is to find the known defamiliarized. It is as if, at the moment of his public commitment to the body of New York, he reverses the entrance into the symbolic order and comes apart again. Critics have enjoyed Wharton's slip in the first printing which opened the wedding with the words of the burial service.[22] (Archer, too, might have learned from his anthropology that "the bridegroom's soul is apt to fly away at the wedding.")[23] But the funereal hints go farther than simply placing a tombstone on marriage to May; instead they seem to take Archer altogether out of the social world. Details, even of ordinary language (Archer's heart "stopped beating," the sight of the "apparition," the "fantastic figure" of Medora Manson, 1161), take on more spectral resonance. Archer wonders whether he is hallucinating. Possibly he is—but the text itself seems, too, to be flickering with glimpses of a different kind of discourse, as social surfaces become "unutterably strange." It is in passages like this, when Archer seems to be pushing toward a different kind of self (one, impossibly, beyond the social), that the mimetic mode of realism, where detail metonymically holds in it the larger scene, seems to feel beneath it other pressures, as the novel of manners shifts into the fantastic. In the terrain of fantasy, Allon White argues, "Corporal disintegration is the reverse of the constitution of the body during the mirror phase and it occurs only at those times when the unified and transcendent ego is threatened with dissolution."[24]

We do not have to be familiar with French psychoanalytic theory to see this process at work in *The Age of Innocence*. In Archer's world, identity is formed within social consciousness, and when Archer is confronted with a challenge to his categories he begins to come apart, losing his sense of himself, his language, position, bodily space. Some readers would agree with Archer that to be locked in the family is to be buried alive, but the text also suggests, conversely, that *loss* of social being is a form of death. In *A Son at the Front*, the war novel Edith Wharton laid aside to write *The Age of Innocence*, her painter, Campton, cannot see when the frame goes from round his world; Archer, too, does not know how to look at things. When Ellen asks if he takes the family view, he can only wander across the room and stare with "void eyes" (1104); he loses his voice in the family—"they never quote you when they talk about its being her duty to go home" (1255)—and his most ordinary words sound like "a strange language" (1198). Imagery of graveyards, tombs, and vaults surrounds him, as his body dies, cut off from the circulation of the collective. Dropped from any source of meaning, he is open to possession: "demons" and "inner devils" move in to haunt him (1288).

The text calibrates this in violent figures of racking bodily disturbance which run against the composed detail through which the social world is narrated. It notes Archer's loss of control as he blushes, laughs hysterically, winces, slams down his fist, leaps from his chair, flings open a window, frightens people with his gaze. Inside his head, the confusion he feels at the altar is a symptom repeated time and again, as Archer's brain whirls and the blood beats in his temples. (Mrs. Mingott's stroke hovers in the text in these moments, long before it channels itself through her.) Displacing Archer from the New York drawing room, the text produces hints of different spaces altogether. Emptied of its certainties, Archer's mind becomes an "empty and echoing place" (1181), an interior where doors slam (1180)—or an even wilder landscape, where blood rushes to the temples "as if he had been caught by a bent-back branch in a thicket" (1214), or he pitches from a precipice (1153), or an evening sweeps by, "running and running like a senseless river that did not know how to stop" (1286). Here, Archer loses his foothold entirely: he feels as if he had "slipped through the meshes of time and space" (1197) or "as if he floated somewhere between chandelier and ceiling" (1281). This topography of the unreal exists for readers only through the narration, but Archer begins to act as if it could become material, in fantasies of flight ("His own fancy inclined to Japan" [1158], of "plunging" (a favorite term) out of the here and now, or of reversing time and returning to childhood.

Many of the episodes readers find most resonant are ones which concentrate these motifs, where the landscape is at once internal and external (or as Wharton expressed it rather more poetically, "an event in the history of a soul").[25] There is space here for only one example: the encounter between Archer and Ellen in the Patroon's house. The episode is a wonderful instance of the fusion in the text of smooth surface and deep disarray, and of a space which is both public and private, enacting at the same time a fantasy and a critique of individual freedom. (Monsieur Rivière may speak of "quant à soi," but it remains a myth.) The house itself occupies multiple levels of space—psychological, social, and historical—and (with Ellen in a red cloak, looking like "the Ellen Mingott of old days," 1119) becomes a fairy-tale gingerbread cottage for two lost children: a fantasy of privacy and escape. This is the original Dutch governor's cottage and, as Chandler emphasizes, represents the guarantee of leisure-class power itself—in its original stamp, built in 1612—virtually on the edge of historical time in the colonial settlement of the United States.[26] Much of its fascination is this suggestion that Archer and Ellen can go back, escape from their history and begin again. (The famous last paragraph of *The Great Gatsby* reaches out to that same historical moment, the sighting of the unspoiled continent.) Wharton duplicates the desire in the biographies of the characters—to Archer, Ellen looks as she did when they were children—and beyond this lies the dream of escape from any social category at all. Impossible though we know this is, here, for a moment, where the house looks "as if magically created" for them, there is the illusion that the "miracle" will happen (1122): that they will meet in a fairy-tale world transcending time and history.

But, as we have seen, because society has taught the individual how and what to feel, once Archer loses touch with his social role he has lost himself. Here the text presents him as completely paralyzed. He desires intensely but cannot act: he moves away from the hearth to look out at the snow. It is an attempt to bring life back to rule; "black tree-boles against the snow" (1122) have style and form and suggest prison bars, as Newland tries to close up his awkward senses. The inner pressure blurs the distinction between outer and inner worlds. Archer's perception is radically disarranged: first he sees Ellen and the fire, as he will see her lifelong, imposed on everything, like an image imprinted on a white sheet. And then, in the same mode, just as he feels he is about to break all the rules, he sees the banker Beaufort. As Chandler reminds us, this ironic arrival keeps the mythic world entangled with the commercial one of Beaufort's version of the "perfect little house" (1123).[27]

But social comedy also veers at the same instant into darker fantasy. We know that Beaufort is the strongest image for Archer of lust and impropriety but also a figure fascinating for its difference. From unknown origins, Beaufort offers the possibility of multiple, alternative selves, created through money, women, languages, foreign places, and new careers. He even speaks Ellen's dialect, inaccessible to Archer. As Archer suggests, Ellen likes Beaufort "because he's so unlike us" (1207). The narrative precipitates him at pressured moments, as his "unexpected figure" (1039) shadows Archer's encounters with Ellen. Even a thought of Ellen can produce him: Archer "saw the lady of whom he was thinking seated in a box with the Beauforts" (1108). In the Patroon's house, in the context of stirred emotion and disturbed vision, Beaufort seems to arise from Archer himself, a strange externalization of his guilt, projected onto the snow in the shape of his dark rival.

The moment stays with Archer, powerful and haunting: "he could never hear the name without the sharp vision of Beaufort's heavy figure, opulently furred and shod, advancing through the snow at Skuytercliff" (1223). In Wharton's ghost stories and elsewhere, she was interested in the double, the Other who is the dark side of the self.[28] In "Afterward," the ghost is specifically an economic and moral one, who rises up to haunt the man whose wealth is founded on his labor. Instead of a book entitled *The Economic Basis of Culture*, the rich man meets his material unconscious in the shape of a gray figure, face shaded by a hat. This is how the text consistently represents Beaufort: muffled, faceless or threatening, "darkly projected against a blaze of light" (1096). One answer, then, to the persistent question of who Beaufort "really" is might be that he is a version of Archer—a self who enacts all that Archer cannot.

Contesting the same slot, socially and psychologically, Archer feels "invisibility ... non-existence" (1123) in the banker's presence. He winces when Ellen joins their names, but the coupling happens again and again, as meeting by meeting, bouquet by bouquet, the men pursue Ellen side by side. Thoughts of Beaufort provoke some of Archer's most profound moments of disturbance; "insinuations about Beaufort made him reckless" (1226). All of his questions to Ellen deny the identity but confirm it also, coming to a head when he asks directly whether Beaufort is to replace him. His conscious ambition is to make Ellen see Beaufort as he "really was, with all he represented—and abhor it" (1077); his darker one, to become him. It is impossible for Archer to take Ellen without taking on the role of Beaufort. (At dinner, the talk about Beaufort's extinction warns him of his own.)

The deeply held assumptions about the behavior of a gentleman, the morality that is felt in the blood, mean that Wharton cannot write Archer an ending with Ellen. When she experimented with offering her lovers some life together, she could not complete the story. In the published text, Archer cannot think beyond the limits of his society: conversation with Ellen leaves him "dumb" and "dazed" with "frozen tears" (1245–7). (A gentleman, even when facing the unthinkable, he lowers his voice, so that his wife's coachman will not hear.) Nor can he become the figure of Beaufort. To ensure a future, the figures who threaten structural collapse, to self and to society, must be expelled from New York and from the narrative. To write otherwise would be to pronounce an end to the values of a class. An uncategorized woman (not married, divorced, single, or mistress) has no place in the culture: Ellen is sent to Paris. Beaufort's excesses must be rebuked while society heals itself. New York redescribes Mrs. Mingott's stroke as an attack of indigestion and wipes out the scandal. Beaufort is "heard of in Constantinople, then in Russia; and a dozen years later ... in Buenos Ayres" (1295). Neither exile is seen again directly in the final chapter. Within this closed space, the options for the self are firmly controlled: in banishing desire and excess, it resists fragmentation and so never tests the possibilities for different forms of being: Archer is reintegrated into a stable, if frozen, identity. Holding to known forms, the text, too, lets go of other modes of representation and comes home to the bounds of realism. Another kind of novel (fantastic, modernist, or contemporary feminist) might see fragments as a liberation from traditional forms, from constructs of class, gender, and "character."[29] Here, social, psychological and narrative order cohere.

If the novel ended with May's announcement, we would be left seeing the leisure class as an effective self-regulating system. In a nineteenth-century novel, a coda in the present tense might confirm the choices and suggest that now, at last, all was in place. Instead, *The Age of Innocence* throws everything into the air. First, there is, the surprise of the final chapter, which sweeps the 1870s into the distant past and seems to overturn all its values. The immediate impact is of dramatic social transformation, of emotions released, in exuberant images of mobility, in behavior, appearance, physique, and relationships. With telephones and Atlantic crossings, the boundaries seem to be gone. The modern generation has swept away "the signposts" and "the danger signal" (1300), to create a world where "all the social atoms spun around on the same plane" (1296). But then there comes a secondary jolt, when we realize that, from the reader's position with the gulf of World War I between, even this vision of the contemporary is itself now an irretrievable past. (The war, Wharton's letters tell us, insists on a historical imagination: neither novelist nor reader can simply ignore the fact that the novel is set in the prewar years.) Perhaps, then, within the narrative, the continuities matter more than the changes? How much change, indeed, is there? Does the last chapter project the demise of the leisure class or its survival? Where, if at all, are the gains—and the losses?

The complex crosslights make any of these questions difficult, even impossible, to answer. The narrative performs a careful balancing act—"After all, there was good in the old ways.... There was good in the new order too" (1291–2)—and it takes this farther in a sequence of figures who, among them, embody what previously would have seemed impossible reconciliations. Though by their very existence they seem to turn Archer's old New York into the ruins of Troy, equally they might be seen as successful adaptations of that world, replete with the new blood and new money Mrs. Mingott recommended, maintaining its cultural heritage in the face of the twentieth century.

The text does not directly restore those it has expelled, but to a certain extent it legitimates their energies. Where their counterparts in a nineteenth-century novel might have been decisively extinguished, Beaufort and Ellen live on in new social spaces and maintain their influence. Though kept at a distance (he is dead by the end of the novel), Beaufort, we hear, is allowed both another fortune and another marriage (this time producing a child), and Ellen's life in Paris, as recent feminist criticism suggests, points toward new roles for women, even if it is not the novel's task to take them up. In her apartment, empowered by an allowance from Mrs. Mingott, living separately from her husband, she is not a gothic heroine imprisoned in a tower, Isabel Archer in a dark house, or another nineteenth-century rebel, doomed and dead.[30] (She is more like Ida Lewis, the heroic lighthouse keeper we heard of living in her Lime Rock tower [1185] or, as critics remark, Edith Wharton herself, a wealthy, independent expatriate in Paris.) Archer preserves Ellen as a picture in his head, but the text allows the reader to imagine more dynamic possibilities.

But this final chapter gives more space to characters new to the text. Just as *The House of Mirth* produced Netty Struther, who offers a solution (at least in fantasy) to many of the contradictions of the rest of the novel, so *The Age of Innocence* generates answers in figures who carry, in nonexplosive versions, forms of energy blocked in the main narrative.

The most commented on is, inevitably, Fanny Beaufort, who emerges to confound Lefferts's ironic prophecies by supplying one of "Beaufort's bastards" (1284) to be married to Archer's first-born son. In Fanny's multiple parentage (she has been raised by an unlikely team of Beaufort, Fanny Ring, Ellen Olenska, and Mrs. Jack Welland), the narrative brings back its exiles and incorporates them into the social structure. In an "almost cousinly relationship" with Archer's children (1295), Fanny provides a "foreign" marriage from within the safety of the endogamous group; happy to look like an Isabey miniature in emeralds and pearls but at home with Debussy and with Paris theaters, she safely combines the modern with the ancestral, and it is into her hands that the family heritage is placed when Janey makes her bridal gift of Mrs. Archer's jewels.

Will the jewels be safe with Fanny? Though Archer registers a trace of doubt—"Fanny Beaufort, whatever one might think of her" (1293)—the reader would imagine so. In presenting a society that thrives on the vigorous "bastard" blood, *The Age of Innocence* is not showing us social overthrow, or even much readjustment. Mary Archer may be more tolerant than her mother and interested in philanthropy, but she grows up to a Grace Church wedding, not, say, to work in a settlement house. Edith Wharton was not Upton Sinclair: responding to his novel *Oil*, she agreed that corrupt capitalists would make anyone desire "some radical change in the organization of society," but she loathed his socialist solutions and his overtly political writing (*Letters*, 501). Her narrative, in contrast, preserves an image of "civilized living," supported on money and tradition, while regulating its unacceptable versions.

In negotiating this delicate middle way, both art and politics come back into service, cleansed of "unpleasant" (or subversive) associations. Dallas Archer inherits his "vague leanings towards 'art'" (1290) from his father but translates them into a profession. Where Archer's taste led him merely to the right desk and the right engagement ring, Dallas's is potentially more far-reaching; architects have tremendous power to reshape or reproduce social forms. Dallas remains in exclusive regions, but his work, nevertheless, registers change: in the first description of his current project, we learn that he is directly creating spaces in which the newly rich can operate. The "millionaire grocers of the suburbs" insist on "Colonial" houses (1290); Dallas's clients will be housed with better taste. Dallas can be sent to Europe to look at Italian gardens, perhaps with Wharton's recently published *Italian Villas and Their Gardens* in his pocket, and can be relied upon to house a young millionaire in a lakeside palace that matches Mr. van der Luyden's: "People had always been told that the house at Skuytercliff was an Italian villa" (1118). But if class boundaries can be stretched to Chicago, what is left? Dallas belongs "body and soul to the new generation" (1298); he has no more nuance than Beaufort and a breezy lack of regard for psychological interiors. Does he represent the end of his class, the erasure of all its values? or is he a fresh beginning—working within its sphere, with a cultural memory of how things used to be?

Whatever Dallas is, his social function is to channel new energies into older forms. As Beaufort remained safe while contained within the norms of New York, so his successors need controlling through older principles. Cultural practice does this one way, but the 1900s needed more immediate forms of supervision. In the 1870s, Archer's anxieties about the boss, the emigrant, and the financier never take shape in action. He remains the gentleman, vapid and inert, shrugging off Winsett's advice to "roll up your sleeves and get right down into the muck" (1115). (In a house with perfect plumbing, one never has to.) In the 1900s, the novel (like this essay, in its final pages), at last produces its hidden hero, and its most important dinner guest, who bangs a clenched fist on the table, gnashes his eyeglasses, and attempts to stir the leisure class into action.

There can be few readers who would predict Theodore Roosevelt as Archer's compensation for Ellen Olenska. If she becomes "the composite vision of all that he had missed" (1291), Roosevelt emerges as his reward for staying in place. On the level of character, we might suspect that Archer would have preferred, like Monsieur Rivière, to have known Maupassant, but in terms of the direction of the narrative, Roosevelt is far more interesting. Most obviously, he retrieves the image of the gentleman; here, in his most character-building form, is the manly, active opposite of Archer's wavering emptiness, bringing into the text exemplary patrician origins, best-selling books, scholarliness, literary enthusiasm, physical prowess, and legendary charisma—as a hero, even a last-minute one, he has perfect credentials. Indeed, his face would even pass into the ethnic pattern books as the ideal of the American type: "Active, progressive, industrious, full of business and thought" (1910).[31] And as president (and patriarch), he would maintain the advocacy of the upper-class family, worrying about "Race Suicide" and urging the leisured elite to breed.

Through this muscular paragon, the novel offers a different model of a social agent, reinstating a vigorous public voice turned on more disorderly enemies than a single woman. We hear it directly in the text, making its appeal for an effort of herculean housekeeping: "You're the kind of man the country wants, Archer. If the stable's ever to be cleaned out, men like you have got to take a hand in the cleaning" (1290). Within the general glow of knowing the president, Archer's memory frames a moment in 1899 or 1900, during Roosevelt's brief career as governor of New York. Although the timing may have been dictated by verisimilitude (a base in Albany makes dinner invitations more convenient than one in the White House), the speech is impeccably placed to recall the novel's broader concerns. Roosevelt not only echoes Ned Winsett but sets the example: as governor, he took on the bosses and set about regulating the evils of capital. As president, he repeatedly spoke in the terms of Archer's New York, deploring excessive growth and blatant irregularity but alive to the benefits of new commercial wealth. Though he is wrong about Archer's efficacy in the state Assembly, he guides him into a new identity as "a good citizen" (1291) (a rhetoric which was beginning to expand the concept of "Family") and a writer for a reforming weekly. Later, Roosevelt might well have found one of his new men in Dallas: it was an architect, Herbert Croly, whose book *The Promise of American Life* (1909) provided a philosophical base for Roosevelt's own reforming program.[32]

In his immediate incarnation in the narrative, Roosevelt is a deus ex machina, produced to save gentility in peril; in hindsight, he looks more like the last specimen of his kind. He was, we know, Edith Wharton's own model of a statesman, a close friend and also a family member through marriage to one of her network of cousins. After his death in January 1919, she drew on anthropology to write a commemorative poem, in which, as her biographer tells us, using a legend from *The Golden Bough*, she ferried him to meet friends in the land of the dead.[33] For Wharton, this hero certainly left traces in the blood; she reported, in an image alarming to the 1990s, that each of her encounters with him "glows in me like a tiny morsel of radium."[34]

The Age of Innocence was composed and first read in the aftermath of Roosevelt's death and in the immediate wake of World War I. We frame the ending remembering the multiple losses that occurred in the gap between the end of the novel and the moment of reading: not only the loss of Roosevelt but the destruction of the prewar world and all that Wharton valued in it. Even Dallas bears a strong resemblance to the cheerful young men killed in the war whom Wharton, at the same time, was painfully memorializing in *A Son at the Front*. This knowledge makes the rest of the novel, in turn, radically unstable. In *A Son at the Front*, Wharton worried about the heritage for art. (Her "son" has two fathers, a banker and a painter.) To look back to the past is a highly ambiguous act: reviewing sketches he had made of his son, the painter feels that he is digging up the dead. A memorial may merely recycle old forms, or it may produce new ones. In these years, Wharton wondered whether she could go on writing: "the world I had grown up and been formed by had been destroyed in 1914, and I felt myself incapable of transmuting the raw material of the after-war world into a work of art."[35]

If a subject has been fabricated through one kind of discourse, when society changes that subject is disembodied, loses its voice. Interested in staging *The Age of Innocence*, Wharton seems concerned with settling interpretation, re-creating a solid image of the past. But in narration, the novel resists stability, pursuing old traces, fragments of a dead world, reassembling them even while they vanish like the "visions of the night" (1126). For its hero, to know at last that he had been read aright releases him, taking "an iron band from his heart" (1299), retroactively making his life coherent. The novel remains more difficult: a moral tract, rewarded by the Pulitzer trustees; a memorial to Realism and to an extinct social order; a piece of covert modernism, radically taking apart old forms; "the spoils of the ages" (1289), waiting for the opening night of a multi-million-dollar movie at the end of the century. All these (and more) cross and recross a reading: "Is New York such a labyrinth?" Ellen wonders. "I thought it so straight up and down—" (1076).

NOTES

1. *The Age of Innocence* in *Edith Wharton: Novels*, ed. R. W. B. Lewis, Library of America Edition (Cambridge: Cambridge University Press, 1985), 1076. All references are to this edition and are given in the text.

2. Edith Wharton to Mary Cadwalader Jones, February 17, 1911, *The Letters of Edith Wharton*, ed. R. W. B. Lewis and Nancy Lewis (London: Simon & Schuster, 1988), 439. Hereafter cited in the text.

3. Edith Wharton, *The Writing of Fiction* (1915; New York: Octagon, 1966), 7.

4. Ian Burkitt, *Social Selves: Theories of the Social Formation of Personality* (London: Sage, 1971), 29.

5. Ludmilla Jordanova, *Sexual Visions: Images of Gender in Science and Medicine between the Eighteenth and Twentieth Centuries* (Hemel Hempstead, U.K.: Harvester, 1989), 67.

6. Elizabeth Fee, "The Sexual Politics of Victorian Social Anthropology," in *Clio's Consciousness Raised: New Perspectives on the History of Women*, ed. Mary S. Hartman and Lois Banner (New York: Octagon, 1976), 86–102.

7. John F. McLennan, *Primitive Marriage: An Inquiry into the Origin of the Form of Capture in Marriage Ceremonies*, ed. Peter Rivière (1865; Chicago: University of Chicago Press, 1970), 91.

8. Edith Wharton, *A Backward Glance* (New York: Appleton-Century, 1934) 55.

9. Elsie Clews Parsons, *The Family: An Ethnographical and Historical Outline with Descriptive Notes, Planned as a Text-book for the Use of College Lecturers and of Directors of Home-Reading Clubs* (New York: Putnam, 1906), 7–8. Wharton's anthropology may also be discussed in more modern terms. See, for instance, Mary Ellis Gibson, "Edith Wharton and the Ethnography of Old New York," *Studies in American Fiction* 13.1 (1985), 65–8, and Judith Fryer, *Felicitous Space: The Imaginative Structures of Edith Wharton and Willa Cattier* (Chapel Hill: University of North Carolina Press, 1986), 116–42.

10. Cited by Margaret Visser, *The Rituals of Dinner: The Origins, Evolution, Eccentricities, and Meaning of Table Manners* (New York: Grove Weidenfeld, 1991), 76.

11. For more on Mr. Jackson's taste buds, in the context of manners, money, and types, see Richard Godden, *Fictions of Capital: The American Novel from James to Mailer* (Cambridge: Cambridge University Press, 1990), 12–16.

12. Edward Westermarck, *The History of Human Marriage*, 2nd ed. (London: Macmillan, 1894), 264–5. This monumental work was much reprinted.

13. For general arguments on these lines, see Amy Kaplan, *The Social Construction of American Realism* (Chicago: University of Chicago Press, 1988), and Godden, *Fictions of Capital*.

14. Lady Troubridge, *The Book of Etiquette*, vol. 1 (U.K.: Associated Bookbuyers, 1926), 46. Archer's wedding followed "English" models.

15. Julia Ward Howe, *Reminiscences, 1819–1899* (1899; New York: Greenwood, 1969), 406.

16. Elsie Clews Parsons, *Social Rule: A Study of the Will to Power* (New York: Putnam, 1916), 55.

17. Martha Banta's formulation, placing May and Ellen in a brilliant and encyclopedic survey of American types: *Imaging American Women: Ideas and Ideals in Cultural History* (New York: Columbia University Press, 1987), 448–9.

18. For examples of "strong" readings of May, see Susan Goodman, *Edith Wharton's Women: Friends and Rivals* (Hanover, N.H.: University Press of New England, 1990), 96–104, and Mary Suzanne Schriber, "Convention in the Fiction of Edith Wharton," *Studies in American Fiction* 11.2 (1983), 195–7.

19. Banta, *Imaging American Women*, 448–9.

20. Candace Waid, *Edith Wharton's Letters from the Underworld: Fictions of Women and Writing* (Chapel Hill: University of North Carolina Press, 1991), 12.

21. Marilyn R. Chandler's suggestion in *Dwelling in the Text: Houses in American Fiction* (Berkeley and Los Angeles: University of California Press, 1991), 159.

22. R. W. B. Lewis, *Edith Wharton: A Biography* (London: Constable, 1975), 430.

23. Elsie Clews Parsons, *The Old-fashioned Woman: Primitive Fancies about the Sex* (New York: Putnam, 1913), 263. Parsons is reviewing the extensive discourse of "The Jeopardized Male."

24. Allon H. White, "L'éclatement du sujet: The theoretical work of Julia Kristeva," cited in Rosemary Jackson, *Fantasy: The Literature of Subversion* (London: Methuen, 1981), 90.

25. Wharton, *Writing of Fiction*, 84.

26. Chandler, *Dwelling in the Text*, 171.

27. Ibid., 172.

28. See Kathy A. Fedorko, "Edith Wharton's Haunted Fiction: 'The Lady's Maid's Bell' and *The House of Mirth*," in *Haunting the House of Fiction: Feminist Perspectives on Ghost Stories by American Women*, ed. Lynette Carpenter and Wendy K. Kolmar (Knoxville: University of Tennessee Press, 1991), 80–107.

29. See Jackson, *Fantasy*, 61–91.

30. See, for example, readings by Katherine Joslin, *Edith Wharton* (Basingstoke, U.K.: Macmillan, 1991), 89–107; Sandra M. Gilbert and Susan Gubar, *No Man's Land: The Place of the Woman Writer in the Twentieth Century*, vol. 2: *Sexchanges* (New Haven: Yale University Press, 1989), 123–68; Fedorko, "Edith Wharton's Haunted Fiction," 81–2.

31. V.G. Rocine, *Heads, Faces, Types, Races* (1910), cited (with an accompanying illustration) in Banta, *Imaging American Women*, 121.

32. Gwendolyn Wright, *Moralism and the Model Home: Domestic Architecture and Cultural Conflict in Chicago, 1873–1913* (Chicago: University of Chicago Press, 1980), 275–7; also cited by ryer, *Felicitous Space*, 31.

33. Lewis, *Edith Wharton: A Biography*, 391–2.

34. *A Backward Glance*, 317.

35. Ibid., 369–70.

CYNTHIA GRIFFIN WOLFF

Studies of Salamanders: The Fiction 1912–1920

Writing *The Age of Innocence* was a nostalgic act: "I showed it chapter by chapter to Walter Berry," Wharton recollects.[92] Like old times at the very beginning—like composing *The Decoration of Houses* under his keenly critical eye. But so many years had passed; the war was over, and things would never really be the same again. Although she still had Walter Berry, others were gone. Dear comrades of the heady wartime days had died: Ronald Simmons, for instance, a young American of whom she had become terribly fond, had perished in 1918; Newbold Rhinelander (from the younger generation on her mother's side of the family) had been shot down over Germany in September of 1918. Vigorous and vital men losing their lives—it wrenched her heart. Even worse, however, was the fragmenting away of that tight group of old friends who had stood in place of a family for so long in her life. Howard Sturgis died peacefully in his sleep in the first month of 1920. And worst of all, in 1916 she had lost Henry James. She didn't even have the chance to bid him good-by, for they had been separated by that raging holocaust of the war. "Yes,—all my 'blue distances' will be shut out forever when he goes," she wrote Gaillard Lapsley in 1915 as James's illness grew worse. "His friendship has been the pride and honour of my life. Plus ne m'est rien after such a gift as that—except the memory of it."[93] Ready at last to come back "for good"—only to have lost so many of those who might

From *A Feast of Words: The Triumph of Edith Wharton*. Second edition © 1995 by Cynthia Griffin Wolff.

meaningfully share the journey with her. She was entirely conscious of the scope of the privation. In 1920, Henry James was still on her mind. Again, she wrote to Gaillard Lapsley in anguish. "My longing to talk with you about Henry is getting *maladive*. No one can *really understand* but you and me—to the extent to which we understand—so four-dimensionally."[94]

Thus she found herself very much in the midst of her memories of James while she was engrossed with *The Age of Innocence*. She and Edmund Gosse had become involved in extensive and complicated negotiations with James's family over the editing of his letters in 1920. Wharton's and Gosse's candidate to supervise the work was James's young friend, Percy Lubbock, but Mrs. William James so thoroughly detested Edith Wharton that negotiations had to be carried out with appalling subterfuge. Wharton, therefore, was forced to hold herself uncomfortably aloof from the memorial proceedings. Nevertheless, she was an inventive woman. She was making a spiritual pilgrimage home, and she was going to take her old friend Henry James with her. Why not? He "belonged irrevocably to the old America out of which I also came." He had spent his entire adult life as a European exile, even adopting British citizenship in the last year of his life (which Wharton deplored). They had shared the writing of fiction; they had shared countless hours of fun, that quality so impossible to preserve in a written biography— "the quality ... of sheer abstract 'fooling'—that was the delicious surprise of his talk.... From many of the letters to his most intimate group [letters that Wharton was helping to edit in 1920] it was necessary to excise long passages of chaff, and recurring references to old heaped-up pyramidal jokes, huge cairns of hoarded nonsense."[95] Now, for the last time, the Angel of Devastation would swoop down and carry him off again with her. They would go back "for good" together.

The Age of Innocence had many meanings for Edith Wharton. It borrows more extensively from the ambiance of her childhood world than any other novel she published;[96] and it is explicitly called to the reader's attention that Newland Archer is fifty-seven at the conclusion of the novel, Wharton's own age in 1919 when she began writing it. Yet perhaps the central meaning grows out of the complex way in which the novel beckons to Wharton's dearest friend, Henry James.

The communication begins, most fittingly, with a complicated joke: *The Age of Innocence* is the title of a well-known portrait by Reynolds which hangs in the National Gallery; it is the portrait of a lady—a very young lady, to be sure, a little girl in fact. Nevertheless, the reference converts Wharton's title into a private pun. James's novel *The Portrait of a Lady* was Wharton's favorite among his many books (the only one ever to appear on her list of "favorite books"). In the name of her own novel, Wharton announces the antiphonal relationship between her work and James's in the way that *he* would have understood best. There is no mistaking her intention, for at the same time that she converted the working title of "Old New York" into "The Age of Innocence," she also changed the name of her hero to "Newland" Archer, an American who elects to remain at home in the New World only to have Old World temptations and knowledge come to him. That Newland Archer is intended as a parallel to Isabel Archer is further emphasized by Ned Wimsatt's remark to him: " 'You're like the pictures on the walls of a deserted house: "The Portrait of a Gentleman.' "[97]

These resemblances are merely verbal plays, casual allusions meant to convey deeper connections between Wharton's work and James's. Wharton intended neither parody nor one-to-one borrowing: Newland is not Isabel's exact counterpart—nor is Ellen, though Ellen's marriage and her tragic knowledge certainly do recall Isabel's. Rather, Wharton used these allusions to James much as eighteenth-century satirists used references to classical epics as a way of conveying a sense of moral seriousness and a similarity of concern. If "The Age of Innocence" describes the stable pre–World War I society of old New York to which Wharton was making a private pilgrimage, it also describes a prelapsarian state. Thus while James explores the notion of a "fortunate fall" in *The Portrait of a Lady*, in *The Age of Innocence* Wharton examines the value of choosing not to be corrupted. Moreover, Wharton and James focus their intense moral scrutiny on similar concerns, particularly the problem of the right to individual "freedom" as measured against the binding sanctity of the commitment to the institution of marriage.

In the end, however, Wharton's novel is a balancing companion piece to James's; for while James is interested in exploring the world an American Puritan might discover by moving away from New World prejudices, Wharton's thrust is in the opposite direction, back into the shaping culture in which her American hero was born. Implicit in the imperative to come back "for good" is a notion of maturity very similar to the one that Erik Erikson has articulated for our generation: the full development of self is "a process 'located' *in the core of the individual* and yet also *in the core of his communal culture*, a process which establishes, in fact, the identity of those two identities."[98] Wharton, a self-conscious product of the old New York she recreates, had finally come to realize that the children of that time and place must forever bear its mark, cherish its values, and suffer in some degree its inadequacies. Growth, then, must proceed from an understanding of one's background—a coming to terms with one's past, not a flight from it.

The persuasiveness of Wharton's view is nowhere more powerfully rendered than in her handling of tradition. Wharton had accepted what Charity Royall and Newland Archer were to learn: that "each human life begins at a given evolutionary stage and level of tradition, bringing to its environment a capital of patterns and energies; these are used to grow on, and to grow into the social process with, and also as contributions to this process. Each new being is received into a style of life prepared by tradition and held together by tradition, and at the same time disintegrating because of the very nature of tradition. We say that tradition 'molds' the individual, 'channels' his drives. But the social process does not mold a new being merely to housebreak him; it molds generations in order to be remolded, to be reinvigorated by them."[99] The growth of any society depends upon the growth of the individuals who comprise it. Thus, since social change is inevitably tied to the individual struggle to achieve maturity, social change is, ironically, always rooted in the past; no man can achieve maturity until he has accepted the particular conventions and traditions that have shaped him. If he wishes to alter these conventions and traditions, he can do so *only* by drawing on the strengths of his heritage: he cannot choose his heritage, and he cannot repudiate it without repudiating himself; "an individual life is the accidental coincidence of but *one* life cycle with but *one* segment of history."[100]

The particular traditions of old New York threaten to obscure the reader's vision, even as they threaten to suffocate the hero in *The Age of Innocence*. The crowded collage of drawing rooms and Worth gowns and opera evenings and Newport outings all evoke a compelling illusion of "place," and Wharton's eye for detail is seductive.[101] Yet to focus on place as extrinsic to character is, in the end, to miss the point of the novel. Wharton's narrative vantage is carefully chosen (it is similar to James's in *Portrait of a Lady* and even more like Austen's in *Emma*): the narrator may step outside of Newland Archer's mind to make judgments or draw conclusions; but when we see old New York, we almost always see it through his eyes. The world that seems at first a novelistic tour de force becomes, on closer examination, a mirror of Newland's mind and the very condition of his being. This is his "one segment of history"; these are the traditions that have "molded" him and "channeled his drives." The center of this novel is Newland's problem of being and becoming, given the unalterable traditions of this portion of history, this "place."

The Age of Innocence is Wharton's most significant *bildungsroman* (surpassing even *Summer*). In it she traces Archer's struggle to mature, to become in some continuous and authentic way—himself. She lays before us the present and the possible in such a way that the middle-aged man who concludes the novel seems an admirable and significant outgrowth of the untried youth at the beginning. Her profound acceptance of the kind of limitation described by Erikson is mirrored in the creative use to which she puts the *bildungsroman* tradition; her master was Goethe, whose works she was once again rereading in this postwar period. The theme of *The Age of Innocence* might be captured in the most famous line of *Wilhelm Meister*: "*Here or nowhere is America!*"

Newland Archer does have choices, but they have been limited by the nature of his one portion of history. Thus while Wilhelm's search (and that of most *bildungshelden*) is pursued in a journey, Newland's search is entirely internal. He cannot flee the provincial world of old New York; he must learn to transmute it into something valuable. Newland perceives himself as alienated and without vocation; his ordeal by love teaches him the lessons that Wilhelm learned—acceptance of reality and dedication to generativity. In this novel, the ultimate place is the little rock cottage at Skuytercliff: that home stands for the values that will endure—values of family and honor. Newland is here when he decides not to become involved with Ellen, and later he spends his wedding night with May here. It is not a lofty dwelling— narrow, unaesthetic, almost primitive—it scarcely answers the visions of a romantic adolescent. Yet it is such a place as this that Newland must "find."

The journey is not an easy one. Our first glimpse of him tells us that like Ralph Marvell he is, perhaps by inclination, perhaps by training, an onlooker—indeed, but one in a society that trains its young people to be no more than onlookers, members of an audience that stands to the side of life's great struggles and does not participate in them. To meet him as he prepares to watch a production of *Faust* is consummately, ironically appropriate.[102] Having no occupation sufficient to his energies, Newland has turned them to fantasy: "He was at heart a dilettante, and thinking over a pleasure to come often gave him a subtler satisfaction than its realization. This was especially the case when the pleasure was a delicate one" (2). There is a dangerous vitality in this inner life; his considerable passion, finding no satisfactory outlet, has been sublimated into extraordinary palpable fantasies (old New York gave men like Newland little else to do with their passions).

Unknown to Newland, however, the fantasies that have been nourished by the rich passional needs channeled into them slip quietly back into his perceptions of the actual world, distorting these perceptions and deluding his expectations. "'We'll read *Faust* together ... by the Italian lakes,' he thought, somewhat hazily confusing the scene of his projected honeymoon with the masterpieces of literature which it would be his manly privilege to reveal to his bride.... If he had probed to the bottom of his vanity (as he sometimes nearly did) he would have found there the wish that his wife should be as worldly-wise and as eager to please as the married lady whose charms had held his fancy through two mildly agitated years; without, of course, any hint of the frailty which had so nearly marred that unhappy being's life, and had disarranged his own plans for a whole winter. How this miracle of fire and ice was to be created, and to sustain itself in a harsh world, he had never taken the time to think out" (5).

Archer's naiveté about the configuration of his emotional life is coupled with an empty adherence to convention. With a little effort he might become a good man, for there is nothing vicious in his nature and much that is generous. However, never having examined the rules by which his society lives, his notion of "duty"—as in "the duty of using two silver-backed brushes with his monogram in blue enamel to part his hair" (3)—is a thing easily to be confounded with Larry Lefferts' notions of "form." His reading and his active imaginative life have brought other worlds and other customs to his attention; but his reflex for conformity has been too strongly developed to permit him easily to measure his own traditions against these others. "He had probably read more, thought more, and even seen a good deal more of the world, than any other man of the number ... but grouped together they represented 'New York,' and the habit of masculine solidarity made him accept their doctrine on all the issues called moral. He instinctively felt that in this respect it would be troublesome—and also rather bad form—to strike out for himself" (6). Thus the life of his spirit is infused with only the vaguest apprehension of purpose. There is no self-consciousness in his virtue, and he cannot be said to be "moral" because his admirable acts are informed by no continuous inner sense of conscience.

When we first meet Newland, we may be most impressed by his deficiencies—the absence of available passion and the habit but not the substance of "correct" behavior. Yet these apparently empty places in Newland's life contain the possibility of change. His innate vigor has been shaped but not hardened by the traditions of his background; the final inclinations of his character have yet to be formed, and the eighteen months of the novel's principal duration comprise the period of that transformation. Newland is nearing the conclusion of his apprenticeship in old New York. His adolescence and young adulthood have been times for experiment, for casual alliances and intellectual curiosity. Marriage represents commitment, an irrevocable assumption of his adult roles and an affirmation of the society in which he lives. Newland is not prepared for this commitment, and the moment of the crisis is complicated by "the case of the Countess Olenska" (40).

Ellen is the catalyst that forces Newland's self-confrontation, for had she not appeared, he might have spent his whole life attaching his deepest emotions almost entirely to fantasy. Ellen offers him the opportunity to test his capacity to fulfill these fantasies. She draws forth his passion into a warm flesh-and-blood attachment, and she quickens his "dormant emotional life. If he is ever to be the man he fancies he might become, he can be that man with Ellen Olenska. And yet, his reactions to her are deeply ambivalent.

It is typical of Newland's thinking that he should construe Ellen as a "case"; and this is of a piece with all those other habits of mind that push aside the ordinary complexities of actual human life for the grander sweep of the romantic imagination. He evaluates her exotic plight and her "foreign" appearance with nervous interest: her "pale and serious face appealed to his fancy as suited to the occasion and to her unhappy situation; but the way her dress (which had no tucker) sloped away from her thin shoulders shocked and troubled him" (12). Such a vision embodies the mystery of the unknown and represents all the world that lies beyond the familiar boundaries of Archer's experience. The "case" of a woman so intriguingly distressed appeals to his visionary sense, and his musings on her situation become fused in indefinable ways with his unutterable yearning for a larger realm of experience. Ironically, Ellen in person makes him uncomfortable (just as the fashionable nudity of her gown had unsettled his notions of propriety): her frankness, her wry sense of the absurd, and her easy assumption of intimacy all unbalance him. "Nothing could be in worst taste than misplaced flippancy" (15). Thus while the actual freedom of her manner is distasteful, the abstract "right" to "freedom" that her situation justifies is infinitely appealing to him.

Though Ellen's arrival has had the objective effect of hastening Newland's public commitment to May, it has at the same time made that commitment seem a sentence to death by asphyxiation. When Newland retreats to his study to sort out the various effects of Ellen's appearance, he finds that her case has "stirred up old settled convictions and set them drifting dangerously through his mind" (40). His image of Ellen balances conveniently and simplistically against an image of May as "the young girl who knew nothing and expected everything" (40); and the larger vistas of the twilight world from which Ellen has come diminish the appeal of a marriage that seems no more than "a dull association of material and social interests held together by ignorance on the one side and hypocrisy on the other" (41). Central to these images of the women in Archer's life is some picture of what he is to become himself. This scene in his study is but the first in a series of increasingly terrifying invocations of self; the future stretches before him, "and passing down its endless emptiness he saw the dwindling figure of a man to whom nothing was ever to happen" (228). In fearing acceptance into the "hieroglyphic world" of old New York, Archer really fears anonymity and personal insignificance.

Yet he is hindered more by his own habits of thought than by insufficiencies in the society around him, for his impatience with specific details and intractable actualities follows him in his quest for personal identity. Just as it is easier to deal with the "case" of Ellen than with Ellen herself, so it is easier to pursue an image of personal fulfillment that is uncomplicated by the details of everyday living. Throughout much of the novel Archer longs for a life that moves well beyond the charted realms of the familiar, a life of high emotional intensity and sustained moral and intellectual complexity. The kind of life he only hazily conjectures is a life that is, given the "harsh world" of human experience, available to only a very few; and Archer seems an unlikely candidate for the life that his imagination yearns toward.

Ironically, the danger that his life will be insignificant lies not so much in the probability that he will fail to fulfill these fantasies as in the more immediate possibility that, having failed to fulfill them, he will lack the capacity to give any aspect of his life authenticity. Not all things are possible for a man of Newland's time and place; some ways of life that are unavailable to him are, perhaps, better than any that are. But every real life involves compromises and relinquished hopes—even though some lives require more in the way of sacrifice than others. The problem that Newland faces without fully comprehending it is that his desire to create an ideal self substantially hinders him from infusing some *genuinely possible* self with meaning.

To be specific, if the passion that Ellen has finally released in him is eventually thwarted by his failure to effect a relationship with her, then he might not manage to attach these emotions to any part of the life he actually leads. Like Ralph Marvell, he might drift back into idle, empty dreaming. He might never attain the capacity for sustaining deep and meaningful bonds with others. He might become a hollow man altogether. This danger is the central problem that he faces.

And in this respect, Newland's quandary captures the quintessential problem of all who grew to maturity in the repressive society of old New York. Perhaps he will settle for a set of highly stereotyped personal relationships that serve only to mask a deep sense of isolation and incompleteness. Perhaps he will even go through his entire life never feeling that he is really "himself"—even though everyone else seems to think that he is "somebody." It is a horrifying specter.

Newland's yearning for transcendent experience is, from the very beginning, inseparable from his passion for Ellen; the longing for them suffuses the novel with an exquisite pain. And yet Wharton lets us know, though it becomes fully apparent to Newland only at the end of the novel, that precisely those capacities in Ellen that most attract him are capacities leading to behavior that his innermost being cannot tolerate. Throughout the earlier portions of the fiction, Newland drastically simplifies his notions of Ellen (indeed, as he does those of May as well) so that he need not deal with the complexities of her complete person. Newland fancies her world and the outrages she has experienced in it with convenient imprecision: it is "the society in which the Countess Olenska had lived and suffered, and also—perhaps—tasted mysterious joys" (102).[103] He conjures Ellen outside of any coherent social pattern: she has the "mysterious faculty of suggesting tragic and moving possibilities outside the daily run of experience. She had hardly ever said a word to him to produce this impression, but it was a part of her, either a projection of her mysterious and outlandish background or of something inherently dramatic, passionate and unusual in herself" (113). She is the vague embodiment of all that is lacking in his own life.

Yet Archer and Ellen have not one meeting in which the deep and fundamental antipathies between their ways of life are not apparent. Archer may romanticize Ellen's past in blurred and indefinite terms, but Ellen herself has a complete and quite precise complement of habits, manners, and tastes which are the product of her world; Wharton sets the pattern for an ironic juxtaposition of these habits against Archer's in the initial chapter and continues it throughout the novel. During Archer's first visit to Ellen's home, for example, he is enchanted with the artistry of her drawing room, "intimate, 'foreign,' subtly suggestive of old romantic scenes and sentiments" (69); and in some way (the connection is surely not one of decorative affinity) he is moved to ponder his own highly "American" insistence on "'sincere' Eastlake furniture" (70). He is charmed by her experienced, casual manner and offended by her being "flippant" (72). He is deeply outraged by her association with Beaufort, and he naively supposes that he can terminate the association by making "her see Beaufort as he really was, with all he represented—and abhor it" (75). He claims that she makes him "look at his native city objectively. Viewed thus, as through the wrong end of a telescope, it looked disconcertingly small and distant" (74); yet he leaves in a fury when she greets the Duke and Mrs. Struthers (who is not "received" by the polite world) with as much composure as she had greeted him. Each visit before Archer's marriage is tainted by Ellen's affinity for Beaufort—an attachment which he comprehends fitfully and totally detests.

Even at those times after his marriage when Archer seems most unambivalently to press Ellen to an elopement, he continues to view her more as a "case"—"the compromised woman"—than as another complex human being. Thus on the day of their outing in Boston, Archer marvels at Ellen's self-possession, and then reflects that "a woman who had run away from her husband—and reputedly with another man—was likely to have mastered the art of taking things for granted" (140). Still later, when he greets her on her return from Washington, she shocks him by asking: "'Is it your idea, then, that I should live with you as your mistress—since I can't be your wife?' ... The crudeness of the question startled him: the word was one that women of his class fought shy of, even when their talk flitted closest about the topic. He noticed that Madame Olenska pronounced it as if it had a recognized place in her vocabulary, and he wondered if it had been used familiarly in her presence in the horrible life she had fled from" (292–93).

Unable to accept her social accommodations, Newland unrealistically rejects society altogether. "'I want—I want somehow to get away with you into a world where words like that—categories like that—won't exist. Where we shall be simply two human beings who love each other. Who are the whole of life to each other; and nothing else on earth will matter'" (293). However, if Ellen has learned nothing else, she has learned the terrible and inexorable toll that tradition takes: "She drew a deep sigh that ended in another laugh. 'Oh, my dear—where is that country? Have you ever been there?'" (293).

Ellen has a motley background; she was born of old New York, but has spent her childhood as a European vagabond. These bizarre antecedents give her more flexibility than anyone else in the novel, and though Newland is most vividly impressed with her European connections, Ellen herself is oddly imbued with an admiration for what could only be termed May's world. Ellen's view of this world is naive at first: she sees it simplistically as a place that is "'straight up and down—like Fifth Avenue. And with all the cross streets numbered!'" (74). But she learns of its cruel social isolations, and she learns of the loneliness of living among the "'kind people who only ask one to pretend,'" who don't want to "'hear anything unpleasant'" (75)—and still she respects the complex morality that she (but not Archer) can so accurately calculate.

The young Newland Archer evaluates his world harshly and superficially. He sees its innocence as a stifling and destructive element "the innocence that seals the mind against imagination and the heart against experience" (145)—and it weighs insignificantly against Ellen's world of intrigue. Yet there is much in the novel that suggests intricate harmony where Archer perceives only emptiness and silence. There are silences, to be sure; but they are rich with communication—a kind of totality of understanding that is possible precisely *because* the world of old New York is small and limited. It is a world where one can understand, without being told, that Mrs. Beaufort's presence at the opera on the night of her ball indicates "her possession of a staff of servants competent to organize every detail of the entertainment in her absence" (16); a world where Archer strolling abroad in the evening can ascertain that Beaufort must be about on an errand of "clandestine nature" because "it was not an Opera night, and no one was giving a party" (99). This depth of understanding concerns grave things as well as trivial. The very first action Archer takes in the novel is that of joining May at the opera to show his support of her and the family in behalf of Ellen. It is a kind, emotionally generous gesture, and May understands it without a word's being uttered: "As he entered the box his eyes met Miss Welland's, and he saw that she had instantly understood his motive, though the family dignity which both considered so high a virtue would not permit her to tell him so.... The fact that he and she understood each other without a word seemed to the young man to bring them nearer than any explanation would have done" (14). And so, in many ways, it does.

The novel is filled with instances of May's intuitive flashes of deep understanding. Occasionally these are verbalized, but usually they are not. Her penetration into Archer's growing attachment for Ellen, for instance, is more often revealed in a failure to include him in the family's discussions or in a question that discovers him in a lie. Their relationship is filled with a profound silence, but the very limitations of the code that governs their marriage fill the silence with meaning. The most remarkable instance of this mute dialogue occurs one evening when Archer tells May he must go to Washington and May enjoins him to "be sure to go and see Ellen."

> It was the only word that passed between them on the subject; but in the code in which they had both been trained it meant: "Of course you understand that I know all that people have been saying about Ellen, and heartily sympathize with my family in their effort to get her to return to her husband. I also know that, for some reason you have not chosen to tell me, you have advised her against this course, which all the older men of the family, as well as our grandmother, agree in approving; and that it is owing to your encouragement that Ellen defies us all, and exposes herself to the kind of criticism of which Mr. Sillerton Jackson probably gave you, this evening, the hint that has made you so irritable.... Hints have indeed not been wanting; but since you appear unwilling to take them from others, I offer you this one myself, in the only form in which well-bred people of our kind can communicate unpleasant things to each other: by letting you understand that I know you mean to see Ellen when you are in Washington, and are perhaps going there expressly for that purpose; and that, since you are sure to see her, I wish you to do so with my full and explicit approval—and to take the opportunity of letting her know what the course of conduct you have encouraged her in is likely to lead to" (269).

It is true, as Ellen has observed, that old New Yorkers don't like to talk about "unpleasant" things. But what a wealth of shared knowledge their reticences permit!

Newland perceives May's moments of understanding as mere flickers of light in an otherwise unillumined darkness. The evocation of her as a young Diana is, in Archer's mind, a reductive vision of empty, unknowing, unsoiled virginity. He can deal with her primitive complexity no more than he can deal with the consequences of Ellen's experiences with Old World culture. He supposes that her "faculty of unawareness was what gave her eyes their transparency, and her face the look of representing a type rather than a person; as if she might have been chosen to pose for a Civic Virtue or a Greek goddess. The blood that ran so close to her fair skin might have been a preserving fluid rather than a ravaging element; yet her look of indestructible youthfulness made her seem neither hard nor dull, but only primitive and pure" (180). He doesn't hear or understand even her spoken disclaimer: "'You mustn't think that a girl knows as little as her parents imagine. One hears and one notices—one has one's feelings and ideas'" (147–48).

Given Archer's own abysmal innocence, he is unprepared to counter the marshalled forces of the moral world that May commands. For Diana is the divinity of childbirth and fertility; she presides over the generation of life itself. May might well be ignorant of the more refined customs of decadent European culture; but in her "primitive" purity, she is committed to the most fundamental human processes, and in this commitment she is as ruthless as nature itself. May's devotion to an order by which the family can perpetuate itself is absolute; she is willing to release Archer from his engagement to her (for she is a generous woman), but once he rejects that offer, she dedicates herself to the task of holding him to the morality implicit in old New York's regulation of the process of generation.

Archer knows the rules of this morality; he recites them to Ellen much as a child recites a catechism by rote. Old New York has "'rather old-fashioned ideas.... The individual ... is nearly always sacrificed to what is supposed to be the collective interest: people cling to any convention that keeps the family together—protects the children'" (109–10). And yet they are meaningless to him throughout much of the novel. He sees himself not as an active force in this world—indeed, it is a world whose deep moral structures he little comprehends—but as the victim of its well-mannered brutalities, "a wild animal cunningly trapped" (66). The escape that Ellen seems to offer is, given his romanticized vision of her, not the liberty to choose an alternate moral system; it is a seductively blurred vision of "freedom" in an artistically and intellectually stimulating world whose constraints and moral ambiguities he little imagines.

Ellen's view is altogether different. Her contact with Old World corruption enables her to appreciate the pious primitivism of her American cousins. Even New York's rigidities have meaning for her. "'Under the dullness there are things so fine and sensitive and delicate that even those I most cared for in my other life look cheap in comparison. I don't know how to explain myself ... but it seems as if I'd never before understood with how much that is hard and shabby and base the most exquisite pleasure may be paid'" (243). Much of Ellen's affection for Newland stems from her supposition that he really does embody the goodness of a society she has come to respect. She imputes to him, perhaps, a more self-consciously principled mind than he possesses; the creed he recites in attempting to dissuade her from the divorce acquires in her understanding of it a meaning that Archer cannot yet feel. The Newland Archer who is beloved of Ellen Olenska is a "self" whose emotional commitments are integrally linked to the sentiments he has uttered. "'I felt there was no one as kind as you; no one who gave me reasons that I understood for doing what at first seemed so hard and—unnecessary. The very good people didn't convince me; I felt they'd never been tempted. But you knew; you understood; you had felt the world outside tugging at one with all its golden hands—and yet you hated the things it asks of one; you hated happiness bought by disloyalty and cruelty and indifference. That was what I'd never known before—and it's better than anything I've known'" (172).

We might be tempted to judge Ellen's appraisal of Newland to be as uninformed as his is of her. Certainly she demands a kind of moral substance from him that he cannot yet recognize in himself, for the only Newland Archer that Ellen can admire is a man whose felt sense of duty would not permit him to betray those who have rested their confidence in him. Ellen has taken empty words and imputed significance to them; yet hers is not an act of such wistful longing as we might suppose. She may love a man who does not yet fully exist, but she has fixed her affections on what is potential and possible in Newland; and if he is not yet the man she judges him to be, there are clear indications that he has already committed himself to becoming that man.

The center of Newland's early pieties, the grave enduring traditions of his life, all have to do with family; when he acts without thinking, his automatic behavior affirms the bonds of kinship and familial affection. For May, and in a different way for Ellen, this loyalty is part of a coherent ethical framework, however, Newland does not feel the moral component in his behavior, probably because it is so familiar, so much a part of the "given" of his world, that he can become conscious of it only with great difficulty. The strength of his moral reflex is shown at the beginning of the novel when he rushes to May's box "to see her through whatever difficulties her cousin's anomalous situation might involve her in; this impulse had abruptly overruled all scruples and hesitations, and sent him hurrying through the red corridors to the farther side of the house" (14). The same deep instinctive tie to the norms that sustain the family can be seen in his involuntary revulsion from the "sordid" aspects of Ellen's right to "freedom." His social (and moral) inflexibility is confirmed by the splendid, parochial isolation of every European journey he makes. His inability to envision any realistic alternative to this life is captured in his groping visions of a life with Ellen—somewhere, "his own fancy inclined to Japan" (307).

Yet throughout much of the novel Archer has no emotional contact with that part of his nature (by far the greater part) that is so irrevocably wedded to the customs of New York. Because so little affect attaches to this "self," he cannot experience it as truly and authentically himself; because he so little understands it, he cannot respect or admire it.

What May and Ellen do together in a remarkable unvoiced conspiracy is confront Archer with the realities of his situation and thereby confirm the integrity of his life. Ellen does this by awakening his slumbering sentient self and wrenching his passional life away from pure imagination to an actual person (however romantically construed) and a series of particular situations within which he can measure his true capacities. May does so by offering her own "innate dignity" (196) as a worthy object of his emotional and moral allegiance: "Whatever happened, he knew, she would always be loyal, gallant and unresentful; and that pledged him to the practice of the same virtues.... She became the tutelary divinity of all his old traditions and reverences" (196–97). Thus his growing involvement with Ellen both awakens his deepest passions and ruthlessly outlines his personal limitations. May offers if not passion at least a "glow of feeling" (43) that becomes an "inner glow of happiness" (194) after the marriage; even more, she offers a way of life that is worthy of the passion he has discovered in himself. "She would not disappoint him"; she represented "peace, stability, comradeship, and the steadying sense of an unescapable duty" (208). Eventually, she offers a true and honorable life when his dreams of Ellen are confounded.[104]

Newland is not a stupid man, and he is to some degree aware of the emotional distance between himself and Ellen. As we have seen, all of his encounters with her are marked by the fundamental differences in their natures; and though Archer's longing for Ellen usually blinds him to these differences, he is sometimes able to put their relationship into focus. The most significant readjustment of his values occurs during and after their meeting at Skuytercliff. He is always jealous of Beaufort, consistently plagued by a desire to "correct" Ellen's views of him. When Beaufort interrupts their meeting at Skuytercliff, the old jealousy emerges. Yet this time, the outrage is tempered by an even-minded appraisal of their situation.

> Madame Olenska, in a burst of irritation, had said to Archer that he and she did not talk the same language; and the young man knew that in some respects this was true. But Beaufort understood every turn of her dialect, and spoke it fluently: his view of life, his tone, his attitude, were merely a coarser reflection of those revealed in Count Olenski's letter. This might seem to be to his disadvantage with Count Olenski's wife; but Archer was too intelligent to think that a young woman like Ellen Olenska would necessarily recoil from everything that reminded her of her past. She might believe herself wholly in revolt against it; but what had charmed her in it would still charm her, even though it were against her will.
>
> Thus, with a painful impartiality, did the young man make out the case for Beaufort and Beaufort's victim (137).

Having confronted this painful reassessment, Archer makes what must in part be understood as a conscious decision: he immediately journeys south to see May.

May's sympathetic understanding of his emotional conflict contrasts markedly with the distance that has just been demonstrated between himself and the Countess Olenska, and her offer to release him makes him aware, perhaps for the first time, of the depths of her basic goodness. It is a genuine offer, and when Archer refuses it, his refusal constitutes a pledge to May's world as well as to May. Once the pledge has been made, May and Ellen conspire to hold him faithful.

Terrified by the finality of his acceptance of old New York, Archer impetuously turns to Ellen for some escape, but she answers him now as she is to answer him for ever after: "'In reality it's too late to do anything but what we've both decided on'" (171). Ellen convinces the family to hasten the marriage, and then she moves to Washington, out of Archer's sight. In every subsequent meeting, her theme is the same. She reveres the narrow pieties of old New York, and her faith in Archer's own fidelity is the significant force keeping her safely in America: "'If you lift a finger you'll drive me back: back to all the abominations you know of, and all the temptations you half guess'" (245–46). She actively wills that his love for her be realized not in their union but in a continuing separation that gives substance to Archer's own moral life. She conjures him to "'look, not at visions, but at realities'" (292). Thus when at their last private meeting he urges her to consummate their love, she protests: "'Don't let us be like all the others'" (314). She could no longer respect him or the code of his world, and she would, as she resolutely tells him, be forced back to the indignities of life with her husband—a betrayal of her own renewed moral commitment as well. Little wonder that at that moment when they are closest to the finality of a physical union, "they looked at each other almost like enemies" (316).

The news of May's pregnancy is the final force that drives the would-be lovers apart. Yet there is a real decision implicit in this penultimate act of the drama; for a man without firm moral commitments may almost as easily leave a wife and child as a wife alone. Newland is restrained from leaving not by any objective and external force—but by the deep-rooted conviction that his own moral duty must ultimately be defined by family obligations. The child that May is carrying represents a felt demand that has been internalized and thus that he cannot ignore.

Wharton never supposed that Newland could find happiness with a woman like Ellen; and though there are earlier outlines of the novel in which he does break his engagement to May and marry Ellen, he and Ellen are not happy together. There is no shared sense of reality: she misses the life in Europe that she has always known; he misses the familiar amenities of old New York; and finally they separate and return to their different worlds.

Throughout the novel as finally written, Newland repeatedly tries to define the nature of his "realities." Often he presumes Ellen to have known the real world in her life outside of New York, and his own real experiences are featured as lying outside of May's world and his marriage to her. Yet just as often he finds reality in May's world: "Here was truth, here was reality, here was the life that belonged to him" (140). His renunciation of May's offer of release is a final determination of the limitations of his real life (though his doubts continue); and his behavior towards Ellen, especially after his marriage, betrays the fact that he has genuinely chosen to cast his life in terms of old New York morality. His yearning for Ellen is indescribably intense, yet for the most part it belongs to another world. "That vision of the past was dream, and the reality was what awaited him" (216). He searches out the house that Ellen lives in much as one might visit the hermitage of some transfigured saint. "She remained in his memory simply as the most plaintive and poignant of a line of ghosts" (208); he sustains a private shrine to the man he might have been at a different time and in a different place, "and he had built up within himself a kind of sanctuary in which she throned among his secret thoughts and longings" (265).

His passion is still deeply attached to her, and meetings with her reawaken his longing. Nevertheless, his marriage marks the beginning of a process of distancing; and for the most part Archer is more comfortable with this process as he becomes increasingly conscious of his moral estimation of any other course. "In Archer's little world no one laughed at a wife deceived, and a certain measure of contempt was attached to men who continued their philandering after marriage. In the rotation of crops there was a recognized season for wild oats; but they were not to be sown more than once" (308). The imagery suggests the degree to which Newland has actively accepted the values of May's primitive, natural order, and his humiliation when Larry Lefferts casually includes him into a fellowship of deceiving husbands is vividly acute, for "in his heart he thought Lefferts despicable" (309). In the end, he is forced to realize that there can be no real life for Newland Archer and Ellen Olenska together. And the magnitude of his sacrifice measures for him the value of what he has preserved. He relinquishes his Faustian dreams for the more realistic understandings of a Wilhelm Meister and turns his energies from imagination to the process of generation.

In taking this step, Newland accepts the responsibilities that necessarily precede maturity and individual integrity. He has rejected notions of narcissistic self-fulfillment for the responsibility of "establishing and guiding the next generation";[105] and in solving the problems of love, he has accepted the problems of care. The final results of that choice are evident only at the conclusion of the novel.

The last chapter begins with a confirmation of the values that Archer has chosen. He is seated alone in the library. "It was the room in which most of the real things of his life had happened. There his wife, nearly twenty-six years ago, had broken to him, with a blushing circumlocution that would have caused the young women of the new generation to smile, the news that she was to have a child; and there their eldest boy, Dallas ... had been christened.... There Dallas had first staggered across the floor shouting 'Dad,' while May and the nurse laughed behind the door; there their second child, Mary (who was so like her mother), had announced her engagement to the dullest and most reliable of Reggie Chivers's many sons; and there Archer had kissed her through her wedding veil.... But above all—sometimes Archer put it above all—it was in that library that the Governor of New York ... had turned to his host, and said, banging his clenched fist on the table and gnashing his eye-glasses: 'Hang the professional politician! You're the kind of man the country wants, Archer'" (347–49). Not a great life, perhaps, but a good life and a productive life, a life whose goodness has grown naturally and fruitfully out of the best that Newland Archer's time and place had to offer.

The emotions that Ellen freed have flowed bountifully into family affection, and beyond family into community concerns: he has not been crippled by repression, after all. No longer a Romantic visionary, Newland understands himself, now, with the graceful tolerance of a man who reveres the achievements of his special place in history. "It was little enough to look back on; but when he remembered to what the young men of his generation and his set had looked forward—the narrow groove of money-making, sport and society to which their vision had been limited—even his small contribution to the new state of things seemed to count, as each brick counts in a well-built wall. He had done little in public life; he would always be by nature a contemplative and a dilettante; but he had had high things to contemplate, great things to delight in; and one great man's friendship to be his strength and pride" (349).

The process of distancing himself from Ellen that began directly after his marriage has continued; but he can contemplate that process with a reflective, poignant sense of an irrecoverable loss that has in the end been overbalanced by the value of what has been saved. "Something he knew he had missed: the flower of life. But he thought of it now as a thing so unattainable and improbable that to have repined would have been like despairing because one had not drawn the first prize in a lottery.... When he thought of Ellen Olenska it was abstractly, serenely, as one might think of some imaginary beloved in a book or a picture: she had become the composite vision of all that he had missed" (350). Newland is content, even knowing that his life, like all meaningful lives, has compromised his sense of the ideal. He is not the man he had once dreamed of becoming, but he is a man at peace with himself and a man who has the satisfaction of having become most truly himself in the ways that were available to him. He has not betrayed his own capacities. "Looking about him, he honored his own past, and mourned for it. After all, there was good in the old ways" (350).

And old New York has changed; it had contained the seeds of change all along, in old Catherine Spicer's journey up through society or in Mrs. Struthers' increasing respectability. However, the change has not come wrenchingly, as Archer had once thought it must. Instead, it has developed continuously out of the traditions that molded his youth. In his acceptance of the imperatives of his own life, Archer has helped to shape this change, by loving and guiding the son so like himself and by being what New Yorkers came to call "a good citizen." Above all, there are meaningful connections for Newland Archer between the past and the present: his children know freedoms that he never knew as a youth; but he is an unaffected comrade to his own son, who shares his fundamental decency. May was not entirely wrong in assuming that "whatever happened, Newland would continue to inculcate in Dallas the same principles and prejudices which had shaped his parents' lives, and that Dallas in turn (when Newland followed her) would transmit the sacred trust to little Bill" (351). The new ways have grown out of the old ways, and "there was good in the new order too" (352).

This moment of acceptance speaks directly to the problems that Wharton was finally resolving during the period when she was writing this novel. For her, too, one might say that "there was good in the old ways" and that "there was good in the new order too." The young people she had come to know through her work during the war were, like Newland's children, more candid and less limited by the rigidities of custom. Yet Newland's experience suggests that the validity of old New York's morality could withstand changes—even the more violent changes wrought by World War I. There is continuing value in loyalty, in commitment to family, and in undertaking responsibility for the generation that is to follow. Newland's self-confrontation substantially parallels Wharton's; and the placid man whom we meet at the beginning of the last chapter seems entirely to have come to terms with his own life.

However, for Newland one final test of the integrity of his identity is left. It comes when he has the opportunity once again to meet Ellen Olenska.

Newland is a widower, and Ellen has never remarried; there is no external obstacle to the consummation of the dream they shared almost thirty years earlier. Newland is intoxicated with the possibilities implicit in their meeting—"I'm only fifty-seven," he reminds himself while standing before "an effulgent Titian" (361). Yet at the same time he is overcome with doubts; he has felt his life to be "held fast by habit, by memories, by a sudden startled shrinking from new things" (354). He may feel "his heart beating with the confusion and eagerness of youth" (356) when he contemplates Ellen Olenska, but the image he conjures seems cruelly to mock the man he has become, "a mere gray speck of a man compared with the ruthless magnificent fellow he had dreamed of being" (357).

The anticipated visit to Ellen is overwhelming in its significance; for when Newland ponders it, he can at first find only two possible meanings for him. Either he will discover, at long last, that Newland Archer and Ellen Olenska can make a real life together; or his meeting with her will serve only to prove that he is, indeed, no more than a "mere gray speck of a man." Both of these possibilities would deny the validity of the good, decent, binding commitments that have shaped his life for the intervening years. If he is genuinely insignificant, then he has wasted his life; but if he can now find a viable world to share with Ellen, then he might have accepted his freedom thirty years before when May offered it. The quandary seems impossible thus postulated, but Newland is saved from despair by a final and redemptive visitation from the past.

The great strengths in the tradition of old New York lay in its powerful, unspoken capacity for complex communication (and with that— understanding, even compassion) and in its insistence upon the importance of the family above all else. Newland has reaped the fruits of the second of these in his loving fellowship with his son Dallas. Now Dallas, outspoken embodiment of the "good" new ways, enables his father finally to understand the magnitude of the first.

Dallas wonders aloud whether Ellen wasn't "'the woman you'd have chucked everything for: only you didn't.... Mother said ... the day before she died ... she said she knew we were safe with you, and always would be, because once, when she asked you to, you'd given up the thing you most wanted'" (359). Newland, astounded that May knew his secret sorrow all along, astounded that she has told Dallas, can only reply "in a low voice: 'She never asked me.' 'No. I forgot. You never did ask each other anything, did you? And you never told each other anything. You just sat and watched each other, and guessed at what was going on underneath. A deaf-and-dumb asylum, in fact. Well, I back your generation for knowing more about each other's private thoughts than we ever have time to find out about our own'" (359–60). May has again managed to live up to the height of her intuitive strength. Archer had once presumed to suppose that she would never fail him, and now he discovers that she never did. "It seemed to take an iron band from his heart to know that, after all, someone had guessed and pitied.... And that it should have been his wife moved him indescribably" (360).

One vindication of old New York's code is Dallas himself, the son whose affection for his father encompasses even that father's deepest sorrow. This second vindication, the depth of genuine communication that has informed Archer's life with his wife, causes him to look at the meeting with Ellen in a somewhat different light. He has become, inexorably over the years, the man that he is now—a man who has had an affectionate but not passionate marriage, a man who has been a good father, a man who has used the strengths in his own tradition to mold the traditions that followed him. He has become a gentleman, in the truest usage of old New York. It is an identity that has been infused with renewed meaning for him by Dallas's communication. Madame Olenska, too, has been formed by the traditions of that complex European community to which she fled. "For nearly thirty years, her life—of which he knew so strangely little—had been spent in this rich atmosphere that he already felt to be too dense and yet too stimulating for his lungs.... More than half a lifetime divided them, and she had spent the long interval among people he did not know, in a society he but faintly guessed at, in conditions he would never wholly understand. During that time he had been living with his youthful memory of her" (362). If his youthful and more flexible self could not live with the "real" Ellen Olenska, then even less can the man that he has become. Yet this recognition need not bring sorrow or self-doubt.

Ellen had loved him for his honor, had loved him for being different from herself—committed to what he had called "'rather old-fashioned ideas ... any convention that keeps the family together.'" When she loved him, these things had not yet been fully formed in him, and she had loved the potential and the possible. Now at fifty-seven, Newland has become the man Ellen saw in him; any attempt to recapture the past would be a repudiation of the love that she gave him so long ago and of the man he has finally become. Thus he decides, in the end, not to see her. His message, "'Say I'm old-fashioned: that's enough'" (364) is a tribute to the course he has committed himself to, a private reference to that night long ago when he championed family loyalty. Then the words had been hollow in his mouth. Now the slow accretion of his own life has finally given them substance.

So he waits below her apartment, envisioning her as she was not at their first meeting nor at their last, but at the meeting when he "explained" old New York's code to her. Of all their moments in the past, this one has become the most real to him: she will always be the woman she was that night. Thus it is that he pictures her—"a dark lady, pale and dark, who would look up quickly, half rise and hold out a long thin hand with three rings on it" (364).

Archer can acknowledge that Ellen will always be an unattainable dream for him; he accepts it with nostalgic sentiment, and in this recognition, he confirms the value of his own life as he has led it. He has finally discovered the reality he sought, and it rests in the man he has become; for the rest—"'it's more real to me here than if I went up'" (364).

In the end he has gained more than he has lost: he has not rejected his unique moment in history; he has taken the best of it and built upon it. His final act affirms the coherence of his own identity, and in this assertion of "self," Newland achieves genuine maturity. At this moment he shares the wisdom of all men, past and present, who have achieved integrity: he understands his "one and only life cycle as something that had to be and that, by necessity, permitted of no substitutions; ... he knows that an individual life is the accidental coincidence of but one life cycle with but one segment of history; and that for him all human integrity stands or falls with the one style or integrity of which he partakes." Newland has escaped the narrow limitations of old New York in the only way that was ever *really* available to him, by achieving an inner peace that transcends time and place altogether. For "a wise Indian, a true gentleman, and a mature peasant share and recognize in one another the final stage of integrity."[106]

He watches Ellen's apartment, content to be no more than a spectator to the play of high passions. "At length a light shone through the windows, and a moment later a man-servant came out on the balcony, drew up the awnings, and closed the shutters" (365). The drama is over, and Newland is free to go.

The Age of Innocence began with a sly, good-natured jest—a legerdemain with titles, a playing-off of this novel against James's great early work *The Portrait of a Lady*. Now it concludes with another kind of apostrophe to the master—more gentle and private. A tender reminiscence that James had shared with only a very few of the elect is recapitulated in Newland Archer's final vigil; Edmund Gosse has left a rare published record of James's experience:

> I was staying alone with Henry James at Rye one summer and as twilight deepened we walked together in the garden. I forget by what meanders we approached the subject, but I suddenly found that in profuse and enigmatic language he was recounting to me an experience, something that had happened, not something repeated or imagined. He spoke of standing on the pavement of a city, in the dusk, and of gazing upwards across the misty street, watching, watching for the lighting of a lamp in a window on the third storey. And the lamp blazed out, and through bursting tears he strained to see what was behind it, the unapproachable face. And for hours he stood there, wet with the rain, brushed by the phantom hurrying figures of the scene, and never from behind the lamp was for one moment visible the face. The mysterious and poignant revelation closed, and one could make no comment.[107]

The unapproachable face, that eternally elusive specter. Below, the anguished, lonely sentinel, waiting, waiting. One imagines Edith touching his shoulder affectionately. Dear friend, come home. It's more real down here.

NOTES

92. *A Backward Glance*, 369.

93. Letter to Gaillard Lapsley, December 17, 1915, Wharton Archives, Beinecke Library.

94. Letter to Gaillard Lapsley, Sept. 24, 1920, Wharton Archives, Beinecke Library.

95. *A Backward Glance*, 175, 179.

96. See the introduction by R.W.B. Lewis to *The Age of Innocence* (New York: Charles Scribner's Sons, 1968). See also R.B. Dooley, "A Footnote to Edith Wharton," *American Literature*, XXVI (Mar. 1954–Jan. 1955), 78–85.

97. Edith Wharton, *The Age of Innocence* (New York: D. Appleton Co., 1920), 124. Hereafter, all references to *The Age of Innocence* will be cited in the text, giving page number of this edition.

98. Erik Erikson, *Identity, Youth and Crisis* (New York: W.W. Norton Co., 1968), 22.

99. Erik Erikson, *Young Man Luther* (New York: W. W. Norton Co., 1958), 253–54.

100. Erikson, *Childhood and Society*, 268.

101. Note Edmund Wilson's remark in *The Wound and the Bow* that Edith Wharton was "the poet of interior decoration" (New York: Oxford University Press, 1947), 163.

102. Interestingly enough, when Newland does "get into the drama," he does so by imitating the sentimental renunciation scene of *The Shaughbraun*.

103. The word "mysterious" occurs repeatedly in Newland's musings about Ellen. It perfectly captures her almost incorporeal quality in his life. He does not *explore* the mysteries of Ellen's world; he prefers her to remain a mystery—conveniently blurred and obscured in his perception.

104. There are many implications of this improbable cooperation between Ellen and May. For one thing, it suggests that the values that had been polarized in the depiction of the two heroines of *The Reef* have now been conjoined in some coherent and meaningful estimation of life. In terms of Wharton's personal development, the cooperation is even more significant. In order to come back "for good" to the days of her childhood, Edith Wharton had to accept that part of herself that represented an internalization of Lucretia and Lucretia's values. She had to come to final terms with "Mother"—yes—but even more important, she had to accept that part of herself that imitated Mother and reflected Mother's ways. We have said that in *The Reef* Wharton made a fiction out of the disparate parts of herself—and in that fiction, these parts never come together. In *The Age of Innocence*, she pursues much the same tactic: Newland Archer, Ellen Olenska, and May all represent variations of Edith Wharton's "self"; however, now they are in harmony, and now they can be made to cooperate with each other.

105. Erikson, *Childhood and Society*, 267.

106. Ibid., 268–69.

107. Edmund Gosse, "The Lamp at the Window," in *The Legend of the Master*, ed. Simon Nowell-Smith (New York: Charles Scribner's Sons, 1948), 119–20.

JOHN UPDIKE

Archer's Way

*T*he *Age of Innocence* was begun when Edith Wharton was fifty-seven and published in October of 1920, when she was fifty-eight. She had come to the writing vocation tardily, after an upbringing in New York society and some years of an increasingly unhappy marriage to a Bostonian, Edward Wharton. She was twenty-nine when her first short story was published, and six more years passed before her first book, a nonfiction collaboration called *The Decoration of Houses*, appeared. Yet as the new century settled in, she, despite the many distractions of an active social life and travel schedule, and bouts of ill health on both her and her husband's part, had settled into a daily routine of morning writing and a steady, even copious, production of fiction. *The House of Mirth* in 1905 was her first masterpiece; *Ethan Frome* (1911) and *The Custom of the Country* (1913) followed, among many other well received, if less well remembered, titles. Against the grain of her social class, she had become a thoroughly professional, widely read, critically esteemed writer. Still, the brilliance and fullness of *The Age of Innocence*, coming so relatively late in her career, suggest a special renewal.

For a novelist, the halls of memory and imagination are adjacent spaces. An exemplary work of fiction is generally the fruit of a new grasp the author has taken of the riches within. Toward the end of the war, in Paris, Wharton had remarked to Bernard Berenson, "*Je me cherche, et je ne*

From *The New York Review of Books* 42, no. 19. © 1995 NYREV, Inc.

me retrouve pas." Her search for herself had been a process of many steps, beginning with her ardent exploration of her father's library in the Jones house on West Twenty-third Street. Edith Jones's marriage to the amiable but somewhat feckless and, in the end, mentally unstable Teddy Wharton had been another step, which had left her deeply informed on a favorite theme, the unsatisfactoriness of marriage, especially a socially presentable marriage of mismatched spirits. Teddy Wharton might have been an admirable husband for a less intellectually ambitious and formidably achieving woman than his wife; as it was, they tried each other sorely. Their sex life (for which Edith's prim and imperious mother had prepared her by telling her to look at Greek statues and exclaiming, "You can't be as stupid as you pretend") went from poor to nonexistent; but Edith executed another step, in her self-education, by taking a lover, Morton Fullerton, in 1909.

Her ties to Teddy, who on his side had turned to adultery and embezzlement from his wife's assets, weakened along with her ties to the United States; in 1911 she sold the Mount, a splendid house she had built in Lenox, Massachusetts, not ten years before, and became a Parisian. Her divorce followed two years later. World War I possessed her, as it did her adopted country; manifesting a prodigious organizational prowess, she founded and ran hostels for refugees, workshops for women unemployed because of the war, hospitals for tubercular patients, and a rescue committee for a thousand children of Flanders. But for some battlefield journalism later collected in *Fighting France*, her own work, including several novels, languished, and not just for reasons of time and energy. "These four years," she wrote in 1918, "have so much changed the whole aspect of life that it is not easy to say now what one's literary tendencies will be when the war is over."

Weary of Paris, she bought a small estate twelve miles to the north, named Pavillon Colombe after the two soiled doves, Venetian actresses and courtesans, whose lovers had installed them there in the eighteenth century. Also in 1919, she found and leased a suitable winter home—a ruined convent on a hilltop in Hyères, on the Riviera, which an American architect promised to render habitable. "I am thrilled to the spine," Wharton wrote to a friend. "I feel as if I were going to get married—to the right man at last!"

In these new and congenial settings, then, amid the flurry of creativity with which she tackled fresh challenges of interior decoration and gardening, the writer set herself to fulfill a contract with the American magazine *Pictorial Review*, which offered the great sum of eighteen thousand dollars for the serialization of a novel. Wharton always had several novels cooking at once, but she and the editors settled on a new idea. As R.W.B. Lewis explains in his biography of Wharton,

> It bore the working title "Old New York" and the scene was laid in 1875. The two main characters, Langdon Archer and Clementine Olenska, are both unhappily married. Falling in love, they "go off secretly," Edith explained, "and meet in Florida where they spend a few mad weeks" before Langdon returns to his pretty, conventional wife in New York, and Clementine to an existence, separated from her brutish husband, in Paris.

As the reader will see, the eventual *Age of Innocence* departed from this scenario in a number of particulars, including the chief characters' first names and the situation for which Florida is a background. Dividing her year amid four places of residence, including her last extended stay in her apartment on the rue de Varenne, Wharton pushed the novel forward and delivered it on schedule, in April of 1920; Rutger Jewett, her editor at Appleton and Company, wrote her, "Do you marvel that I bow low before such energy?"

New York society had been her milieu and of course had figured in her fiction before; *The House of Mirth* and *The Custom of the Country* both dramatize the charms and cruelties of the Manhattan upper crust. But she had never before approached the topic so deliberately, with the wisdom of her (and her hero's) "readings in anthropology" and the personal sense of history which the world war had inflicted upon her. According to Berenson, she told him that "before the war you could write fiction without indicating the period, the present being assumed. The war has put an end to that for a long time.... In other words, the historical novel with all its vices will be the only possible form for fiction." The 1870s had been the decade of Edith Jones's growing from the age of eight to that of seventeen; she reached back now across the ocean toward an era long dead, as seen by a self long outgrown. Not that she had ever broken completely with her past; as Louis Auchincloss points out in his *Edith Wharton: A Woman in Her Time*, her fund raising for her war charities had enlisted the rich old families, so that her list of directors "reads like a blue book of New York society."

Distressed by much of the contemporary world, she found the nineteenth century, she wrote a friend, "a blessed refuge from the turmoil and mediocrity of today—like taking sanctuary in a mighty temple." She set her agent and former sister-in-law, Minnie Jones, to researching the dates and details of opera performances, balls, assemblies. Her own memories fleshed out, in *The Age of Innocence*, a precisely etched reconstruction of brownstone New York, of Newport before the great cottages, of Florida in a primitive, idyllic stage of development. The author's voice more than once reminds us that this is a past time, when the telephone is just a gadget and the horse-and-carriage the only conveyance.

Yet the insistent historical details, including characteristically Whartonian particulars of décor and costume, do not distance or muffle the passions and intimate presence of the three principal characters: Ellen Olenska, Newland Archer, and his wife, May. Rather, the historical distance unclutters the carefully lit stage: these New Yorkers stroll up and down Fifth Avenue as if it were a village street, and are always encountering each other, in a world scarcely larger or less economically populated than the Starkfield of *Ethan Frome*. The décor is lush, but the plot is stark; its action is mostly subjective, in the realm of the emotions. Though the poor and unfortunate figured in Wharton's awareness, and movingly appear in *The House of Mirth* and several short stories, the train holding Newland and May on their honeymoon trip to Rhinebeck is describing as simply "shaking off the endless wooden suburbs"; no "social question" is allowed to arise and let the reader doubt the importance of how this man and his two women, amid their material comforts, dispose of their romantic needs. Wharton's wartime reading had gone back to basics—the older German literature, the Old Norse sagas, the New Testament—and the directness of myth entered her new novel.

    The Age of Innocence has classic lines, and reminds us of other classics. Like *Anna Karenina*, it pulses with the sexuality of its polite, thoroughly clad protagonists, and with the awesome sacrilege of Victorian adultery. Like *The Princess of Clèves*, it embodies the romantic paradox expressed by its heroine: "I can't love you unless I give you up." Like *The Scarlet Letter*, it shows a Europeanized woman, married to a sinister older man, beckoning to a son of a Puritan society with the allurements of a richer life "over there." Like much of Henry James, and especially *The Ambassadors*, it deals with the effect of European corruption upon the purer American soul and with the terror of a man, like James's Strether, confronting the fact that he has missed "the flower of life" and is "a man to whom nothing was ever to happen." Surely James was much on Wharton's mind, as he was often a guest in her house and a passenger in her automobile, and the intense—but rarely mannered and never unclear—stylistic refinement of *The Age of Innocence* is some kind of riposte, across the English Channel, to his ghost. And, like *A Farewell to Arms*, by a third American in love with Europe, her novel ends with a man walking back to the hotel alone.

But the new sharpness and the strange poetic *steepness* revealed by the crystalline perspective of this novel owe much, I felt upon a recent rereading, to Proust. Proust and Wharton, though they lived but blocks apart and had a number of friends (including André Gide and Walter Berry) in common, never met; but she was among the early enthusiasts for *Swann's Way*, which came out in 1913. She and Berry had been enthralled by the book, to the point of making the names of the aristocratic Guermantes part of their vocabulary; she sent a copy to Henry James, who was slow to warm but eventually pronounced it "a new vision" by "a new master." She herself wrote, after Proust's death in 1922, that "his endowment as a novelist ... has probably never been surpassed." By the time she was working on *The Age of Innocence*, only the second volume of Proust's immense work (*Within a Budding Grove*, in 1918) had followed the publication of *Swann's Way*, but, though the sprawling social commentary of *The Guermantes Way* was still to come, Wharton had read enough to learn his lesson of social analysis, with his flashes of comedy and presiding philosophical temper.

Proust's simultaneously telescopic and microscopic view; his recognition that grandeur and absurdity coexist; his sense of society's apparent rigidity and actual fragility—these inform Wharton's enchanted caricature of her own tribe, brought to life in her delicately farcical elaboration of Mrs. Manson Mingott's absurd girth and her mansion surreally located among "the quarries, the one-story saloons, the wooden greenhouses in ragged gardens, and the rocks from which goats surveyed the scene." The van der Luydens' mummified sacerdotal status, and Lawrence Lefferts's hard-working hypocrisy, and Mr. Welland's tyrannical hypochondria, and Mrs. Lemuel Struthers's inexorable rise all have the serio-comic savor of Proustian data.

Of course, the material was Edith Wharton's already, but Proust's example gave her a new angle on it, a slant both more impudent and lofty than hers hitherto; her earlier treatments of society are relatively caustic and fearful, still full of girlhood resentments. At a time in her creative life when she needed fresh direction, she learned from Proust the dignity of nostalgia and the value of each character as a specimen, an index to the species and to broad laws of behavior. She learned from him, one might say, how to leap: her impending marriage of the daughter of the kept woman Fanny Ring and the son of the old-breed Archers spans worlds, as did Proust's marriage (still in manuscript) of Gilberte Swann, the daughter of a Jew and a courtesan, to the Marquis de Saint-Loup.

The romantic heart of *The Age of Innocence*, however, beats with an ardor that Proust might endlessly anatomize but could not persuasively recreate. Edith Wharton might be brusque and aloof in person—with a mouth, an unkind observer said, "shaped like a savings box"—but she was a writer of unstinting empathy. Her portrait here of a man in love, with his unconscious slippage, his changeable internal weathers, his resolves and irresolution, his unquellable obsession, though it lacks any specifics of male lust, is extraordinary, and beautifully modulated toward its highest pitch. What could more forcefully express the mystery of erotic bewitchment than Archer's way of forgetting what Ellen looks like, and his telling her, in italics, *"Each time you happen to me all over again."* Ellen Olenska is one of the splendid women of American fiction—alluring, conflicted, vulnerable, blithely and touchingly truthful—and we see her entirely through his eyes, in a few hurried encounters; she speaks a sibylline modicum of words in the course of the novel. May Archer, the third principal, barely escapes the author's impulse to make her a simpleton of upper-class prejudices; but in a few critical scenes she is allowed to move beyond her character into a more generous and intuitive femininity. She is seen as a glorious young archer, literally, and, unlike Archer, she hits her targets; she *acts*. The excited and not unsympathetic warmth that exists between women—in this case, cousins—competing for the same man is conveyed, but always in indirect testimony; our masculine narrator hears of, but never overhears, May and Ellen talking. On the other hand, Wharton confidently gives us a number of stag conversations, over brandy and cigars.

The novel glitters with epigrammatic moments, sequins of comedy—"Mrs. Lovell Mingott had the high color and glassy stare induced in ladies of her age and habit by the effort of getting into a new dress"—and jewels of hard wisdom: "A woman's standard of truthfulness was tacitly held to be lower: she was the subject creature, and versed in the arts of the enslaved." The novel treasures and polishes its incidents, as Archer's mind returns to his few, infatuated glimpses of Ellen, shaping them into fetishes and precious symbols. The recent motion-picture adaptation by Martin Scorsese had no trouble locating its scenes, in the almost allegorical tapestry Wharton had laid out; among the $70,000 which the novel earned for its author in the first two years was $15,000 from Warner Brothers, for the first film adaptation.

No scene is more poignant, more memorably loaded with widening significances, than the lonely lovers' meeting in the old Metropolitan Museum, "a queer wilderness of cast-iron and encaustic tiles"; the two seek seclusion in a deserted room containing the "Cesnola antiquities," fragments of vanished Ilium. Ellen, in the awkwardness of this chaste assignation, wanders over to a case:

> "It seems cruel," she said, "that after a while nothing matters ...
> any more than these little things, that used to be necessary and

important to forgotten people, and now have to be guessed at under a magnifying glass and labeled: 'Use unknown.'"

"Yes; but meanwhile—"

"Ah, meanwhile—"

The historical perspective Wharton achieved—the passions of the past, imprisoned in the conventions of the past—widens here into an archeological vista wherein our poor dry fragments will be someday labeled "Use unknown." Our lives, so full of feeling and yearning and egotism, and of the beauty and magnetism with which Nature equips us to accomplish her ends, are but a magnificent "meanwhile," whose most glowing possibilities must often be sealed with a renunciation. *The Age of Innocence*, beneath its fine surface, holds an abyss—the abyss of time, and the tragedy of human transience.

HELEN KILLORAN

The Age of Innocence:
Branching Thematic Allusions

Like *The House of Mirth*, *The Age of Innocence* is a favorite novel.[1] Winner of the 1921 Pulitzer Prize, it has been much read by critics, and judging from what is revealed by the literary allusions, for the most part it has been well read. Nonetheless, some surprises emerge from echoes of the outside world, and from the wildness and dark places of the novel, churning under the surface of its literary allusions. Three primary types of allusions are represented: structural, clustered, and "branching" thematic allusions.

The function of two "structural allusions," Gounod's *Faust* and Dion Boucicault's *The Shaughraun*, have been described by Wagner, Gargano, and Moseley.[2] Most of the remaining allusions are thematic allusions that cluster into four major groups: themes of innocence, themes of living death, themes of revolt, and themes of inaccessible love. While thematic and structural allusions are not new developments, the title may be the first instance of a "reverberating art allusion," an allusion to a painting that appears to allude to an earlier painting of the same name. Sir Joshua Reynolds's title *The Age of Innocence* echoes Louis Gabriel Blanchet's satirical painting of mischievous children (1731). Wharton further developed reverberating art and literary allusions in *The Glimpses of the Moon*. The primary beauty of *The Age of Innocence* is its four related clusters of branching thematic allusions that reveal more themes symbolized by the Sphinx and the Furies.

From *Edith Wharton: Art and Allusion*. © 1996 by the University of Alabama Press.

Newland Archer precipitously announces his engagement to May Welland in order to protect her "innocence" from the influence of her sophisticated cousin, Ellen Olenska, who, having escaped an abusive husband, expected her old New York family to help her obtain a divorce. Instead, the family, through Archer, advises her to remain married. Reluctantly, she follows their advice, but the two fall in love. Nevertheless, Archer marries May. After several clandestine meetings, Newland and Ellen realize that they must either elope or separate forever. Before they can decide, May announces her pregnancy to Ellen, then throws an elaborate farewell banquet in Ellen's honor, effectively expelling her from old New York society. A generation later, when both are widowed, Newland finds himself in Paris on a bench beneath Ellen's window, unable to meet her though he has dreamed of her for twenty years. He decides that he has missed "the flower of life" and that she is more real to him in his mind.

There are several literary allusions to innocence, the most obvious occurring in the novel's title. In addition, allusions to "The Babes in the Wood" (*AI* 47), Drake's "The Culprit Fay" (*AI* 102), Washington Irving's *The Alhambra* (*AI* 146), Balzac's *Contes drôlatiques* (*AI* 85), and Gounod's *Faust* (*AI* 3) all support the theme of innocence. The questions are to what extent is the theme satirical, and who is innocent of what?

Most readers interpret the word "innocence" sexually, but there are two types of innocence in the novel, sexual and social. May is described by Newland Archer as the innocent child he wishes would not possess the "innocence that seals the mind against imagination and the heart against experience!" (*AI* 146). He recognizes that "all this frankness and innocence [is] only an artificial product" (*AI* 46). As if describing the children in the Blanchet painting, he muses: "Untrained human nature was not frank and innocent; it was full of the twists and defenses of an instinctive guile" (*AI* 46). May is socially, if not sexually, experienced. Her polished social skills attract Newland: "She was always going to understand; she was always going to say the right thing" (*AI* 14). "Nothing about his betrothed pleased him more than her resolute determination to carry to its utmost limit that ritual of ignoring the 'unpleasant' in which they both had been brought up" (*AI* 26). Even so, she is sexually more aware than Newland supposes: "You mustn't think that a girl knows as little as her parents imagine. One hears and one notices—one has one's feelings and ideas" (*AI* 149). A detail often raised about May's innocence is that she saves her marriage by behaving deceitfully, lying to Ellen Olenska about her pregnancy. This is not sexual deceit but social deceit about a sexual subject supported by the social code of old New York.

Ellen's sexual innocence is in question not only because of her separation from the count, and "a shadow of a shade" on her reputation (*AI* 26), but because she is willing to face the hard realities of an affair with Newland and offer to "once come to you" (*AI* 312) then return to Europe. Nevertheless, at first she is innocent of the social codes of New York. And while May is rather less sexually innocent than Newland imagines, Ellen is probably somewhat more innocent. The "shadows and shades," the hints of an affair with M. Rivière, who helped her escape from her husband, can be neutralized by examining the allusion to Fitz-Greene Halleck and Joseph Rodman Drake, apparently a gay couple, who wrote a number of poems together. A member of the Knickerbocker Group, Drake was the author of "The Culprit Fay," a poem about a fairy the size of an insect who must perform heroic deeds to expiate the crime of allowing an innocent human maiden to see him. The hint of homosexuality in the situation of a male fairy who must avoid women creates irony in the following passage: "Mrs. Archer and her group felt a certain timidity concerning these [literary] persons. They were *odd*, they were uncertain, they had things one didn't know about in the background of their lives and minds .... and Mrs. Archer was always at pains to tell her children how much more agreeable and cultivated society had been when it included such figures as Washington Irving, Fitz-Greene Halleck and the poet of 'The Culprit Fay'" (*AI* 102, emphasis mine).

Old New York viewed "such unhappy persons as Joseph Drake, author of 'The Culprit Fay,' balanced between 'fame and infamy' as not quite of the best society, and writing not quite the best poetry."[3] Like the "long-haired men and short-haired women" who filled the house of the Blenkers (*AI* 220), M. Rivière had ventured unsuccessfully into authorship (*AI* 199). If his words are read doubly, he seems to be one of the "unhappy" persons who are nonetheless full citizens elsewhere: "Things that are accepted in certain other societies," he says to Newland, "or at least put up with as part of a general convenient give-and-take—become unthinkable, simply unthinkable" in America (*AI* 253). If he had had an affair with Ellen Olenska, her husband would hardly have made Rivière his emissary. All told, especially since she is married, Ellen seems sexually experienced but socially innocent, at least in old New York.

But the most innocent character is Newland Archer, who does not understand M. Rivière. Strictly, Archer is not sexually innocent, having sown his wild oats with Mrs. Thorley Rushworth, but neither that "mild agitation" nor his "sincere but placid" love for May prepares him for the passion he feels for Ellen. His initial ambivalence between his sympathy toward her and his assumption that she is guilty of those "shadows and shades" may be similar to the ambivalence expressed by Fitz-Greene Halleck in his poem "To Ellen," which furnishes the possible source for Ellen's name: "Are there two Ellens of the mind? / Or have I lived at last to find / The Ellen of my heart?"[4]

The allusions to Halleck and Drake are underscored by the allusion to Washington Irving's *The Alhambra* (*AI* 146), which includes a tale of three innocent princesses imprisoned in a tower to protect them from men. The imprisonment has the opposite effect, and they escape.[5]

That Edith Wharton had a humorous attitude toward two sexually innocent marriage partners can be inferred from a comment in her notebook concerning an earlier version of the plot: "At last he and Ellen fly together (contrast between bridal night with May & *this one*)."[6] The thinking behind the note seems borne out by the content of the allusion to Balzac's *Contes drôlatiques* ("humorous tales"), which features two stories, "Innocence" and "The Danger of Being Too Innocent." The latter is a ribald story about the marriage of a boy and girl who had been kept so perfectly pure that their bumbling attempts to discover what is supposed to happen in the bedroom provide amusement.[7]

That context turns Newland's minimal sexual experience toward irony: "He could not deplore ... that he had not a blank page to offer his bride in exchange for the unblemished one she was to give to him. He could not get away from the fact that if he had been brought up as she had they would have been no more fit to find their way about than the Babes in the Wood" (*AI* 46–47).

"The Babes in the Wood" is a rather gruesome tale, *The Children in the Wood*, an old ballad from the Percy collection in which a wicked uncle abandons two infants to die in the woods.[8] The issue of the survival of the innocent applies not only to Ellen but to Newland Archer because he has the child's inability to distinguish between "vision" (or fantasy) and reality. He is innocent of understanding social reality, so that May can manipulate the system dexterously while Newland is blind to her maneuvering.

Both socially and sexually naive as the novel opens, Newland Archer is daydreaming over an operatic performance of Gounod's *Faust*, based on Goethe's play. The scene features innocent fourteen-year-old Marguerite just before she is sexually victimized by the fifty-year-old Faust, whom the devil has provided with the body of a noble youth. Without distinguishing fiction from reality, Archer then shifts his gaze from one stage to another, the opera box opposite, in which he admires May, imagining that she can be a "miracle of fire and ice," then notes the entrance of Ellen Olenska (*AI* 7), which results in a dramatic impulse. He rushes to the box to "protect" May by announcing their engagement early. This very impulse sets in motion a pattern of events that prevents his ever linking with Ellen, and the same medieval sense of honor motivating that impulse will prevent him from deserting his pregnant wife.

At their wedding, a stage show itself, Newland muses that "real people were living somewhere, and real things happening to them ..." (*AI* 182, Wharton's ellipses). Though May at first represents the fiction of chivalric romance, she soon represents the real. When he first sees May at St. Augustine, Florida, Newland thinks: "Here was truth, here was reality, here was the life that belonged to him" (*AI* 141).[9] But it's a reality in which beautiful fictional things do not happen: The advancement of their wedding date was a dream to May. "It was like hearing him read aloud out of his poetry books the beautiful things that could not possibly happen in real life" (*AI* 147). After Newland sees Ellen at the pier in Newport, he makes a dramatic exit patterned after the Boucicault play, realizing, "Reality was what awaited him in the house on the bank"—May (*AI* 215). It's a safe and familiar reality: "The whole chain of tyrannical trifles binding one hour to the next, and each member of the household to all the others, made any less systematized and affluent existence seem unreal and precarious" (*AI* 217). But he cannot give up hope for beauty and passion, so gradually he replaces the reality of May with a fictional dream life with Ellen: "He had built up within himself a kind of sanctuary in which she throned among his secret thoughts and longings. Little by little it became the scene of his real life, of his only rational activities.... Outside it, in the scene of his actual life, he moved with a growing sense of unreality ... so absent from everything most densely real" (*AI* 262). Ellen tries to show him the practical ramifications of his desires: "We'll look, not at visions, but at realities." But he replies, "I don't know what you mean by realities. The only reality to me is this" (*AI* 289). May, an expert at interpreting the reality represented by "arbitrary signs," recognizes the meaning of Archer's absentness when, "absorbed in other visions, [he] had forgotten his promise" to drive home with May after meeting Ellen with May's carriage (*AI* 293). "Could it be possible that the sense of unreality in which he felt himself imprisoned had communicated itself to his wife?" (*AI* 324). It had, and she acted out of her social experience to protect herself from any resulting "unpleasantness."

What Newland Archer loses by remaining in his innocent dream world is indeed "the flower of life," and to him Ellen had "become the composite vision of all that he had missed" (*AI* 347). Twenty years later, Newland thinks that Ellen is the flower of life he missed—and inexplicably chooses to continue to miss (even after inspiration by an "effulgent Titian") when he decides, "It's more real to me here than if I went up" (*AI* 361). Evidence suggests, however, that the "flower of life" that Newland missed is something altogether different, the clue to which can be found in the stories by Balzac.

"Innocence" is an anecdotal joke about children clamoring to see a nude Adam and Eve by Titian. When one child asks how to tell Adam apart from Eve, the other replies, "You silly! ... to know that, they would have to be dressed!"[10] But the anecdote contains a passage about children that Wharton seems to have felt apt: "Watch them playing, prettily and *innocently* ..., and you will agree with me that they are in every way lovable; besides which they are flower and fruit—the fruit of love, the *flower of life*.... Do not expect a man to be innocent after the manner of children, because there is an, I know not what, ingredient of reason in the naïveté of a man, while the naivete of children is candid, immaculate"[11] (emphasis mine).

By living in dreams, chivalric fictions, and books, Newland Archer missed—if indeed he did miss it—the ability to live awake and fully "the real things of this life" that he learned about, ironically, in his library. His memories of May's pregnancy announcement, christenings, the babies' first steps, the engagement and marriage of his daughter, the future of his children, even his friendship with President Roosevelt, are all set in his library (*AI* 344). It is not in Ellen that he has missed the "flower of life" but in his children. Somehow even sadder is the thought that Newland has not missed the "flower of life" but thinks he has.

The failure of Newland Archer and other innocent Americans to live fully awake—a theme that Wharton took up again in *Twilight Sleep*—is emphasized through allusions to *La sonnambula* (*AI* 58), and a cluster of allusions to Tennyson (*AI* 46), Labiche (*AI* 128), and Poe (*AI* 137) that have two themes in common, death-in-life and voyages of exploration: "Incredible dream: ... struck from all three allusions to Edgar Poe and Jules Verne" (*Around the World in Eighty Days*) (*AI* 137, 337). The themes take several forms, from passive resistance, frozen motion, sleep, and sleepwalking to live burial (a theme that occurs in Wharton's work disturbingly often), but together they represent a new kind of cluster—thematic allusions containing more than one theme, or "branching thematic allusions."

In *La sonnambula* (1831), a comic opera by Vincenzo Bellini, complications arise when the heroine sleepwalks into the wrong bedroom the night before her wedding. Wharton's allusion to it underscores the many instances of the sleepy passivity of persons from old New York such as May, who prefers not to travel, such as Mrs. Archer and Archer himself at the conclusion of the novel, who, like Melville's Bartleby, "prefer not to" try to meet new people (*AI* 103), and like the van der Luydens, who escape to their country home when problems surface. In fact, much of the "action" of the novel involves forms of passivity.

Newland, for instance, had attempted to interest May in Tennyson's "Ulysses" and "The Lotus Eaters" without success: "When he had gone the brief round of her he returned discouraged" (*AI* 46). The allusion to "Ulysses" is ironic. Late in life Ulysses "cannot rest from travel"; he must "drink life to the lees" (*Ulysses*, ll. 6–7) and begin a new journey, which late in his life Newland refuses to do. He has become used to living in half dreams of Ellen like "The Lotus Eaters," who found how "sweet it was to dream of Fatherland, / Of child, and wife, and slave" (*Lotus Eaters*, ll. 39–40), and "How sweet it were, hearing the downward stream / With half-shut eyes ever to seem / Falling asleep in a half-dream! (*Lotus Eaters*, ll. 99–101) like Archer, "stopped at the sight [of Ellen at the pier] as if he had waked from sleep. That vision of the past was a dream" (*AI* 215). When May greets Archer in the library after his last meeting with Ellen, he is sitting "without conscious thoughts, without sense of the lapse of time, in a deep and grave amazement that seemed to suspend life rather than quicken it.... What he had dreamed of had been so different that there was a mortal chill in his rapture." May enters and remarks, "I believe you've been asleep!" (*AI* 314).

At May's farewell banquet for Ellen, in passive acceptance that never changes later in life, Archer thinks: "'It's to show me ... what would happen to me—' and a deathly sense of the superiority of implication and analogy over direct action, and of silence over rash words, closed in on him like the doors of the family vault" (*AI* 335-36).

Figuring even more prominently in the novel is the cluster of allusions to voyages of exploration that bring together "Ulysses'" theme of exploration and the theme of wakeful dreaming or living death of "The Lotus Eaters." Wharton directly mentions *Le voyage de Monsieur Perrichon* (1860) by Eugène Labiche. The play is a comic farce, the climax of which involves a fall into a glacial crevasse. The author casts old New York in January as that glacial crevasse: "Archer had seen, on has last visit to Paris, the delicious play of Labiche, *Le Voyage de M. Perrichon*, and he remembered M. Perrichon's dogged and undiscouraged attachment to the young man whom he had pulled out of the glacier." Ironically, he thinks, "The van der Luydens had rescued Madame Olenska from a doom almost as icy" (*AI* 128–29). But Ellen, who actually makes van der Luyden dinners "a little less funereal" (*AI* 87), risks being pulled into the crevasse, for Mrs. van der Luyden has been "rather gruesomely preserved in the airless atmosphere of a perfectly irreproachable existence, as bodies caught in glaciers keep for years a rosy life-in-death" (*AI* 53).

May is constantly described as cool, frosty, or chill. She blows out lights, she is associated with dying fires, and Newland seems doomed to catch the paralyzing cold. After his separation from Ellen, he leans out the window of his library for some air, but May admonishes him that he will freeze to death. "'Catch my death!' he echoed; and he felt like adding: 'But I've caught it already. *I am* dead—I've been dead for months and months'" (*AI* 295). Images of precipices, abysses, and vortices connect the Labiche themes to Poe's "The Maelstrom" (*AI* 116).

In Poe's *The Narrative of Arthur Gordon Pym*,[12] an "intraauthorial allusion" (a reference to another work by the same author), Pym stows away on a ship hiding in a coffinlike box in the hold, a symbolic live burial. After reaching an island, he is buried in a landslide and a number of adventures later sails "uncharted waters toward the South Pole," passing glaciers and icebergs but discovering a warm land with a black landscape at the edge of a chasm that features strange hieroglyphics:

> A range of singular looking indentures in the surface of the marl ... might have been taken for the intentional ... representation of a human figure.... the rest of them bore also some little resemblance to alphabetical characters.... We now found ourselves [in a wild place where] the surface of the ground in every other direction was strewn with huge tumuli, apparently the wreck of some gigantic structures of art.... Scoriae were abundant, and large shapeless blocks of the black granite, intermingled with others of marl. (Poe's note: The marl was also black; indeed, we noticed no light-colored substances of any kind upon the island.) [186]

Newland feels that marriage is a "voyage on uncharted seas" when in fact it's a journey preplanned by society. The image of warm black vegetation occurs during Archer's talk with May when she asks him frankly if there is some one else. "He lower[s] his head, staring at the black leaf-pattern on the sunny path at their feet" (*AI* 148), and lies. "They lived in a kind of hieroglyphic world, where the real thing was never said or done or even thought, but only represented by a set of arbitrary signs" (*AI* 45), and "there were moments when [Newland Archer] felt as if he were being buried alive under his future" (*AI* 140). His entire life is spent "in a deep and grave amazement that seemed to suspend life rather than quicken it. 'This was what had to be, then ... this was what had to be,' he kept repeating to himself, as if he hung in the clutch of doom. What he had dreamed of had been so different that there was a mortal chill in his rapture" (*AI* 314, Wharton's ellipses). The death-in-life theme is supported by another intraauthorial allusion. In this case the allusion to Washington Irving's *The Alhambra* crosses over to "Rip Van Winkle," the legendary resident of the Catskills who slept twenty years. Behind that story lies the motif of the American Revolution symbolized by the hieroglyph of the tavern sign renamed for George Washington by crossing out "George III." It seemed to have occurred while old New York, Washington Irving's "Knickerbocker" country, was asleep, as does the invasion of old New York by the Titans in *The Custom of the Country*.

The plethora of literary and art allusions in *The Age of Innocence* splits into two major categories with branching thematic clusters to the French and Italian revolutions. In a "branching thematic cluster" the members of a cluster fork to form two subtopics. In this case an encompassing "umbrella" allusion to revolutions alludes either to the French Revolution or to the Italian Revolution.

Allusions to the French Revolution begin with general references to Thackeray (*AI* 34, 46, 103), whose *Vanity Fair* takes place during the French Revolution. Allusions point, like May's arrows, to Dickens's *A Tale of Two Cities* (*AI* 34), again about the French Revolution, to David's *The Coronation of Napoleon* (*AI* 98) and Meissonier, another painter of Napoleon (*AI* 209), and to Michelet, historian of the French Revolution (*AI* 194), among others. These allusions support three ideas: Newland Archer's inclination toward a social and intellectual revolt that is reflected in his reading, the futility of Ellen's being "wholly in revolt" against her past (*AI* 139), and such scarcity of revolt in old New York that it becomes worth commenting about Mrs. Welland in "one of her rare revolts against fate" (*AI* 280). A line from *The Custom of the Country* sums up the theme's irony, citing the "myth of 'old families' ruling New York from a throne of Revolutionary tradition" (*CC* 193). The several allusions to revolt range from the comparison of Grandmother Mingott to Catherine the Great, who ran European revolutions from the Russian throne, to the Frenchman M. Rivière, who helped Ellen revolt against her husband. A sly allusion to Ralph Waldo Emerson in Professor Emerson Sillerton's name adds to the list of those who do "revolutionary things" (*AI* 220). These revolutionaries are contrasted to Archer when the poet-journalist Ned Winsett, who is "starving to death" for ideas, is associated with a statement by M. Rivière. "You see, Monsieur, it's worth everything, isn't it, to keep one's intellectual liberty, not to enslave one's powers of appreciation, one's critical independence? It was because of that that I abandoned journalism, and took to so much duller work: tutoring and private secretaryship. There is a good deal of drudgery, of course; but one preserves one's moral freedom" (*AI* 200).

The second twig of the branching thematic allusions to revolt generally concerns Italy—the novels with an "Italian atmosphere" like those of Ouida, George Eliot's *Middlemarch*, which features the Casaubons' Italian honeymoon (*AI* 139), the Italian travel memoirs of Baroness Bunsen (*AI* 192), and Hawthorne's *The Marble Faun* (*AI* 34). Ellen returns to New York with Italian possessions.

The allusions branch again. The first subcategory is the political aesthetic revolutions of the Italian Renaissance: Dante and Petrarch (*AI* 70), the background for *Romeo and Juliet* (*AI* 307), Renaissance painters Botticelli and Fra Angelico (*AI* 71), art critics, historians, and novelists of the Italian Renaissance like the Goncourts (*AI* 104, 199, 201), Walter Pater (*AI* 71), Paul Bourget (*AI* 104), Vernon Lee and John Addington Symonds (*AI* 71), and, of course, Columbus, the Italian Renaissance discoverer of America (*AI* 154).

The second subcategory of references to "Italian revolt" is a set of allusions to the Victorian Pre-Raphaelite Brotherhood, Rossetti (*AI* 139), Swinburne (*AI* 85), and Morris (*AI* 103). The Pre-Raphaelites looked to Raphael and the Italian Renaissance for inspiration to revolt against the prevailing Victorian aesthetic.

Then the allusions to revolution branch as well. One branch supports a theme of inaccessible, unsatisfied, or forbidden love. A diagram would resemble branches, or roots, of a tree. The "branching allusions" seem furthermore meant to reflect the branches and roots of literary and social families.

Naturally, Newland Archer's desire to revolt against his family and old New York is a result of his longing for Ellen Olenska's love. While to Ellen New York is a chilly heaven and her old life hell—"I'm sure I'm dead and buried, and this dear old place is heaven" (*AI* 18)—Archer's version of heaven is a romantic European country where ideas like "mistress" don't exist. He wants to elope with Ellen:

> "I want—I want somehow to get away with you into a world where words like that—categories like that—won't exist. Where we shall be simply two human beings who love each other, who are the whole of life to each other; and nothing else on earth will matter....
>
> "Oh, my dear—where is that country? Have you ever been there.... I know so many who've tried to find it; and, believe me, they all got out by mistake at wayside stations: at places like Boulogne, or Pisa, or Monte Carlo" [*AI* 290].

For Newland Archer, Italy at first seems to be that magic world, since he connects it with Ellen. The theme is reflected in the rooms in which he fantasizes bedroom scenes from plays—the revolutionary Catherine Mingott's "ceilings on which an Italian house-painter had lavished all the divinities of Olympus" (*AI* 212). When he is dreaming about May, Newland thinks, "We'll read *Faust* together ... by the Italian lakes ..." (*AI* 7, Wharton's ellipses). But the Italian escape would probably have been as disappointing as Dorothea Brooke's Italian honeymoon if it had occurred. But it doesn't occur because of May's capacity to stand her ground against change: "They had not gone to the Italian Lakes: on reflection, Archer had not been able to picture his wife in that particular setting.... Once or twice, in the mountains, Archer had pointed southward and said: 'There's Italy'; and May, her feet in a gentian-bed, had smiled cheerfully, and replied: 'It would be lovely to go there next winter, if only you didn't have to be in New York'" (*AI* 194).

Ellen's warnings about "wayside stations" are scarcely necessary, for the impetus against elopement, against "revolution" of any kind, is built into Archer's chill, sleepy old New York roots. His feet, like May's, are firmly planted. In response to Winsett's desire to emigrate, he reacts with all his "old inherited ideas": "Emigrate! As if a gentleman could abandon his own country! One could no more do that than one could roll up one's sleeves and go down into the muck. A gentleman simply stayed at home and abstained" (*AI* 126). Later in life, he and May take the "old-fashioned tour" of Europe, but he declines to join his children in Italy (*AI* 351). The novel's implied hope is that the new generation is more open to change than the old.

That Newland prefers living in a dream state much like Platonic love rather than the real "heaven" of an actively happy life is supported by literary allusions to Shakespeare (*AI* 307), Irving (*AI* 102, 146), Dante (*AI* 70), Petrarch (*AI* 70), Mérimée (*AI* 103, 200), Rossetti (*AI* 139), Morris (*AI* 103), and Vernon Lee's *Euphorion* (*AI* 71). Each item alludes to lovers separated by circumstances beyond their control. Romeo and Juliet are separated by a family feud, Irving's princesses are imprisoned in a tower, Dante and Petrarch are separated from Beatrice and Laura by death, and curmudgeonly Mérimée is kept from his *Inconnue* by geography.

Two other allusions, one to Flaubert (probably *Madame Bovary* is meant) and one to Rossetti's *The House of Life* are more specifically about extramarital love. Rossetti's *The House of Life* is a sequence of love sonnets thought to be addressed to the wife of the artist William Morris. Madame Bovary, of course, was, like Newland Archer, a dreamer trying to escape her mundane existence through reading and extramarital romance. Finally, Vernon Lee's *Euphorion*, a collection of "studies of the antique and the mediaeval in the Renaissance," features a long essay on "Mediaeval Love," according to which the ideal Platonic love of Dante's *Divine Comedy* was made possible by a foundation in courtly love poetry that actually reflected the love of the knight for a *married*, rather than an eligible, lady.[13]

Since Rossetti was influenced by poetry of courtly love, and Wharton knew that, it is not surprising to find that the sonnets of *The House of Life*, like "Love's Lovers," reflect the frustrated longings of unsatisfied love and do so using the images of Cupid and blindness upon which Wharton elaborates in *The Age of Innocence*:

Love's Lovers

Some ladies love the jewels in Love's zone
And gold-tipped darts he hath for painless play
In idle scornful hours he flings away;
And some that listen to his lute's soft tone
Do love to vaunt the silver praise their own;
Some prize his blindfold sight; and there be they
Who kissed his wings which brought him yesterday
And thank his wings to-day that he is flown.

My lady only loves the heart of Love:
Therefore Love's heart, my lady, hath for thee
His bower of unimagined flower and tree:
There kneels he now, and all-unhungered of
Thine eyes gray-lit in shadowing hair above,
Seals with thy mouth his immortality.

In his search for Ellen in the Blenkers' garden, Archer finds a "wooden Cupid who had lost his bow and arrow but continued to take ineffectual aim" (*AI* 224). More successful with the bow and arrow is May, who, though like Mrs. Beaufort she pretends to be blind to her husband's "private weaknesses," is sharp-eyed enough to win the jeweled arrow at the Beaufort's garden party: "That's the only kind of target she'll ever hit," Beaufort says ironically, for May, several times described as the goddess Diana, aims at Ellen Olenska, whose last name means "deer," and hits the bullseye (*AI* 211).[14]

The thematic allusions cluster into four major groups supporting themes of innocence, living death, revolt, and inaccessible love, several of the allusions sharing double themes. Naturally, the themes are interdependent. A state of innocence can be monotonous, a living death, but that is also a description of the state of sin according to Medora Manson: "To me the only death is monotony. I always say to Ellen: Beware of monotony; it's the mother of all the deadly sins" (*AI* 208). A revolt leading to adulterous love is sin, but the novel forces the reader to question sexual or social innocence if, by definition, it must be blind to "unpleasantness" and exclude intellectual stimulation, experience, and appropriate change.

Even though Archer claims to want change (he has a "haunting horror of doing the same thing every day at the same hour" [*AI* 84]), in the museum, a place of intellectual stimulation, he and Ellen are already buried in a necropolis with the sarcophagi and mummies (*AI* 311). To justify his desire to revolt, Archer psychologically projects his own feelings onto May, wondering whether the "deadly monotony of their lives had laid its weight on her also" (*AI* 193). But because of the influence, culture, and training of old New York, an ideal love with someone like Ellen is inaccessible to a man whose every revolutionary idea dissolves at its first contact with habit. When, on his honeymoon, he sees some of the women who "ought to be free," he finds them "queer cosmopolitan women deep in complicated love affairs" (*AI* 196). And "if one had habitually breathed the New York air there were times when anything less crystalline"—like the Italian "way-stations" of Pisa and Bolougne—"seemed stifling" (*AI* 95).

In this way, thematic allusions to literary topics of innocence, death-in-life, revolution, and inaccessible love reinforce these major motifs of the novel. Ironically, in *The Age of Innocence*, Newland Archer *needs* enough Furies to stir him out of his daydreams "un-hungered." And as Emerson Sillerton keeps track of the branches of a firmly rooted family, his name recalls Emerson's "The Sphinx":

> Out of sleep a waking
>   Out of waking a sleep
> Life death overtaking;
>   Deep underneath deep?

> ["The Sphinx," stanza 2, ll. 13–16]

The theme of innocent childhood as the "flower of life," and the "fate of the manchild" ("The Sphinx," stanza 2) contrast to the danger (real or not) implied by the allusions to homosexuality. All the while "historic allusions" and "allusion[s] to democratic principles" (*AI* 3), allusions to allusions, and allusions to a code at the beginning of the novel (*AI* 38, 39) lead to hints of a message at the end in a cross-novel repetition of the phrase, "I've got a message for you" (*AI* 354).

Trapped in a variation of the dilemma, Newland Archer fails to recognize that neglect of cultural education results in living death and that neglect of sexual education endangers children by leaving them prey to Faustian pederasts, and that it ruins the lives of adults who base marriages on mistaken assumptions. Representing Americans, Newland Archer, "Whose soul sees the perfect / Which his eyes seek in vain" (*Sphinx*, stanza 10, ll. 79–80), is blind to the knowledge that while his children are one "flower of life," there are many others in maturity, like the cultural riches of Europe and the potential love of Ellen Olenska. *The Glimpses of the Moon* elaborates on the marriage based on mistaken assumptions, as it introduces the next clue to the code, adds pieces to the neglected child puzzle, and unexpectedly reintroduces the rape theme.

NOTES

1. Edith Wharton, *The Age of Innocence* 1920 (New York: Scribner's, 1970). Subsequent citations in the text refer to this edition.

2. Linda W. Wagner, "A Note on Wharton's Use of *Faust*," *Edith Wharton Newsletter* 3 (1986): 1, 8; James W. Gargano, "Tableaux of Renunciation: Wharton's Use of *The Shaughran* in *The Age of Innocence*," *Studies in American Fiction* 15 (1987): 1–11; Edwin M. Mosley, "*The Age of Innocence*: Edith Wharton's Weak *Faust*," *College English* 21 (1959): 156–80.

3. Edith Wharton, *A Backward Glance* (New York: Scribner's 1934), 68.

4. Fitz-Greene Halleck, *The Poetical Writings of Fitz-Greene Halleck with Extracts from those of Joseph Rodman Drake* (New York: D. Appleton, 1869), 228–30.

5. Washington Irving, "The Three Beautiful Princesses," in *The Alhambra* (New York: G. P. Putnam, n.d.). See the discussion of this allusion in Chapter 7.

6. Alan Price, "Edith Wharton's *The Age of Innocence*," *Yale University Library Gazette* 55 (1980): 26.

7. Honoré de Balzac, "Innocence," in *Contes drôlatiques* (New York: Random House, n.d.), 528.

8. Margaret Drabble, ed., *The Oxford Companion to English Literature* (New York: Oxford University Press, 1985), 192.

9. See also the allusion to *The Confessions of St. Augustine* in Chapter 10, in *The Gods Arrive*.

10. Balzac, 526.

11. Ibid.

12. Edgar Allan Poe, *The Narrative of Arthur Gordon Pym* (New York: Hill & Wang, 1960).

13. Vernon Lee, *Euphorion: Being Studies of the Antique and the Mediaeval in the Renaissance*, vol. 2 (London: T. Fisher Unwin, 1884). Vernon Lee argues that the poetry grew out of conditions in which great numbers of knights and soldiers were garrisoned where the wife of the ruling nobleman and her servants were the only women permitted.

14. "Ollen," a red deer, *The Compact Edition of the Oxford English Dictionary* (New York: Oxford University Press, 1985). This detail may further allude to a painting of Thomas Townshend and Colonel Acland by Sir Joshua Reynolds called *The Archers* (1770). Recently, David Holbrook speculated that May's archery scene was taken from George Eliot's *Daniel Deronda*. See David Holbrook, *Edith Wharton and the Unsatisfactory Man* (New York: St. Martin's Press, 1991), 130.

JILL M. KRESS

The Price of a Conscious Self in
Edith Wharton's The Age of Innocence

"I have often thought that the best way to define a man's character would
be to seek out the particular mental or moral attitude in which, when it
came upon him, he felt himself most deeply and intensely active and
alive. At such moments there is a voice inside which speaks and says:
'This is the real me!' And afterwards, considering the circumstances in
which the man is placed, and noting how some of them are fitted to
evoke this attitude, whilst others do not call for it, an outside observer
may be able to prophesy where the man may fail, where succeed, where
be happy and where miserable."

—William James

In this letter, written in 1875 to his wife, the newly-married William James
reflects on the ways in which one might trace one's own character, one's
"deepest" self, as it were, in order to define it.[1] The process by which we gain
access to that self appears to be twofold: we hear an inner voice speaking and
later consider what produces it and what it means. "This is the real me!" the
voice inside exclaims fervently. The self thereby discloses itself, announcing
its reality, to a rapt audience of one. James's demonstrative pronoun, vague
as it is, appears to offer conclusive evidence for a distinctive self, "intensely
active and alive." Moreover, the self appears explicitly identified by its
consciousness of itself, a consciousness that signals its reality. And yet, James
immediately follows this instinctive voice with a remarkably detached,

From *The Figure of Consciousness: William James, Henry James, and Edith Wharton.* © 2002 by
Routledge.

philosophical reflection on "circumstances." The moment James mentions "circumstances," or where the man is "placed," the energy of the letter moves further and further outward, so much so that it requires an "outside observer" to determine the fate of the self. Understanding character no longer requires attention to an inner voice, but rather, to an ability to "fit" together situation and "attitude"—a term that suggests that identity rests not upon deep inner recesses, but upon one's manner. James's letter goes on to discuss the balance between "holding [one's] own" and "trusting outward things to perform their part," revealing the fundamental contest between that inner voice and the conditions under which it might pronounce itself.

The dramatic rendering, in William James's letter, of an inner voice and its accompanying adjustments in attitude reveals a split in the discourse of consciousness that the philosopher had tremendous trouble reconciling. Though the letter dates from the earliest part of his career, before the publication of *The Principles of Psychology* (1890), it reflects a central preoccupation in all of James's work: the division between a consciousness that locates itself inside us and a consciousness that pervades the natural and the social world. It is a tension we have seen repeatedly acted out, across genres, within every text of this study; it is this tension that characterizes the history of consciousness. The inner voice in James's letter, which represents the conscious mind, effectively precipitates the outward action, suggesting his investment in that voice as the essence of one's identity. On the other hand, his initial sense that we might understand ourselves by "seeking" out what *attitudes* produce this inner exclamation indicates James's ambivalence about the origin of identity. It is striking that he speaks of "defining a man's character" given the confusion that critics have often enjoyed over who, among the James brothers, emerges as the philosopher and who the fiction writer. Indeed, the sketch that William provides reads like the germ of a novel, with its character waiting to be "placed" inside the action, his denouement open either to success or failure, happiness or misery. It sounds, moreover, remarkably like Henry James's conception of *The Portrait of a Lady*, which, he insists, "consisted not at all in any conceit of a 'plot' ... but altogether in the sense of a single character." A single character, moreover, whom James admits he "locked up" as a "precious object" for fear that she might get into the wrong hands.[2] The fiction of his fellow novelist of manners, Edith Wharton, appears to tell a different story. Her work explicitly brings to bear the force of "circumstance" that both William and Henry James work to keep separate or contained. Though Wharton expresses fascination and even sympathy for her characters; more often than not, she suggests that for her, storytelling consists of the conflict between characters and the forces surrounding them, forces that come from the social and cultural sphere.³ Probably the most famous account of these influences comes in her consideration of the subject of *The House of Mirth*, her sense that a novelist might reveal the values of a society by exposing what it destroys.⁴ Thirty years after the publication of her most popular novel, Wharton reflects on that subject again, stating assuredly: "when there is anything whatever below the surface in the novelist's art, that something can be only the social foundation on which the fable is built." This statement characteristically implies that the Wharton novel, at bottom, is purely social, excavate it all you will. But as Wharton continues the discussion of her art, she qualifies the social to make way for the soul.

> [T]he other, supreme preservative of fiction is whatever of unchanging human nature the novelist has contrived to bring to life beneath the passing fripperies of clothes and custom. The essential soul is always there, under whatever disguise; and the storyteller's most necessary gift is that of making its presence felt, and of discerning just how fair it is modified and distorted by the shifting fashions of the hour.⁵

In naming "unchanging human nature" as the basis for her work, Wharton overturns the "social foundation" she previously cited and rests the weight of fiction on more elusive ground: the pursuit of the soul. The Wharton text, not unlike those of her contemporaries in science and psychology, searches for a language to characterize authentic human experience. Though we see the language of the soul repeatedly emerging in nineteenth-century scientific studies of consciousness, such language was once the province of religious texts. The evolutionary scientists combine discussions of the soul with biological and psychological discourse in order to explore the human mind. And Wharton's novels, in their concern over personal psychology, social determinism, cultural criticism, the spiritual and philosophical dimensions of identity, reveal this peculiar heritage. T.J. Jackson Lears explains that in order to understand American modernists, "one has to acknowledge that for them the category of the authentic had more than aesthetic significance. Some of its roots can only be called religious."⁶ It is not surprising, then, that Wharton should imagine her work as a novelist in terms of uncovering this spiritual core. "Essential," "unchanging," and "always there," the soul becomes a substantiated being, the most potent presence inhabiting a story. The soul "preserves" fiction, by which I assume Wharton to mean, saves it, from the "passing fripperies" of a fickle society. Yet it might be hard to find; it might even (purposely?) be "disguised," a hint, on the author's part, that sounds like a tip for her readers.

As Wharton concludes her meditation on the fiction writer's hunt for the soul, she states that part of the work of the novelist consists of "discerning" what modifications and distortions that soul has undergone, hinting, suggestively, that it may not be quite so "unchanging" after all. At the close of this passage, Wharton comes round, syntactically and perhaps philosophically, to the "fashions of the hour"; but the soul continues to be a throbbing presence, one that both writer and reader must anticipate.

Though Wharton here attests to the power of the soul, which seems, always, to be located "beneath" or "underneath" changing customs, fickle times, clothes, or the body that wears the clothes, her fiction repeatedly questions such formulas. In fact, Wharton makes it impossible to sustain readings that separate cultural furnishings, fashionable manners, or social knowledge from anything we might expect to find "underneath" them, anything, that is, like a conscious self. The discourse of consciousness in the Wharton text makes the clothes stand for the self, and reveals the soul to be socially inscripted. An interior untouched by social codes, consciousnesses set apart as private, are suspicious categories for Wharton, challenged and unsubstantiated in her texts. Indeed, Wharton's fiction expressly demonstrates the hazards of self-consciousness for characters made up of social stuff; as such, she remains intensely skeptical of its power and its reality. Because Wharton details the "circumstances" of her characters in terms, especially, of the ubiquitous force of social class, the process by which she defines them shows precisely how they are bound. In *The Age of Innocence*, any sense of a personalized consciousness will be incorporated into society. In *The House of Mirth*, as I have argued, characters must learn to examine not their own insides, but the spectacle of women displayed around them. Since her female characters, especially, receive scrupulous training over their appearance as the only way to achieve a stronger position in society, the reader questions those rare moments when Wharton allows her characters a "voice inside" that exclaims the "real me." Indeed, the word "real" seems emptied of meaning in Wharton, leaving the reader with immense uncertainty over the status of the self in her world.

As we have seen in the previous chapters, the reversals of metaphor and method that occur within the studies of consciousness themselves—whether written by evolutionary scientist or modern novelist—all reveal this profound ambivalence about what it is that makes a conscious self. Overwhelmingly, the debate over subjectivity at the turn of the century suggests that if consciousness is to sustain one's identity, it must allow for a clear outline around the self, a citadel of one. At the same time, philosophers, sociologists, scientists, and novelists, dealing as they do in language, cannot resist the remaking of their own designs. We are as often confronted with the certainty of an authentic core for the self as we are told that the self is infused with the contents of the world in which it lives. The tensions within every account of consciousness, manifested as they are in conflicting metaphors and figures, make boundaries between public and private fluid. Still, no author in this study (including Wharton) seems ready to abandon entirely the notion that such boundaries might be maintained. The conscious self comes with a price and it is precisely in the negotiations between a self-contained existence and a profound awareness of the social implications of identity where we find Wharton's notions of consciousness evolving.

From her earliest work of nonfiction, *The Decoration of Houses* (1897), to her Pulitzer Prize-winning novel, *The Age of Innocence* (1920), Wharton's preoccupation with structural representations of interior space reveals a deep anxiety about the security of personal identity and self-consciousness. Though her language in *The Decoration of Houses* might be confined to architecture and to the design of domestic interiors, Wharton's insistence upon closed doors and properly proportioned entrances and passageways in the real world of a home informs her understanding of personal, mental "interiors." It is clear, in her book of interior design, that the treatment of openings, doorways and thresholds carries not only aesthetic importance, but also signifies social control.[7] The author that insists, in *The Decoration of Houses*, that "No room can be satisfactory unless its openings are properly placed and proportioned" and "Under ordinary circumstances doors should always be kept shut,"[8] is the same author who will recreate a world impervious to outsiders but full of permeable minds.

Indeed, through her depiction of old New York society, Wharton presents a drastically open version of interior life, a consciousness that looks like mind reading, though she also suggests that the self covets inward escape. Unlike Lily Bart, Newland Archer, the central character of *The Age of Innocence*, spends a great deal of time inside his own head. And though he does not relinquish consciousness as Lily does, neither does he gain from it as, for instance, his literary cousin Isabel Archer, does. There is no richness about consciousness in Wharton's post-war novel, no profit from it, perhaps because there is no safeguard for it. Wharton unveils the social basis of consciousness to such an extent in this novel, that minds become common texts, dangerously available for perusal. Private thoughts refuse to remain hidden, but rather, expose themselves in a language that goes beyond one mind to forge links through social and communal relations. Though it lacks the perfect symmetry of couples that *The Golden Bowl* presents, *The Age of Innocence* resembles James's later novel in its representation of consciousness as shared thinking. Wharton does not overlook the oppressiveness of such alliances, however. Maggie Verver will be granted her secret meditations as the method by which she resituates herself in the world of James's novel. Likewise, as we have seen in *The Portrait of a Lady*, Isabel Archer learns that consciousness includes the social envelope; but her vigil allows her protected mental space. For Wharton, though, the openness of the social system threatens to negate entirely any notion of an inward life, any clear sense of an individual. Newland Archer wonders at one point how the van der Luydens' "merged identities ever separated themselves enough for anything as controversial as a talking-over."[9] This merger of identity, which in the lofty van der Luydens seems haltingly complete, represents the eventual fusion of minds that a shared inner dialogue decrees. Such complete coalescence reveals the potentially stultifying effects of intimacy. Perhaps the ultimate irony of Wharton's text emerges in the conflict between a vigilant enforcement, on the part of "society," of the boundary between public and private,[10] and the inability of any character that has entered this privileged realm, to retain the sense of a personal life. The discourse of consciousness in the Wharton text thus repudiates any explicit form of self-communion for the self exists only through the realization of its role, the confirmation of its place, in society. Archer's question: "What am I?" leads him to the abrupt realization: "A son-in-law—" (1186). His identity is neither contained nor discrete; it is contingent upon his position in the family. There are moments in the novel when the self does create a private refuge, yet here it encounters either emptiness or a mere inversion (which is sometimes an exaggeration) of the social arena. We find no place in the Wharton landscape that sustains a conscious life. As Ellen Olenska—a foreigner and a perpetual outsider—comprehends penetratingly, with a laugh, there is no where in New York where one can be alone (1261).

Newland Archer longs for refuge, nonetheless, in a world of private language and the security of personal thought. In comparison to Wharton's earlier novel, *The House of Mirth*, where characters demonstrate a certain resistance to self-analysis, *The Age of Innocence* gives us characters that long for the kind of solitude that allows for personal reflection. Ellen Olenska's plaintive analysis of the "public" nature of New York society summarizes this desire. She sees that the social world can be reduced to the activities inside one house: "One can't be alone for a minute in that great seminary of a house, with all the doors wide open.... Is there nowhere in an American house where one may be by one's self?" (1120–1). In contrast, *The House of Mirth* follows Wharton's prescription for interior design: a world of closed doors: One might argue, in fact, that the novel enacts a series of enclosures that culminate inside Lily's tiny and solitary boarding house room. The irony of Wharton's early narrative, however, comes as we realize that even though Lily Bart remains a consummately closed and contained character, she does not recognize the value of her privacy. Not only does the virginal Lily rarely open herself to others, but, as Maureen Howard suggests, she also fears introspection.[11] Wharton makes clear that this consummate socialite would prefer *not* to have access to her own self: when Lily "made a tour of inspection in her own mind, there were certain closed doors she did not open."[12] If *The House of Mirth*, in this sense, shows a "closed" self, then *The Age of Innocence* makes these doors radically open.

Wharton repeatedly demonstrates the fallacy of a private, self-enclosed consciousness throughout *The Age of Innocence*, perhaps the most affecting instance of which occurs at the end of the novel. Archer learns that the terrible secret he has harbored, and that he holds inside by an "iron band" around his heart, is really no secret at all. His wife, as he discovers, had "guessed" (1299). It might be more accurate to say that he rediscovers this truth since he recognizes—earlier in the novel, at the farewell dinner for the Countess Olenska—that he is at the center of a "conspiracy" (1282). Furthermore, he suddenly sees at that point that May "shares" New York's belief that he and Ellen are lovers (1286). At the dinner party, we see a consciousness that fails to insulate the self because the mind is too accessible; the "tribe" has unlimited access to one's interior life. And yet, strangely, the "iron band," which Archer recognizes years later, seems to suggest the opposite; that is, it seems to offer Archer some form of protection, one might even say containment, for a self. The release of this fastening on his heart, therefore, seems a characteristically ambivalent gesture on Wharton's part: if it means freedom, its removal leaves him suspiciously adrift.[13]

As Archer's meditations often make clear, *The Age of Innocence* produces characters who appear to present mysterious depths compelling a keener examination than the sort of superficial self-appraisals that we see in *The House of Mirth*. Yet the two novels effectively reverse our expectations about the role of self-consciousness in the formation of subjectivity. Characters like Newland Archer, who attempt to conceal their thoughts, scrupulously cultivating their insides, end up with a public consciousness that is entirely "readable." In contrast, Lily Bart's energy radiates only outward, to her audience and to her appearance. Though she eschews self-analysis, wants to "get away from herself," prefers to "shut out consciousness," she remains, to those around her, a perverse enigma (18; 339). She is obliged to advertise herself and yet the travesty of her fate is that no one reads her right. Newland's misdirected self-investigation and Lily's reluctance to study her self have the same result. It is as if Wharton courts the desire for a rich interior, but chastises her characters for requiring it either by suggesting the precariousness of seeking such personal sanctuary or by exposing it as false.

Wharton relentlessly shows that Archer cannot have private thoughts, cannot close his consciousness to others nor protect it from some higher form of social proprietorship.[14] At first, he relishes the communication he has with his fiancée, May Welland, one that requires no unpleasant words, indeed, one that seldom requires words at all. Such habits and forms of exchange, however, establish a fierce intimacy that conducts Archer and May through a network of social associations beyond their control. When Archer precipitates the announcement of his engagement, he has only to look at May for her to decipher his intention:

> [H]is eyes met Miss Welland's and he saw that she had instantly understood his motive.... The persons of their world lived in an atmosphere of faint implications and pale delicacies, and the fact that he and she understood each other without a word seemed to the young man to bring them nearer than any explanation would have done. (1027–8)

Wharton more famously refers to this type of language as "hieroglyphic" where "the real thing was never said or done or even thought, but only represented by a set of arbitrary signs" (1050).[15] Though Archer here celebrates this inconspicuous form of communication because it brings him "nearer" to his fiancée, in time, he reverses his judgment of May. That same ability he has to read her thoughts eventually fills him "with a secret dismay."[16] Archer laments the very fact of his wife's accessibility: "never in all the years to come, would she surprise him by an unexpected mood, by a new idea, a weakness, a cruelty or an emotion" (1250). Wharton, of course, shows Archer's blindness on this point. What's more, she continually exposes him as a poor reader of women.[17] Consequently, as critics have often suggested, she invites further investigation into the mysteries behind May's blushes. What is disturbing, however, is that Wharton also allows us to read May's thoughts—unchallenged—through *Archer's* consciousness, emphasizing the exactitude of the rules with which they communicate. Wharton delivers an entire monologue—a "mute message" as she calls it— in May's voice. But it is Archer who is given the authority to tell the reader what she "means" (1227). Of course, as I have been suggesting, Wharton overturns consciousness in this novel so that its contents are no longer personal property. Archer does not possess the power to narrate the story of the novel;[18] but he does, at least initially, participate in the communal consciousness of the organism that is New York. We are meant to understand that Archer can "hear" May precisely because she has been trained out of any sort of individuality. Her message follows standard code. What Archer does not see is that he too remains open for the same sort of decoding. The paradox of this permeability of consciousness is, of course, that it destroys rather than nurtures intimacy. The possibility, then, for meaningful relationship, for mutual exchange, disappears.

Archer has no difficulty receiving or relaying the voice of the family—which is identical to the voice of New York—as the novel opens. He understands unspoken signals, such as the "particular curve" of his mother's eyebrows that reminds him to keep silent before the butler (1047). He recognizes distinctions, as only one of his set would, like the difference between being "merely a Duke and being the van der Luyden's Duke" (1064). And though he strays from the family in his ideas about the Countess's marriage, when he meets her alone to deliver his opinions, he finds himself speaking, "in a voice that sounded in his ears like Mr. Letterblair's," about the ruling forces of New York society (1103). Indeed, the Countess's response, "that's what my family tell me," implies that there is no other answer Archer could make (1104). We see Archer's repeated attempts to "strike out" for himself—words that he uses to convince May to hasten their marriage—each met with a countermove that suggests the impossibility of original thought (1081–2). His mother assumes, for instance, as the controversy over the Countess's behavior heightens, that he "sees only the Mingott side" (1086). Aligned with a larger body, Archer's participation in the consciousness of the clan appears explicit and definitive. Moreover, it appears to obliterate any chance that he might think something like his own thoughts. Possibilities for communication and self-communion, dependent as they are on notions of private and public space, become dubious categories in the Wharton novel. As I have noted in the previous chapter, even in its drive for closure, *The House of Mirth* refuses to settle upon a singular conception of consciousness or of the self. *The Age of Innocence*, likewise, unsettles us, though Wharton appears, in her images of open doors and accessible minds, to be considering the possibility of transcending personal consciousness.

Though Archer might misread the thoughts and motivations of the characters (in particular, the women) around him, he provides, as often, a fascinating look at the competing theories of consciousness and selfhood that operate in the text. When Newland attempts to understand Ellen Olenska's "mysterious faculty of suggesting tragic and moving possibilities," he idealizes her character, explicitly romanticizes her past, and attempts to classify her.[19] At the same time, he also speculates more broadly on the origins of identity. Since the term "faculty" suggests both the natural abilities of an organism, such as seeing or hearing, as well as skills derived from practice or habit, Archer initially leaves open the "tragic possibilities" of the Countess as either inherent or learned. Wharton's attention here to the language of evolution, like the many anthropological allusions in the text, gets somewhat convoluted in Archer's mind.[20] As his reading continues, though, he specifies his interpretation in order to locate, as it were, the essence of the Countess: "Archer had always been inclined to think that chance and circumstance played a small part in shaping people's lots compared with their innate tendency to have things happen to them." Madame Olenska, as he says in the same context, "had hardly ever said a word to him to produce this impression, but it was a part of her" (1107). Here circumstances, behavior and social situation all become irrelevant for a woman whose "innate tendency" occasions the dramatic. Wharton uses words such as "innate" and "inherently" to replace Archer's earlier ambivalence regarding Ellen's "faculties" and, consequently, underscores his gloss over the woman whom he calls "quiet, almost passive" (1107). Perhaps more important than Newland's inability to see Ellen as an agent in her own life is the fact that he represents, even in his sentimentalized portrayal, a crucial division in the understanding of personal identity. Archer believes the self to be defined by inborn qualities, not by circumstances or experiences, nor social environment. Certainly, *he* "produces" this elaborate impression of an essentially dramatic woman. And while Wharton may satirize Archer's limited views of identity as an inherent commodity in favor of a socialized self, she will allow Ellen an unqualified moment of self-reliance, indicating the tantalizing possibility of a sustaining interior life.

Readers of *The Age of Innocence* who want to recover the power of women in the novel often lose track of the passionate attachment that Ellen expresses for Archer.[21] In fact, she acknowledges Newland as *the* source of her newfound knowledge. Given the extensive cultural capital that the Countess has gained from her time abroad, it seems strange that Archer, hemmed in as he is, would have something of value to give to the Countess Olenska. Indeed, Wharton represents Ellen's knowledge (intellectual, cultural, relational) as vastly exceeding Archer's. But the sort of knowledge that Archer provides is knowledge that she appears never to have encountered—knowledge that, we are to understand, nourishes the self. After their first, mutual confession of feeling, where Ellen pronounces that she "cannot love" Newland unless she "gives [him] up" (1153), she consoles herself with this thought: "I shan't be lonely now. I was lonely; I was afraid. But the emptiness and the darkness are gone; when I turn back into myself now I'm like a child going at night into a room where there's always light" (1153). The Countess first notes that Archer possesses his knowledge because he has learned to resist the "temptation" of what lies beyond the calm order of New York; thus he has shown her something better than "the things [the world] asks of one"—"better," she exclaims, "than anything I've known" (1152). That Archer's rejection, as she names it, of the "world outside" should motivate the Countess to "turn back into [her]self" seems a peculiar lesson indeed, considering that Archer is rarely allowed that inner refuge himself. Nevertheless, Wharton's suggestion here of an interior life that one might choose in lieu of the surrounding world separates and individuates a self. There appears to be so clear a distinction between inner and outer worlds that turning away from the worldly "tug" (1152) necessarily means "turning into" a self.

Archer listens uncomprehendingly to Ellen's valiant speech outlining her new mode of self-reliance. In fact, Wharton tells us repeatedly that Archer cannot "understand" Ellen, nor can she understand him (1148; 1152; 1153). Archer finds that the Countess's inward retreat "envelops her in a soft inaccessibility" (1153); and though Ellen maintains the boundary between them for reasons of sexual propriety, it is clear that Archer has become unaccustomed to anything like a closed consciousness in others. Though he may inspire the Countess to embrace what she has "never known before" (1152), he does not, himself, register the impact of her words. Turning inward, Ellen suggests a desire to transcend the social world even while the text maintains the impossibility of such a gesture. Moreover, the novel may very well suggest that transcendence for female characters can come about only as a result of transgression.[22] But the Countess has already been "beyond" (1246), and she recognizes that such excesses do not enrich the self. She has paid a high price for stepping outside New York's circle, yet she declines participation in its social game. When Ellen assumes an interior for the self, an inner room "where there's always light," she reinvents Emersonian transcendence by bringing it indoors. She does not enter the woods, nor does she come anywhere near transparency; instead, Wharton seems to accentuate her opacity as a way to retain an individualized consciousness even in the wake of social forces. The Countess embraces a self that carries its own light, though she must explicitly turn inward in order to preserve it.[23]

The problem, however, in reading the Countess's words as an instance of heightened selfhood is that most attempts to hold on to a personal, inward cache in this novel receive ambivalent or blatantly ironic treatment from Wharton. If the novel concedes to a self, it is a self with fluid boundaries, saturated with the contents of the social world. Perhaps the most vivid instance of Wharton's skepticism over an autonomous self in this novel comes in the philosophy of Dr. Carver, founder of the Valley of Love. Wharton plays on the language of nineteenth-century mysticism and mesmerism, both of which William James and Alfred Russel Wallace combined, to the chagrin of their colleagues, with their more "legitimate" studies of consciousness and mental life.[24] Such forays into pseudo-science, represented by Agathon Carver in *The Age of Innocence*, become comical, and as backward as the Gothic script on his calling card. Through her amusing depiction of a man who has made the "illuminating discovery of the Direct Contact" (1141)—with what, we don't know—Wharton aligns herself with scientists, most of whom dismissed popular seances and spiritual communication. She thus presents Dr. Carver, who lives, as Medora Manson reports, "only in the life of the spirit" (1141), conducts "inner thought" meetings (1180), and calls upon the spirit to "List—oh, list!" where it will (1141), as a farcical representative of the discourse of consciousness. When Medora tells her niece, Ellen, that she has received a "spiritual summons" (1147) to be with Dr. Carver, the Marchioness Manson seems, quite absurdly, to represent the flip side of that communal consciousness set on keeping the social order of old New York. Despite all signs of Dr. Carver and Medora's fatuity, though, Wharton will not dismiss completely their brand of spiritualism. Dr. Carver provides, at any rate, something like William James's answer to questions about consciousness in resorting to ephemeral language. When the doctor calls upon the "spirit" to go where it will, he exposes the openness of a system where our "inner thoughts," if we are in tune with such movements, actually resist closure. And if we take "list" to mean harken or attend then his words quite cunningly suggest that survival in a social system such as New York's, relies upon shrewd attention to what is happening around oneself. Outward observance, not inward attention, is the rule. Consequently, though his rhetoric shows inconsistencies, it appears, finally, to indicate a lack of containment for anything associated with the self. He also stands as an alternative to the "blind conformity to tradition" that the novel decries; indeed, his brand of spirituality requires, as the Countess remarks with interest, "all sorts of new and crazy social schemes" (1206).

Ridiculous as he is, Dr. Carver reveals "inner thought" and social action to be inseparable. And perhaps Wharton means for this to be the lesson, as it were, of the novel. Archer will come to understand this, even in his small way, since he does his part in the State Assembly and becomes a sort of locus for social change in his community (1290–1). However, Archer's resistance, throughout most of the novel, his sense that an inner life counts for more, plagues *The Age of Innocence*, continually teasing us with the anticipation of a deeply fulfilling, interior reality. The persistence of the word "real" in Wharton's fiction—one that appears to resist even the most caustic irony on her part—suggests that we might locate an authentic language precisely through the intersection of society and soul. As easy as it is to caricature Archer's quest for transcendence, Wharton continually comes round to the idea, revealing her reluctance to abandon entirely the notion of interiority as a model for subjectivity. Though modern readers have little sympathy for Archer's melodramatic sense that he has missed "the flower of life" (1291), we hold fast to the belief that Ellen Olenska saves something of herself when she removes to Paris. And while we might note Wharton's reversal of certain assumptions about gender—as Marilyn Chandler suggests, she places Archer as the figure trapped in domestic life, a position usually assigned to a female character—it is difficult to know whether this means we might somehow redeem her hero.[25] I have suggested that Wharton appears to allow Ellen a kind of retreat inside herself, one for which, in her mind, she is indebted to Archer. Indeed, the Countess becomes more and more closed even as she enters deeper into New York society. Newland suffers long spells without gaining access to her thoughts, and certainly he never "understands" her as he does one of his own kind. Nor does the reader necessarily. If Ellen indulges in meditative vigils, we are not privy to them. If she takes pains to analyze the messages sent to her by May, or the rest of the family, the reader never knows. We hear simply that Ellen "understands," as May tells her husband, "everything" (1275), a sweeping rhetorical acknowledgment on Wharton's part that is reminiscent of Henry James. But if Ellen understands "everything," Archer seems to understand "nothing." Accordingly, as the novel progresses, he loses his place within the communal mind of New York. As our center of consciousness, he may well be a miserable failure since he cannot read the Countess's gestures and stands paralyzed in the face of his wife's "secret hopes" (1186). What's more, he persists in the fantasy that he might be free of the social forces that make him who he is, all of which unravel before the reader, exposing Archer to our sympathy or our judgment. May's secrets may be deep, but it is the Countess whose privacy— culminating when she returns the key to her potential lover (1278)—closes her off entirely.[26] Though readers of *The Age of Innocence* might imagine that Ellen's withdrawal to some inner space could be more appealing than the restriction that New York offers, Wharton does not let us indulge in such romance. Elizabeth Ammons regards Ellen as a "New Woman," defined by her independence of thought and her desire for freedom, though, unhappily, rejected by America.[27] But such interpretations rely upon privileging the individual over the community—a complicated gesture in the Wharton text. The individual, in Wharton, is never completely free. Indeed, the Countess, of all people, understands that social relations as well as the community that she inhabits shape her identity. Though Ellen eventually lives alone in Paris, she remains linked to New York not only through the support of her grandmother's trust (1278), but also through the parental role she assumes with the more gently transgressive Fanny Beaufort (Archer's future daughter-in-law), a role that brings her connection to the family full circle.

Wharton may be looking with irony at old New York society, but she is also looking with nostalgia.[28] She will not go so far as to suggest that one can live without social forms.

Archer attempts such a life. Because he feels constrained by society, he desires complete removal from it.[29] Yet Wharton makes the idea of his removal inconceivable. Though Archer so often seeks a sequestered place— a place where he might live and breathe a different "air" than what New York manufactures; a "country" where he might indulge in a relationship otherwise considered illegitimate (1245); any other place, "other houses, roofs, chimneys ... the sense of other lives outside his own" (1250)— Wharton reveals the emptiness of this rhetoric at each instance. There is no such country, and Archer has grown accustomed to New York ways, so much so that were he to enter an atmosphere "less crystalline," he would find it "stifling" (1091); he would literally be unable to breathe. What's more, even an escape "inside himself" does not yield the privacy that he fancies. The most elaborately personalized "place" to which Archer retires does appear, at first, to be protected space. But the novel undermines the security of Archer's privacy even as he believes himself to be indulging in it.

> [H]e had built up within himself a kind of sanctuary in which she throned among his secret thoughts and longings. Little by little it became the scene of his real life, of his only rational activities; thither he brought the books he read, the ideas and feelings that nourished him, his judgments and his visions. (1224)

Wharton explicitly creates this space "within" Archer, hinting that he has, in fact, acquired a consciousness that is private. The sanctuary becomes a sort of glorified inward library full of sentimentalized visions that arise out of the books he has read.[30] Newland, in one memorable instance, enhances this feeling of enclosure as he follows the image of the Countess inside the "enchanted pages" of a volume of verse by Rossetti appropriately called "The House of Life" (1125).[31] And though Archer might be content remaining in this sacred place, Wharton makes clear that he will do so at the expense of his existence. Closed doors in *The Age of Innocence* do not provide privacy so much as they signify annihilation, as when Archer feels, with a "deathly sense," "the doors of the family vault" closing in on him (1283).

Though he positions the Countess securely on a throne inside his head, Newland loses his own footing in the outside world, as Pamela Knights convincingly argues, moving about "with a growing sense of unreality," startled to find that anyone "imagines" he is actually there (1224).[32] More importantly, if thinking of the Countess appears, in one electric episode, to produce the inner sanctuary for Newland, elsewhere when he thinks of her, his mind literally empties out. This split in the manifestation of his consciousness reveals the trouble Archer has in holding on to any definitive self: is his interior a sanctuary (replete with images for worship) or a vacuum? Occupied with his familiar routines, he can indulge in the security of an identity anchored by habit, where his daily activity serves as a "link with his former self" (1178). But even that sense of a "former" self indicates a splintering that Archer has yet to come to terms with, mostly because he clings to the idea of the mind as the stronghold for a singular self, a notion that Wharton's text disputes. When reflections of Ellen "[make] of his mind a rather empty and echoing place," or an interior with reckless, slamming doors (1179–80), we begin to see the price that Archer will pay for his refuge. At Newport, surrounded by people alive to the business of socializing, Archer seems distinctly out of place; to him the activity appears shocking "as if they had been children playing in a grave-yard" (1179). As Newland experiences the evacuation of his mind, he reads the world around him as an inversion of the dead space inside him. Social activity, significantly, appears to desecrate that hallowed ground.

In a scene that sheds light on the nature of his sanctuary, Archer attempts to create another private space for himself—not a mental space, this time, but a physical space—in the real world of his home. The moment comes after the farewell dinner for Ellen, an event that forces upon Archer, "in a vast flash," his position in "the centre of countless silently observing eyes and patiently listening ears" (1282). Wharton tells us, quite plainly, "[H]e had come up to the library and shut himself in" (1287). Taking the sentence out of context, however, occludes the clever placement of the action and the fact that Wharton encompasses Newland's reclusive moment, literally, inside an intrusion. The rupture to the fantasy of an enclosed self, a break that comes about after he is reminded of the tribe that rules his life, is rendered quite subtly here. Though it has the character of a stage direction, we hear of Newland's position as if it were an afterthought. That is, Wharton does not set the scene with his attempt to absent himself, but, rather, with May's assertion of her presence. Indeed, we do not even observe Newland alone until May enters, and revokes his privacy. Wharton begins her scene with May's abrupt question, spoken "from the threshold of the library," a question that "rouses him with a start." May's voice precipitates the action. So immediately we see that Archer cannot "shut himself in," that such a motion seems incongruous from the start, given May's appearance. Newland's wife stands at the entryway of his room, unbeknownst to him and eventually enters his library, a space clearly designated as his personal chamber. Wharton's meticulous attention to the purpose of doors in *The*

Decoration of Houses is instructive here. In detailing the terms for home design, Wharton repeatedly laments the "absence of privacy in modern houses," offering a critique of domestic life along with her assessment of interiors.

> [E]ach room in a house has its individual uses: some are made to sleep in, others are for dressing, eating, study, or conversation; but whatever the uses of a room, they are seriously interfered with if it be not preserved as a small world by itself.[33]

The door, of course, is what "preserves" the integrity of the room, specifically by making its boundaries distinct. However, Wharton makes clear that Newland cannot keep this room closed off from outside intrusion.[34] We learn in the final chapter of the novel that Archer's library is "the room in which most of the real things of his life had happened" (1289). Wharton accompanies that statement with a list of occurrences such as birth announcements, engagements, christenings, pre-wedding arrangements, career discussions, a child's first step and first words, indicating that the library has lost its "individual," sacred purpose. The room no longer stands as its own little world, a place with one distinct "use," because it must contain all of Archer's worlds.

To return to the previous scene of May's interruption, we see, then, the futility of Archer's attempt to "shut himself in" this room or anywhere, even though it is designated as "his." We wonder, even, if this room has a door since May's voice opens the scene and obliterates any illusion of privacy that Archer might maintain.[35] May does, as we see, request permission to enter this space that Archer has declared as his own—a room he can furnish and decorate as he pleases—but Archer cannot keep intimacy with himself even here. The scene, in fact, carries on with the progressive encroachment of his wife who ends up "warmly and fragrantly hovering over him" (303). What "shuts" Archer in, is, of course, the news of May's pregnancy, a fact that makes public their intimacy. In approaching the threshold of his study, May refuses Archer the closed consciousness that he so desperately seeks; that is, her opening question acts as a transgression, a breach in the circle that Archer has tried to draw around himself. It is significant that May asks, ultimately, as she breaks the news that they are to have a child, " 'You didn't guess—?' " (1288). May assumes that Archer has read the signs—her fatigue, her languid attitude (1248), a face "paler than usual" (1266), perhaps even her "unnatural vividness" (1266)—and conjectured that she is pregnant. She assumes, in short, and thereby almost succeeds in redeeming, the shared inner dialogue with which they began their courtship. Hence her penetrating look into her husband's eyes, to which Archer uncomfortably submits, before he "turns" his own eyes away: "he felt that his wife was watching him intently" (1288). In this sense, May's oft-mentioned "transparent eyes" may indicate the sacrifice of her own privacy, her vigilant attempt to maintain a joint consciousness with her husband at the expense of a closed interior.[36]

Despite May's attempts to keep communion with her husband, Archer loses his ability, or rather, relinquishes his capacity to participate in the consciousness of New York. Yet the novel asserts that his position inside this social repository must be maintained. He must, it seems, empty himself out in order to remain a viable participant in the community. Like William James's receptacle "in which, through which, and over which minds join,"[37] and the imaginary conversations that govern *The Golden Bowl*, the consciousness that Wharton's novel establishes requires attention to social forces as the only way to retain a self. It is a disquieting lesson for the twentieth-century American novel, given our culture's commitment to debased versions of Emersonian individualism.[38] Society may reclaim Archer's thoughts as public, not personal, property; but the process is a vexed one in the Wharton novel. The contortions acted out on the psyche—and sometimes the body—of her main character as he tries to make his inner world "real" reflect the friction within Wharton's imagination of the novel: is it founded on society or the soul? We diminish Wharton's project as a writer when we abandon the more elusive part of this theory; as Carol Singley suggestively argues, Wharton is a writer not only of society but also of spirit.[39] And yet, Wharton herself continually challenges the possibility that the spirit or inwardness might be viable categories for identity. More specifically, she questions whether such categories are "real."

Wharton both deploys and disables the discourse of realism as it applies to interior life. Certainly, Newland Archer's confusion over the "real" reflects his growing detachment from the society that sustains him. Moving back and forth, for instance, between the scene with the Countess by the shore and the view of May "sitting under the shameless Olympians and glowing with secret hopes" (1186), Archer enacts a dizzying series of reversals about "reality" that continue until the final chapter of the novel. The resonance of the word "real" in this text, reminiscent of the meditation on the "real" self I have examined in *The House of Mirth*, underscores the preoccupation Wharton has with questions of identity and existence. As difficult as it is to pin down Archer's perception of what is "real," given his desperate vacillations between the dream world and reality, it is precisely those vacillations that make evident the complications of Wharton's project for the conscious self. If the discourse of consciousness, in some respects, replaces religious discourse in its search for authentic self-expression, interior dimensions of human character, and the experience of the soul, there is something imperative about keeping this language elusive. The problem, of course, is that Wharton and her contemporaries distrust the capacity of language to represent experience; authors of consciousness want to cultivate language's creative capacity without entirely losing control over it. With this in mind, perhaps we might consider Wharton's continual refuge in the word "real"—"real people," "real things," "real self," "real life," "the last shadow of reality"—as more than irony. Perhaps Wharton's relentless repetition of the term shows a desire to maintain some control over language, to rein in the capacity for words to mean too many things. Wharton recognizes, certainly, the various inversions of meaning that language undergoes, inversions that become heightened in the face of the division between personal and social life. Claire Preston suggests that this linguistic demarcation in Wharton's fiction "represents an impoverishment of vocabulary, in which the opposite of a thing is formulated merely as its own cancellation."[40] In these moments, words continually—almost automatically—turn inside out. The notion of reality, then, becomes fluid intimating that an exchange between the two worlds may be the crux of identity. Staring at Ellen, waiting for her to turn to him, Archer is suddenly confronted with the sense that this vision is only a "dream"; "reality" awaits him with May and a family ruled by clocks and dinners. But once Newland enters the Welland house, the "density" of the atmosphere, the overt luxury of its "heavy carpets," the "stack of cards and invitations"—all signs of the influx of the social world—make that life the "unreal" one. And the brief scene on the shore, significantly, becomes "as close to him as the blood in his veins" (1187–8). He transposes these scenes, in other words, resisting the pull of the social world, so that the episode he reconstructs, the image he holds of the Countess, literally enters into him, and becomes an interiorized reality.

Archer's desire to make the life inside his consciousness the only "reality," his attempts to keep the social world as remote as a backdrop, come through most powerfully in his impulsive visit to the remote cottage at Skuytercliff, where the van der Luydens have taken Ellen on "retreat." When Archer decides to meet the Countess, he is deceived into thinking that he will find a deeper intimacy with her, perhaps even with himself, here. Their encounter begins, after all, with a flirtatious sense of mind reading where Ellen confesses she "knew" he'd come (1120). Though Wharton rewrites that confident communication a moment later when they each declare they cannot speak the other's language (1120). Wharton seems to assign Ellen a more penetrating vision since she sees that no house in America affords a spot for seclusion: one is perpetually "on stage" in its society (1121), a metaphor that suggests one might be one's "real" self if only some private space could be found. Newland does not deny or defend what Ellen calls the "public" nature of New York; instead, he takes recourse in the fantasy that the van der Luyden's Patroon house, unlocked only for the day, will provide a thoroughly private moment for them. And Ellen too, after all, "ran away" to this place, indicating that she conceives of it as an escape ("I feel myself safe here" [1116])[41] despite her keen awareness of the openness of American society. Newland indulges in extremes, however. He believes they have found a "secret room" (1122) that might protect and conceal them, and insofar as the room stands for the self, he hopes it will contain the feelings he struggles to articulate. The house, as he sees it, waits expressly for him and Ellen, "as if magically created to receive them" (1121). And here, Wharton's language collapses into vagueness: "if the thing was to happen, it was to happen in this way, with the whole width of the room between them, and his eyes still fixed on the outer snow" (1122). The "thing" most likely is the Countess's motion toward an embrace that Newland imagines, that he "almost" hears; and, arguably, the vagueness is all his. But the fact that Wharton keeps this thing unnamed preserves the sense that the deepest imaginings, the most real moments, defeat our powers of description. The immediacy of Archer's feeling where "soul and body [throb] with the miracle to come" (1122) utterly bursts, of course, at the sight of Julius Beaufort. Newland's dramatic gesture in "throwing open the door of the house" (1122), therefore, appears ridiculous. The society that they suppose they have left looms in the snow-covered shelter of the Patroon house. Even the most exclusive, the most secluded houses, Wharton suggests, cannot secure intimacy.

Though Skuytercliff appears to offer the possibility of "escape" from the social world to a safer spot, a place where, as the Countess remarks, they might have a "quiet talk" (1121), Beaufort's entrance, with the din of New York at his heels, closes the gap between public and private space to the point of obliteration. It is no surprise, then, that Beaufort's interruption should carry them into a conversation about the telephone, a technology that requires directness of communication and, as Wharton shows in the final chapter, makes evasion nearly impossible.[42] Certainly, in a novel that turns upon calculated ellipses, punctuated silences, "implication and analogy" (1282), conversation becomes a valuable commodity. Archer esteems good conversation such as the kind he finds with Ned Winsett; it allows him, the narrator tells us, to "take the measure of his own life" (1114). And he seems quite moved by the talk he has with the French tutor, Monsieur Rivière, especially by the idea of "intellectual liberty" that he details when they first meet. "[I]t's worth everything, isn't it, to keep one's intellectual liberty, not to enslave one's powers of appreciation, one's critical independence?" (1174).

Rivière tells Archer that he left journalism in order to "preserve" his "moral freedom," a concept that is directly linked to his ability, as it were, to "speak" his mind. Elaborating on the notion of moral freedom, "what we call in French one's *quant a soi*," the Frenchman tells Archer, "when one hears good talk one can join in it without compromising any opinions but one's own; or one can listen, and answer it inwardly. Ah good conversation—there's nothing like it, is there?" (1174). The sense that one can "preserve" one's freedom by choosing when and what to speak; that one might "answer inwardly" without compromising oneself, works against the transparency of mind that the social world of New York dictates. In that respect, it is remarkably "foreign." We see, in the way that Archer is immediately drawn to the notions of the Frenchman, the allure of a mind that can open or close itself; that can speak for itself. Like the French phrase, *quant a soi*, which indicates guardedness or a desire not to be read, Rivière's speech oddly shows self-protection as the ultimate form of personal freedom. And we might assume, since this inspiring speech comes from the voice of a writer who affirms the importance of "critical independence," that Wharton would endorse such a mode of life. What is troubling about it, however, is how quickly we learn that Monsieur Rivière is far from independent. The limitations placed upon him by his social position seriously interfere with the authority he derives from his free mind. Indeed, he confesses, in this same conversation, that the idea of ending his days living in a garret is "chilling to the imagination." Social class, which relegates the Frenchman to the garret, invariably infringes upon—that is, literally diminishes—the space in which he can circulate. What's more, it hints at a lifeless existence for him or at least a deadening of that which he most reveres: the imagination. When Rivière shows up later in the novel, as Count Olenski's messenger, we see the effects of his limited power. He comes, literally, to speak for the Count. The moment he speaks for *himself* (in a conversation that reveals to Archer how far removed *he* is from the family negotiations), Rivière sacrifices his position (1218). Furthermore, as Medora Manson assures Archer, the home that the Countess abandoned, in addition to its material opulence, has "brilliant conversation" (1143), making the value of such talk immediately suspect.

Wharton constructs an open consciousness in this book, but communication falters nonetheless, partly because it is difficult to know what kind of "talk" to trust in *The Age of Innocence*. There is little room for meditation, for something like a self talking to itself, in the strained world that Wharton presents. It is telling that when such inner conversations do occur, they often consist in "conjectures" about the thoughts or actions of another, a gesture that inevitably brings minds closer together. When Archer wonders, at one point, what has been keeping his wife, he finds such guesswork allows him to enter yet another mind, her father's: "He had fallen into the way of dwelling on such conjectures as a means of tying his thoughts fast to reality. Sometimes he felt as if he had found the clue to his father-in-law's absorption in trifles; perhaps even Mr. Welland, long ago, had had escapes and visions" (1248). Archer's consciousness here aligns itself with Mr. Welland's, through their mutual "absorption." More specifically, Newland's speculations about the contents of another man's mind afford a distinct link between his thoughts and another's, a sort of mental cross-checking that keeps this society orderly. The mind, thus defined by its relations, is never independent or autonomous. Thoughts of May lead Newland to thoughts of his father-in-law in an unstinting logic that reveals the impossibility of escaping some collective social accord. Newland, as we have seen, strains to remove himself from this system of shared thinking; he perhaps senses that such an order not only obliterates privacy, but also threatens to erase all difference, as if his inner life were automatically to duplicate his father-in-law's. After all, Archer recognizes with exasperation how May begins "to humour him like a younger Mr. Welland" (1227). May's gestures to "relegate" him to "the category of unreasonable husbands" (1187) certainly correspond as rigidly to Newland's insistence on making his wife represent a "type rather than a person" (1164). Identity, constructed in these instances through strict classification, becomes distinctly homogeneous, repetitious even, as if to suggest that there are only so many "types" society knows. Hence the exigency of Newland's wish to operate outside the "silent organization" that holds his world together (1285), a wish significantly figured as an attempt to move beyond "inarticulateness."

Finding agency apart from the clan proves difficult for the characters inside the "powerful engine" that is New York (1074). Archer realizes during his encounter with Ellen in Boston, that to remove himself from the communal consciousness he must withstand an interruption, a gap between thought and articulation, that literally disables his voice. "[H]e really had no idea what he was saying: he felt as if he were shouting at her across endless distances" (1198). Though Wharton configures Newland's detachment in the melodramatic tropes of flustered and frustrated courtship, she also suggests that consciousness, as one's relation to oneself, gets profoundly severed here. The voice, as one vehicle for self-expression, falters when divorced from communal utterance. Archer resists the only form of consciousness endorsed by his society; that is, he attempts to extricate himself from it, retreating to his "sanctuary," hiding in May's brougham, flitting off to Boston, tucking himself away in his library, meeting the Countess secretly in the museum. He even dreams, as he tells May, of going "ever so far off—away from everything"—to Japan (1287–8). What he finds, as a result of all his maneuvers, is a self divided against itself. Wharton explicitly configures this division as an estrangement of voice: he seems to be speaking "a strange language" (1198); "he could not trust himself to speak" (1218); "the sound of his voice echoed uncannily" (1273); "he could not find his voice" (1274). Moreover, Newland hears other voices without recognizing their meaning or being able to identify them; the talk, at the final dinner party for Ellen, sweeps past him "like some senseless river running and running because it did not know enough to stop" (1285). Similarly, he does not recognize Countess Olenska's voice when he contrives to meet her in Boston, despite his habit of lingering over images of her. "The words hardly reached him: he was aware only of her voice, and of the startling fact that not an echo of it had remained in his memory" (1199).

Though the novel advances toward a virtual depletion of the inner life—we continually witness its absorption, its consumption, by the public world—the great leap in the final chapter over twenty-six years appears to open up a space for private reflection. It is difficult to know how to read this motion, however, considering the exhaustive gestures of the rest of the narrative, which work against any notion of authentic self-expression, any "inner voice" or "real me." Still, at the close of this novel, we find Archer in his library, in the midst of solitary contemplation. Wharton highlights this seclusion through contrast: Archer has just returned from a crowd—"the throng of fashion" (1289)—that has been circulating through the galleries of the Museum, and that seems to represent the society from which he has long wished to extricate himself. Yet the associations that visit him in his library do not exactly ground him, or stabilize his identity; they seem rather strangely to dislodge him. Newland remains metaphorically suspended while he reviews his past: "There are moments when a man's imagination, so easily subdued to what it lives in, suddenly rises above its daily level, and surveys the long windings of destiny. Archer hung there and wondered...." (1294; ellipsis original). This is not the first time we've witnessed Archer in this odd state. At the bon voyage dinner for the Countess, he appears to be "float[ing] somewhere between chandelier and ceiling"; Wharton calls this condition "imponderability" (1282), thus disabling Newland's consciousness and making him decidedly unable to think. The gesture toward suspension is not unlike the indefinite closure that Wharton achieves in *The House of Mirth*. An ellipsis, similarly, keeps Lily "hanging." Even *before* she finds a certain mental hiatus with the sleeping drug, Lily imagines herself in limbo, detached from all that is real: "But this was the verge of delirium ... she had never hung so near the dizzy brink of the unreal" (339). The difference is that Lily stands at the edge of an abyss while Archer's position—in the final chapter at least—allows him to rise above what he has been used to seeing. Precarious as this dangling state might be, the repeated use of the ellipsis interestingly indicates that it is also nonverbal. Wharton thereby echoes a prevailing sentiment regarding the inadequacy of language among writers seeking to define a conscious self. Words cannot authentically translate the experience of Archer's "wondering" or Lily's "delirium" because there is no language equivalent to the varied manifestations of consciousness.

The picture of Archer's imagination "rising" and hanging above its daily level literalizes the idea of the "free mind" that Monsieur Rivière pronounces in the text. As we have seen, it is a displacement that brings with it an exacting cost. When the mind lifts itself beyond "what it lives in," it may acquire proportionate moral elevation; but it seems clear that one cannot remain long in such a pendulous state. In his Preface to *The American*, Henry James addresses this idea of "experience liberated, so to speak; experience disengaged, disembroiled, disencumbered, exempt from the conditions that we usually know to attach to it." James explicitly states that such a model allows one to operate in a medium that relieves experience of its "relations"; but the balloon of experience, as James describes it, belongs to the realm of romance, a mode that he realizes crept into his narrative unawares.[43] The Wharton novel strains against realism but will not abandon it for romance.[44] Wharton cannot fully endorse a self apart from "relations," yet her multiple ellipses (there are seven) in the final chapter suggest her fascination with the gaps that such a self might fill.

Archer alights from his suspended condition, as it were, in Paris. And perhaps the foreignness of this place along with the fact that he is accompanied by a son untrained in the old ways, "unconscious of what was going on in his father's mind" (1299), allows him to move beyond the claustrophobic compass of New York. But his decision not to enter the Countess's home; his belief that uncertainty is equivalent to passion ("Only, I wonder—the thing one's so certain of in advance: can it ever make one's heart beat as wildly?" [1296]), like his sense that "thinking over a pleasure to come" gives a "subtler satisfaction than its realization" (1018) shows a perverse desire to remain in the suspended state, to make that anticipatory condition the whole reality. "'It's more real to me here than if I went up,' he suddenly heard himself say; and the fear lest that last shadow of reality should lose its edge kept him rooted to his seat" (1302). As opposed to the closing moments of *The House of Mirth* (rendered not through *Lily's* voice, but via a narrative voice), this moment delivers Archer's vision in Archer's spoken words. Such a maneuver on Wharton's part has prompted many readers to divert any ambivalence regarding the potential for authentic inner reality onto Archer. As such, Archer is either a victim of society's constraints or a victim of his own constrained vision.[45] But the ambivalence is also

Wharton's. For a novel intensely devoted to transparency of consciousness, this final moment, showing characters entirely closed off from one another's thoughts appears to enact a strange reversal.

While reading Wharton's fiction through the facts of her biography is a tricky business, we might learn something by paying attention to the figurative language she employs across genres. It seems important, at this juncture, to remember that she fills *A Backward Glance* with references to "inner voices," "real" selves, the "acquisition" of her "real personality," the discovery of "authentic human nature," the "inmost self," and her "inner world," all terms which it seems clear she intends without irony.[46] Indeed, these references make for some of the most deeply felt emotion in the text, a response that Wharton appears quite self-consciously to invite. At the same time, she records entirely unsentimental examples of her keen critical eye, like her earnest inquiry to Henry James about the characters inside his *Golden Bowl*. Disturbed by what she sees as a lack of "atmosphere" in James's late novels, the sense that they are "more and more severed from that thick nourishing human air in which we all live and move," she approaches James with this "preoccupation." "I one day said to him: 'What was your idea in suspending the four principle characters in 'The Golden Bowl' in the void? What sort of life did they lead when they were not watching each other ...? Why have you stripped them of all the *human fringes* we necessarily trail after us through life?'"[47] Wharton's language in both instances reveals, with characteristic sharpness, a theory of consciousness remarkably balanced on its edge. The "human fringe," which we trail behind us, itself an echo of William James's language for consciousness, seems to spill from us despite our efforts to contain ourselves. And it is for Wharton material indispensable to fiction. At the same time, as we see penetratingly, even poignantly in *A Backward Glance*, she will not abandon the possibility that language can render authentically some core of the self that she alternately names the soul, the inner life or one's *real* self. Though she could imagine the "suspended" existence, Wharton will not attempt to sustain it in the way she sees James's fiction uncomfortably poised. But it is really the same anxiety over language, over the central question of translating one's conscious life into words, that brings Wharton and James to linguistic "suspension." Both authors, writing as they do at the intersection of society and selfhood, struggle to find a language adequate to inward reality; it is a problem vital to the modern novel as well as the new psychology at the turn of the century.

Perhaps, too, as I have suggested with respect to the evolutionary writers to whom William James's philosophy of consciousness owes so much, the impulse to record the conscious life necessarily carries with it a profound fear of the loss of creative power. This concern might explain the phenomenon so familiar in the modern novel of leaving the ending, as Henry James would have it, *en l'air* as well as the almost obsessive impulse toward revision that we have seen among scientific texts intent on defining consciousness. Both gestures indicate the impossibility of settling upon any one answer, any singular term, any positive fate for consciousness or for the characters whose lived experience we follow. The language for consciousness, as we have repeatedly seen, vacillates in these texts between the certainty of inner life as the essence of identity and the sense that we come to know ourselves through our relationships and through the inevitable imprint of the social world. All of these texts are preoccupied with the desire to locate an authentic expression for the life of the mind; and in some sense, all of them fail to do so—an awareness that the authors sometimes painfully relate. The history of consciousness, soaked through as it is by the cultural environment, reveals itself through a complex series of metaphors that move in and out of, but never rest upon, one linguistic system. Unwilling to relinquish the language of the soul, novels, scientific studies, texts of psychology and social psychology combine spiritual and social influence as they bring consciousness into being. The belief in the "real me," the sense that interior life is (and must remain) a mystery that we are awakened to again and again, rubs up against the sense that who we are is bound by social ties, collective responsibilities, and our history within a community. The narrative of consciousness does not resolve this split, but rather, intensifies it, maybe even elevates it so that it becomes *the* question and thereby the legacy of the culture of the modern mind.

NOTES

1. *The Letters of William James*, edited by his son, Henry James (Boston: Atlantic Monthly Press, 1920), 1.199–200. As the letter continues, James defines the feeling accompanying what he calls the "characteristic attitude," that is, the encounter with the "real me." "I feel a sort of deep enthusiastic bliss ... which translates itself physically by a kind of stinging pain inside my breastbone (don't smile at this—it is to me an essential element of the whole thing!), and which, although it is a mere mood or emotion to which I give no form in words, authenticates itself to me as the deepest principle of all active and theoretic determination which I possess" (1.200). By locating the "feeling," ultimately, inside his breastbone, as a physical sensation, James materializes what is otherwise immaterial and intangible; he will struggle with this same mind/body split throughout *Principles of Psychology* and later essays examining the conscious mind.

2. Henry James, *The Portrait of a Lady*, volumes 3 and 4 (New York: Charles Scribner's Sons, 1908), vii; xii.

3. Though Wharton critics have generally been attuned to the forces of gender and social class in her fiction, Elizabeth Ammons asserts that we must add race to the list. Ammons argues that both the erasure and the presence of race in Wharton's writing (especially the representation of whiteness as racial) needs to be addressed and that we

cannot continue to approach her work as if race were not an operative category in it. See Elizabeth Ammons, "Edith Wharton and the Issue of Race" in Millicent Bell, ed., *The Cambridge Companion to Edith Wharton* (New York: Cambridge University Press, 1995), 68–86.

4. About the origins of *The House of Mirth*, Wharton writes: "In what aspect could a society of irresponsible pleasure-seekers be said to have, on the 'old woe of the world', any deeper bearing than the people composing such a society could guess? The answer was that a frivolous society can acquire dramatic significance only through what its frivolity destroys…. The answer, in short, was my heroine, Lily Bart." See Edith Wharton, *A Backward Glance* (New York: D. Appleton Century Company, 1934), 207. For more on *The House of Mirth*, see chapter five.

5. *Edith Wharton: The Uncollected Critical Writings*, ed., Frederick Wegener (Princeton: Princeton University Press, 1996) 265; 267. Wharton's introduction accompanied the Oxford University Press, "World Classics" edition of *The House of Mirth*, published in 1935.

6. See "Looking for the White Spot" in T.J. Jackson Lears, *The Power of Culture: Critical Essay in American History* (Chicago: University of Chicago Press, 1993), 15. Lears focuses his discussion of the modernist discourse of authenticity on a study of Sherwood Anderson. He argues that "the white spot," a Transcendentalist notion of a pure space that exists between the individual and God, becomes, for Anderson, a symbol of intense communion with another person. Thus, it might be "the way that modern people experience authentic spiritual life—now that the question of 'immortal life' had become too embarrassing to discuss" (31). Though Lears begins the essay with an acknowledgement that the ideal of authentic self-expression has been cast aside now that we recognize it as a "cultural construction," his analysis of Anderson shows that we need not automatically discard the discourse of authenticity.

7. In her discussion of the architecture of The Mount, one of Edith Wharton's homes, Sarah Luria claims that doors reveal "an inwardly projected domestic order [that] seems determined to probe the inner life as it is to defend its sanctity" (309). She argues that Wharton's domesticity is inseparable from her work and that the design of her house made possible the space she needed to create her life's work. Though Luria claims that Wharton's architectural creed allows her to maintain private space in her own home, the novels so deeply complicate the tensions between public and private space that it seems likely the issue remained a vexed one in Wharton's own life. See "The Architecture of Manners: Henry James, Edith Wharton, and The Mount," *American Quarterly* 49 (1997): 298–327.

8. Edith Wharton and Ogden Codman, Jr., *The Decoration of Houses* (1897; reprint, New York: Charles Scribner's Sons, 1901), 23; 49.

9. *The Age of Innocence* in *Edith Wharton: Novels*, ed., R.W.B. Lewis, (1920; reprint, New York: Library of America, 1985), 1057. All subsequent references will be to this edition of the text.

10. A wonderfully telling example of this scruple comes as Archer contemplates the Mingott clan's act in bringing the Countess "out": "he was glad that his future wife should not he restrained by false prudery from being kind (*in private*) to her unhappy cousin; but to receive Countess Olenska in the family circle was a different thing from producing her *in public*, at the Opera of all places" (1024; my emphasis).

11. See Maureen Howard, "The Bachelor and the Baby: *The House of Mirth*," in Millicent Bell, ed., *The Cambridge Companion to Edith Wharton* (New York: Cambridge University Press, 1995), 137–156.

12. *The House of Mirth* in *Edith Wharton: Novels*, ed., R.W.B. Lewis, (1905; reprint, New York: Library of America, 1985), 85. I am grateful to Jennifer Klein Hudak for making clear to me Lily's intensely closed nature here.

13. My understanding of the dissemination of Archer's consciousness owes much to Pamela Knights's essay, "Forms of Disembodiment: The Social Subject in *The Age of Innocence*" in Millicent Bell, ed., *The Cambridge Companion to Edith Wharton* (New York: Cambridge University Press, 1995), 20–45. Knights makes note of Wharton's interest "in what happens to the self when separated, by will or circumstances, from the world that has formed it" and states that the author's examination of Archer in *The Age of Innocence* "parallel[s], in its own terms, contemporary debates about the social basis of consciousness" (21).

14. James Robinson was the first to make explicit the sense that Archer cannot divorce himself from society and maintain a self. Robinson argues that Archer is a creature of the old ways, and "cannot break away from them without destroying himself psychologically in the process" (4). See James A. Robinson, "Psychological Determinism in *The Age of Innocence*," *Markham Review* 5 (Fall 1975): 1–5. Pamela Knights complicates this argument in helpful ways through her attention to disembodiment.

15. Emerson, too, uses the notion of the hieroglyphic in conjunction with communication, but specifically, communication with oneself. In *Nature*, he claims that there are no questions we cannot answer, "whatever curiosity the order of things has awakened in our minds, the order of things can satisfy. Every man's condition is a solution in hieroglyphic to those inquiries he would put." Thus, he suggests that we might look for answers inside ourselves, though, troublingly, what we find is a "hieroglyphic," something mysterious and difficult to decipher. See Richard Poirier, ed., *Ralph Waldo Emerson* (Oxford: Oxford University Press, 1990), 3.

16. Archer's dismay at the loss of this more delicate form of "nearness," which he shares with May in place of any sexual intimacy before their marriage, might explain his "curious indifference to [the Countess's] bodily presence," even as he is on the verge of a love affair with her. Wharton sets Archer's indifference toward the sensual Ellen inside a moment where he sits "with her face abandoned to his gaze.... The face exposed her as much as if it had been the whole person, with the soul behind it" (1208). Though Wharton may be suggesting a demureness on the part of Archer that rivals May's and that goes as deep as his love of tradition, it seems important to consider his wish here for an intimacy beyond the body. If we dismiss the possibilities for such intimacy as mere prudishness or sentimentality, we ignore the complications of Wharton's idea of the self—conflicted as is—her sense that fiction must bring to life both the "social picture" *and* the soul.

17. For a rich discussion of Archer's blindness and misreadings, see Emily J. Orlando, "Rereading Wharton's 'Poor Archer': A 'Mr. Might-have-been' in *The Age of Innocence*," *American Literary Realism* 30 (Winter 1998): 56–76.

18. As Pamela Knights puts it, he is Wharton's "specimen rather than her spokesman." Knights, 21.

19. See Martha Banta's study, *Imaging American Women: Ideas and Ideals in Cultural History* (New York: Columbia University Press, 1987) for a comprehensive discussion of the typology of American women.

20. Most discussions of Wharton's social Darwinism center on *The House of Mirth*, though the rest of her fiction, certainly, shows the influence of Darwin's theories as well as his language. For a fine discussion of these influences, see Claire Preston, *Edith Wharton's Social Register* (New York: St. Martin's Press, 2000), 49–60. Also, see Nancy Bentley, "'Hunting for the Real': Wharton and the Science of Manners" in Millicent Bell, ed., *The*

Cambridge Companion to Edith Wharton (New York: Cambridge University Press, 1995), 47–67 for further discussion of Wharton's use of anthropology, primitivism and what Bentley calls "culture consciousness" in the novel.

21. Clare Virginia Eby cautions readers to modify what she calls the "dominant" interpretations of the novel that overstate both Wharton's sympathy for her central character and "the power of New York women." See Clare Virginia Eby, "Silencing Women in Edith Wharton's *Age of Innocence*," *Colby Quarterly* 28 (June 1992): 93–104.

22. Julie Olin-Ammentorp and Ann Ryan make this point in their study of *The Custom of the Country*. See "Undine Spragg and the Transcendental I," *Edith Wharton Review* 17 (Spring 2001): 1–8.

23. The fact that Ellen Olenska ends up, at the close of the novel, in a room where "a light shone through the windows" (1302), a room that remains closed to Archer (and to the reader), shows Wharton's ambivalence, to the end, over the privacy of the Countess's inner realm.

24. See Alfred Russel Wallace, *On Miracles and Modern Spiritualism* (London: James Burns, 1875) and William James, *Varieties of Religious Experience: A Study in Human Nature* (New York: Random House, 1929). Chapters one and two also provide a fuller discussion of Wallace and James.

25. Marilyn Chandler seems quite ready to do so. She reads Archer's enslavement to society as a variation on the theme of entrapment that feminist critics have recognized in women's stories of domestic life. But she explicitly replaces the female character a feminist reading would be set on redeeming with Wharton's male center: "It would be hard to accuse Wharton ... of partiality to one sex over the other, as some have tried to do. Her complaint is always with structures and systems, institutions and customs—products of human desire and human politics, entrapping all in them, even those who most assiduously work for their preservation." See Marilyn Chandler, *Dwelling in the Text: Houses in American Fiction* (Berkeley: University of California press, 1991), 178.

26. Kathy Miller Hadley suggests that Wharton purposely draws the reader's attention to the "untold stories" of May and Ellen. She claims that Archer's "obsessive curiosity" about Ellen's life invites the reader to speculate about it, an activity that, she asserts, undermines the structure of the novel and its focus on Newland Archer. See "Ironic Structure and Untold Stories in *The Age of Innocence*," *Studies in the Novel* 23:2 (1991): 262–272. Gwendolyn Morgan makes a similar gesture in calling May the "unsung heroine" of the novel; she joins other critics in redeeming May as a character that transcends the behavioral formulas of old New York. See Gwendolyn Morgan, "The Unsung Heroine—A Study of May Welland in *The Age of Innocence*" in Pat Browne, ed., *Heroines of Popular Culture* (Bowling Green: Bowling Green State University Popular Press, 1987), 35; Evelyn E. Fracasso, "The Transparent Eyes of May Welland in Wharton's *The Age of Innocence*," *Modern Language Studies* 21:3 (1991): 43–8; Linette Davis, "Vulgarity and Red Blood in *The Age of Innocence*," *The Journal of the Midwest Modern Language Association* 20 (1987): 1–8; and Elsa Nettels, *Language and Gender in American Fiction: Howells, James, Wharton and Cather* (Charlottesville: University Press of Virginia, 1997) for similarly redemptive readings of May.

27. Elizabeth Ammons, *Edith Wharton's Argument with America* (Athens: The University of Georgia Press, 1980) 146. Ammons's argument depends upon her conviction that Wharton was committed to a feminist critique of the role of women in America throughout her entire career. Kathy Fedorko, likewise, reads Ellen as "the aware feminine self," "a woman comfortable with autonomy, with her body, with self-knowledge" (69). Fedorko claims that Wharton "press[es] the limits of rationality, to utter the unutterable

about sexuality, cage, death, fear, and especially, the nature of men and women" in her work (ix). The fact that Fedorko's argument rests upon Wharton's use of gothic elements in her fiction, especially her ghost stories, shows how complicated this maneuver might be in a novel (mostly) devoted to realism. Susan Goodman, *Edith Wharton's Friends and Rivals* (Hanover: University Press of New England, 1990), shows a different spin on the question of female autonomy, taking issue with studies that claim Wharton's work places women in isolation. Goodman argues that Wharton's "heroines" define themselves through their connections with other women; but she still assumes a "female community" set apart from the larger social body.

28. John Updike claims that Wharton learned from Proust "the "dignity of nostalgia." Updike finds that Wharton owes much to Proust, whom she admired, but never met: "Proust's simultaneously telescopic and microscopic view, his recognition that grandeur and absurdity coexist; his sense of society's apparent rigidity and actual fragility—these inform Wharton's enchanted caricature of her own tribe" (18). See John Updike, "Archer's Way," *The New York Review of Books* 42, no. 19 (1995 November 30): 16, 18.

29. Kenneth D. Pimple states that when Archer falls in love with Ellen and contemplates abandoning May, "he does not for an instant think of challenging society, but only of fleeing it" (147). In his essay, Pimple also makes the point that Wharton's books give us an "exceedingly rare glimpse of the traditions, mores and beliefs of a privileged segment of nineteenth-century America whose doors were firmly closed to any outside observer" (138). Calling to mind the advice Wharton herself gives in *The Decoration of Houses*, Pimple's observation reveals further subtleties regarding Wharton's ambivalence about the privacy of/in the world she presents in her fiction. See "Edith Wharton's 'Inscrutable Totem Terrors': Ethnography and *The Age of Innocence*," *Southern Folklore* 51 (1994): 137–152.

30. Hildegard Hoeller's reading of Wharton is informative here. Though she does not discuss *The Age of Innocence*, her study suggests that Wharton's fiction is best understood as a dialogue between two genres: sentimental fiction and realism. She stresses the fact that Wharton plays with sentimental love plots at the same time that she destabilizes them with the economies of realism. If, as I have suggested, the word "real" appears to be emptied of meaning in Wharton, then the detailed rendering of Archer's "real life" in the sanctuary is merely ironic. However, I am more interested, along with Hoeller, in the ways that Wharton maintains the tension between two discourses—whether they be sentimentality and realism or the language of the "real self" versus the socialized self—until the end. See Hildegard Hoeller, *Edith Wharton's Dialogue with Realism and Sentimental Fiction* (Gainesville: University Press of Florida, 2000).

31. For a provocative reading of this scene see Orlando, 58–9.

32. See Knights for a fuller discussion of Archer's "disembodiment" or loss of being.

33. Edith Wharton, *The Decoration of Houses*, 22. Wharton refers, in various places, to the "newness" of the couple's house, which seems to align it with the modernism that she criticizes. At one point she even indicates that their home exemplifies an express resistance to the uniformity of architecture in New York. The Archers live in "a newly built house in East Thirty-ninth Street. The neighborhood was thought remote, and the house was built in a ghastly greenish-yellow stone that the younger architects were beginning to employ as a protest against the brownstone of which the uniform hue coated New York like a cold chocolate sauce; but the plumbing was perfect" (1072). This wry look at his own future dwelling comes as a result of Archer's response to Ellen's interiors; so it is difficult to tell whether he admires or laments the newness. The fact that he twice dwells on the strange color (1072; 1178) and here calls it "ghastly" indicates his distaste for this departure from

form. But Archer does like the latest trends, even as he clings to traditions. The engagement ring he chooses for May has "the new setting ... but it looks a little bare to old-fashioned eyes" and he dreams of decorating his library with "plain new bookcases without glass doors" (1072), a plan that he follows through with despite family disapproval.

34. Claire Preston suggests that these intrusions—mere interruptions in the beginning of the story—have become "institutionalised in a room of their own." Preston, 42.

35. The room does, in fact, have a door. If we follow Archer's string of memories in Chapter 34, we hear that his son Dallas, as a young boy, "first staggered across the floor shouting 'Dad,' while May and the nurse laughed behind the door" (1289).

36. I cannot help but wonder if Wharton's recurrent description of May's "transparent eyes" might be referring playfully to Emerson's famous "transparent eyeball." If this is the case, May's self-effacing nature ("I am nothing. I see all") might, in a perverse reworking of Emerson's code, indicate the only form of consciousness available in the world of *The Age of Innocence*.

37. William James, *Essays in Radical Empiricism* (New York: Longmans, Green and Co., 1922), 85. See chapter four for a discussion of this essay, "A World of Pure Experience," with respect to Henry James's *The Golden Bowl*.

38. Kristin Boudreau asserts the abiding power of Emerson's rhetoric in her study of recent film versions of Hawthorne and James. See Kristin Boudreau, "Is the World Then So Narrow? Feminist Cinematic Adaptations of Hawthorne and James," *The Henry James Review* 21 (2000): 43–53. Robert Weisbuch repeats this sentiment in "James and the American Sacred," *The Henry James Review* 22 (2001): 217–228. He claims that James asserts a Hawthornian self, as opposed to an Emersonian one, a self that participates in the world and is defined by it. However, it seems as if Emerson's language has more staying power since Weisbuch (inadvertently?) echoes the philosopher's rhetoric ("Build, therefore, your own world") when he states that "Isabel chooses to *make her world*" (226; my emphasis).

39. Singley's book is a comprehensive study of "the dimensions of Wharton's religious, spiritual and philosophical search in the context of American intellectual thought and religious history" (xi). See Carol Singley, *Edith Wharton: Matters of Mind and Spirit* (New York: Cambridge University Press, 1995).

40. Preston makes this point with respect to Wharton's binary of "nice" and "not-nice" or the "not-x" phrase in general: "The semantic opposite of 'x', expressed as the category 'not-x', is a descriptive evasion which relieves the mind of imaginative, verbal, or social exercise. This evasion is a kind of restrictive antithesis which in semantic terms leads nowhere" (2). Preston's discussion of *The Age of Innocence* turns on this binary opposition. See Preston, 1–8.

41. Irving Howe astutely notes that even Ellen Olenska, despite her obvious experience and sophistication, "affirms the value of social innocence" in the novel. Here and elsewhere, the Countess indicates a desire to come under the shelter of New York. Howe cites the instance where the Countess tells Archer: "I want to do what you all do— I want to feel cared for and safe" (1074). She also, later in the novel, tells him: "I promised Granny to stay with her because it seemed to me here I should be safer" (1263). See Irving Howe, "Perception, Communication and Growth as Correlative Themes in Edith Wharton's *The Age of Innocence*," *Agora: A Journal in the Humanities and Social Sciences* 2, no. 2 (1973): 71.

42. In Newland's telephone conversation with his son, Wharton reveals this directness: "Dallas seemed to be speaking in the room: the voice was as near by and natural as if he had been lounging in his favorite armchair by the fire." At the same time Wharton

makes the voice a force that presses upon another ('Think it over? No sir: not a minute. You've got to say yes now'), she also implies something about its detachment by calling attention to Dallas' voice as if it stood apart from him: "The voice began again" (1293). The sense that Dallas' voice is almost too direct, too forceful might indicate a certain longing on Wharton's part for more subtle forms of communication.

43. Henry James, *The American*, volume 2 (New York: Charles Scribner's Sons, 1907), xvii–xviii.

44. Pamela Knights maintains that the novel resists stability, that "when Archer seems to be pushing toward a different kind of self (one, impossibly, beyond the social)... the mimetic code of realism ... seems to feel beneath it other pressures, as the novel of manners shifts into the fantastic" (35). Also relevant here is Hildegard Hoeller's engaging discussion "Economy and Excess: Realism and Sentimental Fiction Reconsidered" (her book's introduction). She asserts, quite aptly for *The Age of Innocence*, that the realist narrative, as opposed to the sentimental, "is more likely to be struggling against its own form, which tends to remind us of the very fact that it is artificial, artistic, constructed." See Hoeller, 25–37.

45. Cynthia Griffin Wolff argues that Archer triumphs over society in his acceptance of reality, a reading that rests upon the belief that he has been its victim. Emily Orlando and Claire Preston offer arguments for the contrary. For these readers, Archer's only victimization is self-imposed. See Wolff, *A Feast of Words*, 323–5; Orlando, 72–73 and Preston, 24.

46. See *A Backward Glance*, 89, 104, 112, 127, 173, 197 respectively.

47. Wharton continues by saying that James was surprised at her question, "and I saw at once that the surprise was painful, and wished I had not spoken. I had assumed that his system was a deliberate one, carefully thought out, and had been genuinely anxious to hear his reasons. But after a pause of reflection he answered in a disturbed voice: 'My dear—I didn't know I had!'" *A Backward Glance*, 190–1.

Chronology

1862	Edith Wharton is born Newbold Jones in New York City on January 24 to Lucretia Rhinelander Jones and George Frederic Jones. She is the youngest and only female sibling.
1866	Her family moves to Europe where she learns French, German, and Italian.
1872	Edith's family returns to New York.
1876	She writes *Fast and Loose*, her first, unpublished novella.
1878	Lucretia Jones arranges a private printing of Edith's *Verses* (juvenilia).
1879	One or more poems are published, at the recommendation of Henry Wadsworth Longfellow, in *Atlantic Monthly*.
1880–82	Edith travels to Europe with her parents. Her father dies in southern France in 1882. She is briefly engaged to Newport socialite Henry Stevens.
1885	She marries Edward Wharton and they move into a cottage on her mother's Newport estate. From then on, she and her husband spend half the year in Europe, mainly in Italy, France, and England.
1889	The couple rents a house on Madison Avenue in New York City.
1890	*Scribner's* publishes "Mrs. Manstey's View," her first short story.

1891	The Wharton's buy a house in New York City on what later becomes Park Avenue.
1895–97	Edith suffers from periods of depression. In 1897 she publishes *The Decoration of Houses*, written in collaboration with Ogden Codman, Jr.
1899	She publishes *The Greater Inclination*, her first collection of short stories.
1900	Wharton publishes *The Touchstone*, a novella.
1901	The Mount, which would be her home in the U.S. until its sale in 1911, is built in Lenox, Massachusetts. In 1901 her mother dies. She publishes *Crucial Instances*, a collection of short stories
1902	*The Valley of Decision* is published, her first long novel.
1903	Wharton meets Henry James, with whom she develops a lifelong friendship. She publishes *Sanctuary*, a novella.
1904	Wharton publishes *The Descent of Man*, a collection of short stories, and *Italian Villas and Their Gardens*.
1905	Wharton publishes *Italian Backgrounds* and *The House of Mirth*.
1906	The play version of *The House of Mirth* opens in New York.
1907	Wharton establishes a second home, a rented apartment, in Paris. She publishes *The Fruit of the Tree*, a novel.
1908–10	Wharton has an affair with Morton Fullerton.
1908	Wharton publishes *A Motor-Flight through France* and *The Hermit and the Wild Woman and Other Stories*. She begins her friendship with Henry Adams.
1909	*Artemis to Actaeon and Other Verse* is published. Her husband admits he has embezzled $50,000 from her trust fund but later makes restitution.
1910	Wharton's husband enters a sanatorium in Switzerland, while she remains in the new Paris apartment. Wharton publishes *Tales of Men and Ghosts*, a collection of short stories.
1911	*Ethan Frome* is published.
1912	*The Reef* is published.
1913	Edith Wharton divorces her husband. She publishes *The Custom of the Country*.
1914–18	Wharton performs work for refugees, for which she is made Chevalier of the Legion of Honor in 1916. She visits the

front lines and writes articles that are collected in *Fighting France, from Dunkquerque to Belforte* (1915). She also edits *The Book of the Homeless* (1916), compiled for the benefit of the war relief. Wharton travels to Algeria, Tunisia, and Morocco; publishes *Xingu and Other Stories* (1916), *Summer* (1917*)*, and *The Marne* (1918); she begins friendship with André Gide. Henry James dies in 1916.

1919–20	Wharton publishes *French Ways and Their Meaning* and *The Age of Innocence*, which wins Pulitzer Prize; also publishes *In Morocco*, travel sketches.
1922–23	Wharton publishes two novels, *The Glimpses of the Moon* (1922) and *A Son at the Front* (1923).
1924–26	*Old New York* (1924), a collection of four novellas, is published along with *The Mother's Recompense* (1925), a novel; *The Writing of Fiction* (1925); and *Here and Beyond* (1926), a collection of short stories; and *Twelve Poems*. Wharton is elected to the National Institute of Arts and Letters.
1927–33	In 1928, Edward Wharton dies. Wharton publishes four novels: *Twilight Sleep* (1927), *The Children* (1928), *Hudson River Bracketed* (1929), and *The Gods Arrive* (1932). She also publishes two works of short stories: *Certain People* (1930) and *Human Nature* (1933).
1934	Wharton publishes *A Backward Glance*, her autobiography.
1935–36	The play versions of *The Old Maid* and *Ethan Frome* are successful in New York.
1936	Wharton publishes *The World Over*, a collection of short stories.
1937	On August 11, Edith Wharton dies of stroke in France. *Ghosts*, a collection of what she considered her best supernatural tales, is published posthumously.
1938	Posthumous publication of *The Buccaneers*, an unfinished novel.

Contributors

HAROLD BLOOM is Sterling Professor of the Humanities at Yale University. He is the author of over 20 books, including *Shelley's Mythmaking* (1959), *The Visionary Company* (1961), *Blake's Apocalypse* (1963), *Yeats* (1970), *A Map of Misreading* (1975), *Kabbalah and Criticism* (1975), *Agon: Toward a Theory of Revisionism* (1982), *The American Religion* (1992), *The Western Canon* (1994), and *Omens of Millennium: The Gnosis of Angels, Dreams, and Resurrection* (1996). *The Anxiety of Influence* (1973) sets forth Professor Bloom's provocative theory of the literary relationships between the great writers and their predecessors. His most recent books include *Shakespeare: The Invention of the Human* (1998), a 1998 National Book Award finalist, *How to Read and Why* (2000), *Genius: A Mosaic of One Hundred Exemplary Creative Minds* (2002), and *Hamlet: Poem Unlimited* (2003). In 1999, Professor Bloom received the prestigious American Academy of Arts and Letters Gold Medal for Criticism, and in 2002 he received the Catalonia International Prize.

CUSHING STROUT has been Ernest I. White Professor of American Studies and Humane Letters at Cornell University. He is the editor of a book on Hawthorne and has written titles such as *The Veracious Imagination: Essays on American History, Literature and Biography*.

DAVID HOLBROOK is Emeritus Fellow of Downing College, Cambridge. In addition to having written a book on Edith Wharton, he has written about the female image in the work of D.H. Lawrence and Charles Dickens.

KATHY MILLER HADLEY is the author of *In the Interstices of the Tale: Edith Wharton's Narrative Strategies*.

JOHN J. MURPHY is Professor of English at Brigham Young University. He is the editor and/or co-editor of books on Willa Cather and has edited the *Willa Cather Newsletter*. He is a member of the Edith Wharton Society.

CLARE VIRGINIA EBY has been Associate Professor of English at the University of Connecticut and is the author of *Dreiser and Veblen, Saboteurs of the Status Quo*. She is one of the editors of *The Cambridge Companion to Theodore Dreiser* and has edited works of Dreiser.

DALE M. BAUER teaches English at the University of Kentucky. He is one of the editors of *The Cambridge Companion to Nineteenth-Century American Women's Writing* and the author or editor of other titles as well.

PAMELA KNIGHTS has lectured in English and American Literature at the University of Durham, England. She wrote the introduction for Edith Wharton's *The House of Mirth* in the Everyman's Library edition and is the editor of *The Awakening and Other Stories*.

CYNTHIA GRIFFIN WOLFF teaches writing at the Massachusetts Institute of Technology. She is the editor of Penguin's edition of *The Age of Innocence* and the author of *Classic American Women Writers: Sarah Orne Jewett, Kate Chopin, Edith Wharton, Willa Cather*.

JOHN UPDIKE has won two Pulitzer Prizes. While most well-known for his novels, he also has written poems, short stories, essays, and criticism.

HELEN KILLORAN teaches at Ohio University, Lancaster. She has published *The Critical Reception of Edith Wharton* and is a past president of the Edith Wharton Society.

JILL M. KRESS teaches English at St. John Fisher College, Rochester, and is the author of *Figure of Consciousness: William James, Henry James, and Edith Wharton*.

Bibliography

Ammons, Elizabeth. "Cool Diana and the Blood-Red Muse: Edith Wharton on Innocence and Art." In *American Novelists Revisited: Essays in Feminist Criticism*, edited by Fritz Fleischmann, 209–24. Boston: Hall, 1982.

Asya, Ferda. "Resolutions of Guilt: Cultural Values Reconsidered in *Custom of the Country* and *The Age of Innocence*." *Edith Wharton Review* 14, no. 2 (1997): 15–20.

Bentley, Nancy. "'Hunting for the Real': Wharton and the Science of Manners." In *The Cambridge Companion to Edith Wharton*, edited by Millicent Bell, 47–67. New York: Cambridge University Press, 1995.

Blackall, Jean Frantz. "The Intrusive Voice: Telegrams in the *House of Mirth* and *The Age of Innocence*." *Women's Studies: An Interdisciplinary Journal* 20, no. 2 (1991): 163–68.

Bloom, Harold, ed.. *Edith Wharton*. Broomall, PA: Chelsea House Publishers, 1986.

Bremer, Sidney H. "American Dreams and American Cities in Three Post-World War I Novels." *South Atlantic Quarterly* 79 (1980): 274–85.

Candido, Joseph. "Edith Wharton's Final Alterations of *The Age of Innocence*." *Studies in American Fiction* 6 (1978): 21–31.

Celly, Anu. "Barricaded by Banalities of Evasion: Women in *The Age of Innocence*." *Indian Journal of American Studies* 28, nos. 1–2 (1998): 37–47.

Coolidge, Olivia E. *Edith Wharton, 1862–1937*. New York: Scribner, 1964.

Cuddy, Lois A. "Triangles of Defeat and Liberation: The Quest for Power in Edith Wharton's Fiction." *Perspectives on Contemporary Literature* 8 (1982): 18–26.

Das, Dilip K. "The American Family in Transition: Some Turn-of-the-Century Images." *Indian Journal of American Studies* 21, no. 2 (1991): 47–54.

Davis, Linette. "Vulgarity and Red Blood in *The Age of Innocence.*" *The Journal of the Midwest Modern Language Association* 20, no. 2 (1987): 1–8.

Dessner, Lawrence Jay. "Edith Wharton and the Problem of Form." *Ball State University Forum* 24, no. 3 (1983): 54–63.

Doyle, Charles C. "Emblems of Innocence: Imagery Patterns in Wharton's *The Age of Innocence.*" *Xavier University Studies* 10, no. 2 (1971): 19–25.

Durczak, Joanna. "America and Europe in Edith Wharton's *The Age of Innocence.*" In *Polish-American Literary Confrontations*, edited by Joanna Durczak and Jerzy Durczak. Lublin: Maria Curie-Sklodowska University Press, 1995. 35–47.

Evans, Elizabeth. "Musical Allusions in *The Age of Innocence.*" *Notes on Contemporary Literature* 4, no.3 (1974): 4–7.

Fracasso, Evelyn E. "The Transparent Eyes of May Welland in Wharton's *The Age of Innocence.*" *Modern Language Studies* 21, no. 4 (1991): 43–48.

Fryer, Judith. "Purity and Power in *The Age of Innocence.*" *American Literary Realism* 17, no. 2 (1984): 153–68.

Gibson, Mary Ellis. "Edith Wharton and the Ethnography of Old New York." *Studies in American Fiction* 13, no. 1 (1985): 57–69.

Godfrey, David A. "'The Full and Elaborate Vocabulary of Evasion': The Language of Cowardice in Edith Wharton's Old New York." *Midwest Quarterly: A Journal of Contemporary Thought* 30, no. 1 (1988): 27–44.

Grenier, Richard. "Society & Edith Wharton." *Commentary* 96, no. 6 (1993): 48–52.

Jacobson, Irving. "Perception, Communication, and Growth as Correlative Theme in Edith Wharton's *The Age of Innocence.*" *Agora: A Journal in the Humanities and Social Sciences* 2, no. 2 (1973): 68–82.

Kekes, John. "The Great Guide of Human Life." *Philosophy and Literature* 8, no. 2 (1984): 236–49.

Killoran, Helen, and Alan Price. "The End of the Age of Innocence: Edith Wharton and the First World War." *American Literature* 69, no. 1 (1997): 1.

Kundu, Gautam. "The Houses That Edith Wharton Built: The Significance of the Van Der Luydens' Italian Villa and the Patroon's Rock Cottage in *The Age of Innocence*." *Indian Journal of American Studies* 13, no. 1 (1983): 127–31.

Lamar, Lillie B. "Edith Wharton's Foreknowledge in *The Age of Innocence*." *Texas Studies in Literature and Language: A Journal of the Humanities* 8 (1966): 385–89.

Martin, Robert K. "Age of Innocence: Edith Wharton, Henry James, and Nathaniel Hawthorne." *Henry James Review* 21, no. 1 (2000): 56–62.

Mayne, Gilles. "About the Displacement of Certain Words in *The Age of Innocence*: A Bataillian Reading." *Edith Wharton Review* 14, no. 2 (1997): 8–14.

McWilliams, Jim. "Wharton's *The Age of Innocence*." *Explicator* 48, no. 4 (1990): 268–70.

Mizener, Arthur. *Twelve Great American Novels*. New York: New American Library, 1967.

Morgan, Gwendolyn. "The Unsung Heroine: A Study of May Welland in *The Age of Innocence*." In *Heroines of Popular Culture*, edited by Pat Browne, 32–40. Bowling Green, OH: Popular, 1987.

Murphy, John J. "The Satiric Structure of Wharton's *The Age of Innocence*." *Markham Review* 2, no. 3 (1970): 1–4.

Niall, Brenda. "Prufrock in Brownstone: Edith Wharton's *The Age of Innocence*." *Southern Review* 4 (1971): 203–14.

Orlando, Emily J. "Rereading Wharton's 'Poor Archer': A Mr. 'Might-Have-Been' in *The Age of Innocence*." *American Literary Realism* 30, no. 2 (1998): 56–77.

Pimple, Kenneth D. "Edith Wharton's 'Inscrutable Totem Terrors': Ethnography and *The Age of Innocence*." *Southern Folklore* 51, no. 2 (1994): 137–52.

Pizer, Donald. "American Naturalism in Its 'Perfected' State: *The Age of Innocence* and *An American Tragedy*." In *Edith Wharton: New Critical Essays*, edited by Alfred Bendixen and Annette Zilversmit, 127–41. New York: Garland, 1992.

Price, Alan. "The Composition of Edith Wharton's *The Age of Innocence*." *Yale University Library Gazette* 55 (1980): 22–30.

Robinson, James A. "Psychological Determinism in *The Age of Innocence*." *Markham Review* 5 (1975): 1–5.

Salecl, Renata. "Love: Providence or Despair." *New Formations: A Journal of Culture/Theory/Politics* 23 (1994): 13–24.

———. "I Can't Love You Unless I Give You Up." In *Gaze and Voice as Love Objects*, edited by Renata Salecl and Slavoj Zizek, 179–207. Durham, NC: Duke University Press, 1996.

Saunders, Judith P. "Becoming the Mask: Edith Wharton's Ingenues." *Massachusetts Studies in English* 8, no. 4 (1982): 33–39.

Scheick, William J. "Cupid without Bow and Arrow: *The Age of Innocence* and the Golden Bough." *Edith Wharton Newsletter* 2, no. 1 (1985): 2–5.

Taubin, Amy. "Dread and Desire." *Sight and Sound* 3, no. 12 (1993): 6–9.

Tintner, Adeline R. "Jamesian Structures in *The Age of Innocence* and Related Stories." *Twentieth Century Literature* 26 (1980): 332–47.

Trumpener, Katie, and James M. Nyce. "The Recovered Fragments: Archeological and Anthropological Perspectives in Edith Wharton's *The Age of Innocence.*" In *Literary Anthropology: A New Interdisciplinary Approach to People, Signs and Literature*, edited by Fernando Poyatos, 161–69. Amsterdam: Benjamins, 1988.

Turk, Ruth. *Edith Wharton: Beyond the Age of Innocence*. Greensboro, NC: Tudor Publishers, 1998.

Van Gastel, Ada. "The Location and Decoration of Houses in *The Age of Innocence.*" *Dutch Quarterly Review of Anglo-American Letters* 20, no. 2 (1990): 138–53.

Wagner, Linda W. "A Note on Wharton's Use of Faust." *Edith Wharton Newsletter* 3, no. 1 (1986): 1, 8.

Wagner-Martin, Linda. The Age of Innocence : *A Novel of Ironic Nostaglia*. New York: Twayne Publishers, 1996.

Wharton, Edith. The Age of Innocence: *Complete Text with Introduction, Historical Contexts, Critical Essays*, edited by Carol J. Singley. New Riverside Editions. Boston: Houghton Mifflin, 2000.

Wharton, Edith. The Age of Innocence *Authoritative Text, Contexts, Criticism*, edited by Candace Waid. Norton critical edition. New York: W.W. Norton & Co., 2003.

Williams, Merle A. "Henry James and the Redemption of 'Awkward' Concepts through Fiction." *Henry James Review* 18, no. 3 (1997): 258–64.

Wolff, Cynthia Griffin. "*The Age of Innocence*: Wharton's 'Portrait of a Gentleman.'" *Southern Review* 12 (1976): 640–58.

Acknowledgments

"Complementary Portraits: James's Lady and Wharton's Age" by Cushing Strout. From *The Hudson Review* 35, no. 3 (Autumn 1982): 405–415. © 1982 by The Hudson Review, Inc. Reprinted by permission.

"*The Age of Innocence*" by David Holbrook. From *Edith Wharton and the Unsatisfactory Man*: 117–138. © 1991 by David Holbrook. Reprinted by permission.

"Ironic Structure and Untold Stories in *The Age of Innocence*" by Kathy Miller Hadley. From *Studies in the Novel* 23, no. 2 (Summer 1991): 262–272. © 1991 by the University of North Texas. Reprinted by permission.

"Filters, Portraits, and History's Mixed Bag: *A Lost Lady* and *The Age of Innocence*" by John J. Murphy. From *Twentieth Century Literature* 38, no. 4 (Winter 1992): 476–485. © 1992 by Hofstra University. Reprinted by permission of the publisher.

"Silencing Women in Edith Wharton's *The Age of Innocence*" by Clare Virginia Eby. From *Colby Quarterly* 28, no. 2 (June 1992): 93–104. © 1992 by Colby College. Reprinted by permission.

"'Edith Agonistes'" by Dale M. Bauer. From *Edith Wharton's Brave New Politics*: 165–178. © 1994 by the Board of Regents of the University of

Wisconsin System. Reprinted by permission of the University of Wisconsin Press.

"Forms of Disembodiment: The Social Subject in *The Age of Innocence*" by Pamela Knights. From *The Cambridge Companion to Edith Wharton*, edited by Millicent Bell: 20–46. © 1995 by Cambridge University Press. Reprinted by permission.

"Studies of Salamanders: The Fiction, 1912–1920," section 9, by Cynthia Griffin Wolff. From *A Feast of Words: The Triumph of Edith Wharton*: 302-326. Second edition © 1995 by Cynthia Griffin Wolff. Reprinted by permission.

"Archer's Way" by John Updike. From *The New York Review of Books* 42, no. 19 (November 30, 1995): 16, 18. © 1995 by NYREV, Inc. Reprinted by permission.

"*The Age of Innocence*: Branching Thematic Allusions" by Helen Killoran. From *Edith Wharton: Art and Allusion*: 56–69. © 1996 by the University of Alabama Press. Reprinted by permission.

"The Price of a Conscious Self in Edith Wharton's *The Age of Innocence* by Jill M. Kress. From *The Figure of Consciousness: William James, Henry James, and Edith Wharton*: 161–186. © 2002 by Routledge. Reprinted by permission.

Index

Age of Innocence, The (Wharton), *see also* specific characters
  allusions in, 141–54, 164
  Bill Archer in, 80, 126
  fear of immigrants in, 73–77
  Fullerton Jackson in, 17–18
  irony in, 5, 16, 22, 33–43, 51, 58, 63, 71–82, 100, 116, 143, 149, 152–53, 160, 172
  compared to *A Lost Lady*, 45–53
  Mary Archer in, 80, 125
  narrator, 33, 37, 49, 61–62, 84, 92–93, 100–6, 112
  compared to *The Portrait of a Lady*, 1–11, 110–12, 130
  publication of, 34, 133, 189
  Mrs. Rushworth in, 18–19, 28–29
  social contextualizatism of eros in, 45–53
  social innocence in, 83–108
  social silence of Old New York in, 55–69, 143
  structure of, 33, 35, 90, 159
  Mrs. Thorley Rushworth in, 143
Alhambra, The (Irving), 148
Ammons, Elizabeth
  Edith Wharton's Argument with America, 73–74
Anna Karenina (Tolstoy), 136
Artemis to Actaeon and Other Verse (Wharton), 188
Auchincloss, Louis
  Edith Wharton: A Woman in Her Time, 135

Backward Glance, A (Wharton), 1, 57, 64, 71, 178, 189
Bauer, Dale M., 192
  on social irony in *The Age of Innocence*, 71–82
Baym, Nina
  on the American male hero, 34
Berry, Walter, 71, 109, 137
Bloom, Harold, 191
  introduction, 1–2
  on Wharton's nostalgia, 1–2
Blum, Virginia
  on *The Age of Innocence*, 38
Boas, Franz
  The Mind of Primitive Man, 81
Book of the Homeless, The (Wharton), 189
Brace, Charles Loring
  The Dangerous Classes of New York and Twenty Years' Work Among Them, 73
Buccaneers, The (Wharton), 72, 82, 189
Burkitt, Ian, 84

Cather, Willa
  A Lost Lady, 45–53
  My Mortal Enemy, 48
  "Nebraska: The End of the First
     Cycle," 47
  Not Under Forty, 46
  One of Ours, 45, 47
  O Pioneers!, 45
  compared to Wharton, 45–53
Certain People (Wharton), 189
Chase, Richard
  on the American male hero, 34
Children, The (Wharton), 72, 74, 81,
  189
Cooley, Charles Horton, 84
Coronation of Napoleon, The (David),
  149
Cott, Nancy, 64
Croly, Herbert
  The Promise of American Life, 105
Crucial Instances (Wharton), 188
Custom of the Country, The
  (Wharton), 2, 133, 135, 148–49,
  188

Dallas Archer in *The Age of
  Innocence*, 125–26
  marriage, 80
  in Paris, 42, 64, 128
  silence of, 56
  social function, 104–6
*Dangerous Classes of New York and
  Twenty Years' Work Among Them,
  The* (Brace), 73
Daniel Deronda (Eliot), 25
Dante, 149, 151
Daudet, Alphonse, 79
David
  The Coronation of Napoleon, 149
  Decoration of Houses, The
    (Wharton), 109, 133, 188
  language in, 159, 170

Degler, Carl, 73
Descent of Man, The (Wharton), 188
Dickens, Charles
  A Tale of Two Cities, 149

Eby, Clare Virginia, 192
  on social silence of Old
     New York in *The Age of
     Innocence*, 55–69
*Edith Wharton: A Woman in Her
  Time* (Auchincloss), 135
*Edith Wharton's Argument with
  America* (Ammons), 73–74
Eliot, George, 6
  Daniel Deronda, 25
  Middlemarch, 149
  The Mill on the Floss, 25
Ellen Olenska in *The Age of
  Innocence*, 86–87, 90, 113, 136
  and Archer, 114–17, 121, 126–29,
     138, 144–47, 150–53
  consciousness of, 160–79
  husband, 26–27, 30–31, 38, 42,
     88, 142–43, 163
  morality of, 8–9, 11, 13–15,
     17–21, 23–25, 48–49, 51–52,
     56, 58, 61–63, 65, 75–76,
     78–79, 99, 101–3, 105, 120–25
  past, 96, 100, 149
  return of, 5, 7, 36, 149
  self-possession, 117–19
  sexual innocence, 142–43
  tribal expulsion of, 1–2, 28–29,
     42, 55–56, 58–59, 64, 72–73,
     77, 80, 88, 92–95, 97
  untold story of, 33–42
Emerson, Ralph Waldo, 10, 149
Emerson Sillerton in *The Age of
  Innocence*, 90
  bohemianism, 76, 149, 153
Ethan Frome (Wharton), 133, 136,
  188–89

Euphorion (Lee), 151

Fanny Beaumont in *The Age of Innocence*
  engagement, 31, 80, 103, 167
Fast and Loose (Wharton), 187
Feast of Words: The Triumph of Edith Wharton, A (Wolff), 3–4, 8
Fee, Elizabeth, 85
Felicitous Space (Fryer), 37
Fighting France, from Dunkquerque to Belforte (Wharton), 134, 189
Fitzgerald, Scott, 45
Flaubert, Gustave
  Madame Bovary, 151
French Ways and Their Meaning (Wharton), 61, 77, 84, 189
Fruit of the Tree, The (Wharton), 188
Fryer, Judith
  on *The Age of Innocence*, 40–41
  Felicitous Space, 37

"Genocide and Eugenics" (Koonz), 74
Ghosts (Wharton), 189
Gide, André, 137, 189
Gilman, Sander, 74
Glimpses of the Moon, The (Wharton), 141, 153, 189
Gods Arrive, The (Wharton), 189
Golden Bowl, The (James, H.), 159, 171, 178
Gosse, Edmund, 130
Greater Inclination, The (Wharton), 188
Guermantes Way (Proust), 137

Hadley, Kathy Miller, 192
  on Wharton's irony, 33–43
Hawthorne, Nathaniel
  The Marble Faun, 149
Here and Beyond (Wharton), 189

Hermit and the Wild Woman and Other Stories, The (Wharton), 188
Holbrook, David, 191
  on Newland Archer's self-defeat, 13–32
Holmes, Oliver Wendell, 74
House of Life, The (Rossetti), 151
House of Mirth (Wharton), 2, 90, 96, 103, 133, 188
  allusions in, 141, 163
  irony in, 160–61
  New York society in, 135–36, 157–58
  real self in, 171, 176–77
  silence in, 62
Howe, Irving
  on Wharton, 3–4, 8–10
Howe, Julia Ward, 90
Hudson River Bracketed (Wharton), 189
Human Nature (Wharton), 189

Ideas and the Novel (McCarthy), 6
In Morocco (Wharton), 189
Irving, Washington, 151
  The Alhambra, 148
Italian Backgrounds (Wharton), 188
Italian Villas and Their Gardens (Wharton), 104, 188

James, Henry, 46, 71, 109, 137, 159, 177, 179
  death, 189
  The Golden Bowl, 159, 171, 178
  influence on Wharton, 3–11, 14, 20–21, 25, 28, 31, 45, 50, 110–11, 130, 160
  The Portrait of a Lady, 1–11, 110–12, 130, 156, 160
James, William, 84, 110, 155–56, 165–66, 171, 178
Julius Beaufort in *The Age of*

Innocence, 22–23, 37, 80
downfall, 50, 73, 88, 90–91, 93,
  96–97,
  and Ellen, 100–4, 117, 122–23,
  173

Killoran, Helen, 192
  on Wharton's art of allusion,
  141–54
Koonz, Claudia
  "Genocide and Eugenics," 74
Knights, Pamela, 192
  on the social innocence in *The
  Age of Innocence*, 83–108, 168
Kress, Jill M., 192
  on Newland Archer's divided self,
  155–85

Lawrence Lefferts in *The Age of
  Innocence*
    rumors of, 63–64, 76–78, 103,
    114, 125
Lears, T.J. Jackson, 157
Lee, Hermione, 48
Lee, Vernon
  Euphorion, 151
Lewis, R.W.B.
  on Wharton and *The Age of
    Innocence*, 1–2, 11, 45, 46, 57,
    60, 63, 135
Lewis, Sinclair, 45
Longfellow, Henry Wadsworth, 187
Lost Lady, A (Cather)
  compared to *The Age of Innocence*,
    45–53
social contextualizatism of eros in,
  45–53
Lubbock, John, 85
Lubbock, Percy, 110
  Portrait of Edith Wharton, 3

Madame Bovary (Flaubert), 151

Mrs. Manson Mingott in *The Age of
  Innocence*, 22, 76
  Catherine the great, 80, 89,
    149–50
  stroke, 96–97, 99, 102–3
  transformation, 52, 56, 91–92,
    137, 163
"Mrs. Manstey's View" (Wharton),
  187
Marble Faun, The (Hawthorne), 149
Marne, The (Wharton), 189
May Welland in *The Age of
  Innocence*, 89–90, 128, 136, 138,
    161
  assertion of, 169–70, 172, 175
  courage of, 32, 55, 60, 63–65
  death, 15, 30, 42
  family, 14, 125–27
  innocence of, 5–8, 10, 16–24,
    26–27, 29, 39–40, 49–51, 61,
    75, 77, 84, 93–95, 104, 118,
    120–23, 142–53, 162
  pregnancy, 80, 94, 102, 124–25,
    142, 146, 170–71
  untold story of, 33–35, 37–41
  wedding, 113, 115, 119, 142, 163
McCarthy, Mary
  Ideas and the Novel, 6
McClennan, John F., 85–86
Mead, George Herbert, 84
Middlemarch (Eliot), 6, 149
Mill on the Floss, The (Eliot), 25
Mind of Primitive Man, The (Boas),
  81
Mother's Recompense, The (Wharton),
  72, 189
Motor-Flight through France, A
  (Wharton), 188
Murphy, John J., 192
  on social contextualizatism of
    eros in *The Age of Innocence*
    and *A Lost Lady*, 45–53

My Mortal Enemy (Cather), 48

Narrative of Arthur Gordon Pym
(Poe), 148
"Nebraska: The End of the First
Cycle" (Cather), 47
Ned Winsett in *The Age of Innocence*,
111
bohemian, 73, 79, 81, 151
intellectualism, 78, 104–5, 149,
173
Newland Archer in *The Age of
Innocence*, 136, 138
consciousness of, 33–42, 48–53,
55, 60–62, 64, 85, 92, 97–101,
103–5, 110, 112, 114–15,
126–27, 158, 161–63
conventional marriage of, 6–9,
13, 19–20, 22, 31, 35, 37–40,
52, 64, 75–79, 93–95, 98, 111,
113–15, 117, 119, 124, 142,
145, 148, 163
desires of, 93, 100, 116–18, 147,
150–53
divided self, 84–87, 90, 155–85
idea of order, 2
imagination, 17
innocence of, 143–47
compared to Isabel Archer, 1–11
morality, 19, 37, 56–59, 62–63,
120–25, 129–30
self defeat of, 13–32
Norton, Sara, 46
Not Under Forty (Cather), 46

Old Maid, The (Wharton), 189
Old New York (Wharton), 189
"Old New York" in *The Age of
Innocence*, 25, 42, 48, 105–6, 118
changes, 76–78
compass of, 177
consciousness, 126–29, 162, 171

history, 1–2
prosperity, 91
rigidities, 121–24
social silence of, 55–69, 143
society, 5–6, 10, 13, 15, 17,
20–21, 23, 34, 53, 82, 92–99,
101–3, 116, 120, 135–36,
142–44, 146, 148–51, 153,
159–61, 163–68, 173–75
traditions, 36–37, 85–89, 104,
112–15
One of Ours (Cather), 45, 47
O Pioneers! (Cather), 45
"Other Two, The" (Wharton), 72

Parkman, Francis, 63
Parsons, Elsie Clews, 87
Petrarch, 149, 151
Poe, Edgar Allan, 146
Narrative of Arthur Gordon Pym,
148
Portrait of a Lady, The (James, H.),
156
compared to *The Age of Innocence*,
1–11, 110–12, 130
Caspar Goodwood in, 7, 9
irony of, 5
Isabel Archer in, 1–11, 103, 111,
160
Portrait of Edith Wharton (Lubbock),
3
Post, Emily, 87
Preston, Claire, 172
Price, Alan
on *The Age of Innocence*, 34
Promise of American Life, The
(Croly), 105
Proust, Marcel
Guermantes Way, 137
Swann's Way, 137
Within a Budding Grove, 137

Reef, The (Wharton), 81, 188
"Roman Fever" (Wharton), 72
Rossetti, 168
  The House of Life, 151

Sanctuary (Wharton), 188
Sargent, Jon Singer, 49
Scarlet Letter, The (Hawthorne), 136
Shakespeare, William, 151
Sillerton Jackson in *The Age of*
  Innocence, 56, 92
  criticism, 58, 119
Sinclair, Upton, 104
Smith, Henry Nash
  on the American male hero, 34
Son at the Front, A (Wharton), 46,
  99, 106, 189
Spencer, Herbert, 79, 85
Stepan, Nancy, 74
Strout, Cushing, 191
  on Isabel Archer compared to
    Newland Archer, 3–11
Stout, Janis P., 59
Summer (Wharton), 72, 77, 189
Swann's Way (Proust), 137

Tales of Men and Ghosts (Wharton),
  188
Tale of Two Cities, A (Dickens), 149
Thackeray, William Makepeace
  Vanity Fair, 149
Theory of the Leisure Class (Veblen),
  91
Tolstoy, Leo
  Anna Karenina, 136
Touchstone, The (Wharton), 188
Tuttleton, James W., 60
Twelve Poems (Wharton), 189
Twilight Sleep (Wharton), 72, 146,
  189
Tylor, Edwin, 85

Updike, John, 192
  on Wharton's narrative, 133–39

Valley of Decision, The (Wharton),
  188
van der Luydens in *The Age of*
  Innocence
  silence and speech, 56–59, 90,
    92–93, 104, 137, 146–47, 160,
    163, 172
Vanity Fair (Thackeray), 149
Veblen, Thorstein, 57
  Theory of the Leisure Class, 91
Verne, Jules, 146
Verses (Wharton), 187

Mrs. Welland in *The Age of*
  Innocence, 16–17, 76–77, 88–93,
    137, 149
Wharton, Edith, 133–34
  and allusion, 1, 4, 141–54
  birth, 187
  compared to Cather, 45–53
  childhood, 1–2, 46, 84–85, 110,
    135
  chronology, 187–89
  control of tradition, 109–31
  death, 189
  feminism, 56
  irony, 22, 33–43, 71–74, 80, 166,
    168, 172
  Henry James' influence on, 3–11,
    14, 20–21, 25, 28, 31, 45, 50,
    110–11, 130, 160, 167
  narratives, 2, 33, 48, 133–39, 156,
    158–60, 162, 166–67, 174,
    176–79
  and nostalgia, 1–2, 10, 46, 48, 64,
    75, 81, 109, 169–73
Within a Budding Grove (Proust),
  137
Wolff, Cynthia Griffin, 192

A Feast of Words: The Triumph of Edith Wharton, 3–4, 8
   on Wharton's control of tradition, 46, 48–49, 51, 56, 64, 109–31
Woodress, James, 45

World Over, The (Wharton), 189
Writing of Fiction, The (Wharton), 97, 189

Xingu and Other Stories (Wharton), 189